Women's Work in
Post-war Italy

Trajectories of Italian Cinema and Media

Series editor: Flavia Laviosa
Print ISSN: 2632-487 | **Online ISSN:** 2632-488

The book series Trajectories of Italian Cinema and Media intends to engage with diverse academic communities, build new conceptual frameworks and foster a globally-focused and representative corpus of scholarship in Italian cinema and media studies. With the aim of exploring new critical and historical trajectories, this book series will trace the evidence of Italian cinema's international polysemy and polycentrism, define the extent of its inspirational force, examine other cinemas' artistic innovations resulting from their osmosis with the Italian film tradition, and foster comparative analyses of themes and genres between Italian and other world cinemas.

If you wish to propose a manuscript to be included in the series, please contact the series editor Flavia Laviosa (flaviosa@wellesley.edu).

In this series:

Fellini's Films and Commercials: From Postwar to Postmodern, by Frank Burke (2020)
Paolo Sorrentino's Cinema and Television, edited by Annachiara Mariani (2021)
Pasta, Pizza and Propaganda: A Political History of Italian Food TV, by Francesco Buscemi (2022)
The Many Meanings of Mina: Popular Music Stardom in Post-war Italy, by Rachel Haworth (2022)
Women's Work in Post-War Italy: An Oral and Filmic History, by Flora Derounian (forthcoming)
Call Me by Your Name: Perspectives on the Film, edited by Edward Lamberti and Michael Williams (forthcoming)

Women's Work in Post-war Italy

An Oral and Filmic History

Flora Derounian

Bristol, UK / Chicago, USA

First published in the UK in 2023 by
Intellect, The Mill, Parnall Road, Fishponds, Bristol, BS16 3JG, UK

First published in the USA in 2023 by
Intellect, The University of Chicago Press, 1427 E. 60th Street,
Chicago, IL 60637, USA

Copyright © 2023 Intellect Ltd
All rights reserved. No part of this publication may be reproduced, stored in a retrieval system, or transmitted, in any form or by any means, electronic, mechanical, photocopying, recording, or otherwise, without written permission.

A catalogue record for this book is available from
the British Library.

Copy editor: MPS Limited
Cover designer: Tanya Montefusco
Cover image: Film frame from *Anna*. Alberto Lattuada, 1951. Italy.
© 2023 by and between Cristaldifilm of Zeudi Araya Cristaldi Snc (licensor) and Hauser & Wirth (licensee).
Production manager: Debora Nicosia
Typesetter: MPS Limited

Hardback ISBN 978-1-78938-812-1
ePDF ISBN 978-1-78938-811-4
ePUB ISBN 978-1-78938-813-8

To find out about all our publications, please visit our website. There you can subscribe to our e-newsletter, browse or download our current catalogue and buy any titles that are in print.

www.intellectbooks.com

This is a peer-reviewed publication.

Contents

List of Figures	vii
List of Tables	ix
Acknowledgements	xi
Notes on the Text	xi
Introduction	1
SECTION 1: AGRICULTURE – RICE WEEDERS	**23**
1. A Brief History of Rice Weeders in Italy	25
2. Earth and Rebirth: Filmic Representations of Rice Weeders	33
3. Martyrs Without Medals: Oral Histories of Rice Weeders	57
SECTION 2: TEXTILES – SEAMSTRESSES	**81**
4. A Brief History of Seamstresses in Post-war Italy	83
5. Modern Women: Filmic Representations of Seamstresses	88
6. Cinderella Stories: Oral Histories of Seamstresses	112
SECTION 3: RELIGIOUS WORK – NUNS	**133**
7. A Brief History of Nuns in Post-war Italy	135
8. Fallen Women: Filmic Representations of Nuns	140
9. Professed Professionals: Oral Histories of Nuns	165
Afterword	191
Bibliography	197
Filmography	213
Index of Interviews	217

Figures

1.1	Italy's rice belt. Personal drawing, Flora Derounian, 1 January 2017.	26
2.1	US publicity poster for *Riso amaro* (1949). Posteritati, n.a., 1949.	35
2.2	French publicity poster for *La risaia* (1956). Avoir-alire.com, n.a., 1955.	37
2.3	US publicity for *La risaia* (1956). Cinematerial, n.a., 1955.	51
2.4	Elena (Elsa Martinelli) dances in *La risaia*. Still from *La risaia*, Matarazzo, 1955. Italy. © Minerva.	54
3.1	Rita Montagnana, Giuliana Nenni, and Palmiro Togliatti at unnamed event in commemoration of Margotti. Europeana.eu, n.d. Accessed 14 February 2018.	64
3.2	Margotti's image used at unnamed protest. Europeana.eu, n.d. Accessed 2 July 2018.	74
3.3	Margotti's body being transported from the crime scene. Europeana.eu, n.d. Accessed 2 July 2018.	77
3.4	Margotti's daughters at her funeral. Europeana.eu, n.d. Accessed 2 July 2018.	78
5.1	Men pursue the female protagonists of *Le ragazze di piazza di Spagna* in Villa Borghese. *Le ragazze di piazza di Spagna*, Emmer, 1952. Italy. © Cine Produzione Astoria.	94
5.2	Elena and Lucia (Cosette Greco, Liliana Bonfatti) gaze out of the atelier window in *Le ragazze di piazza di Spagna*. *Le ragazze di piazza di Spagna*, Emmer, 1952. Italy. © Cine Produzione Astoria.	94
5.3	Rosetta's (Madeleine Fischer) body is collected in the hyper-public city space in *Le amiche*. *Le amiche*, Antonioni, 1959. Italy. © Trionfalcine.	98

5.4	Lucia (Liliana Bonfatti) cycles through a landscape of ruined buildings and new electricity pylons in *Le ragazze di piazza di Spagna*. *Le ragazze di piazza di Spagna*, Emmer, 1952. Italy. © Cine Produzione Astoria.	102
5.5	The atelier space in *Le ragazze di piazza di Spagna*. *Le ragazze di piazza di Spagna*, Emmer, 1952. Italy. © Cine Produzione Astoria.	102
5.6	Marisa (Lucia Bosè) returns to Garbatella after a ball in *Le ragazze di piazza di Spagna*. *Le ragazze di piazza di Spagna*, Emmer, 1952. Italy. © Cine Produzione Astoria.	106
5.7	Lucia (Liliana Bonfatti) gazes at Marisa (Lucia Bosè) as she models at a ball in *Le ragazze di piazza di Spagna*. *Le ragazze di piazza di Spagna*, Emmer, 1952. Italy. © Cine Produzione Astoria.	107
6.1	Salaries for first-grade workers in *sartorie per uomo/per signora* between 1945 and 1963. Personal drawing, Flora Derounian, 2017.	118
6.2	Average salaries for men and women working in *sartorie su misura* between 1945 and 1963. Personal drawing, Flora Derounian, 2017.	118
8.1	Silvana Mangano on the set of *Anna* (1951). Captured from the documentary Rai Edu, *Sorriso amaro*, 2009. Italy. Doc Italia. *Sorriso amaro*, Rai Edu, 2009.	140
8.2	Letizia's (Anna Magnani) veil becomes unpinned in *Suor Letizia*. *Suor Letizia*, Camerini, 1956. Italy. © Cineriz.	158
8.3	'I haven't lost' says Anna (Silvana Mangano) as she prepares for surgery in *Anna*. *Anna*, Lattuada, 1951. Italy. © Cristaldi.	163

Tables

3.1	List of the documentaries' sponsors and affiliations. Flora Derounian, 2017.	59
5.1	Comparison between Clelia's character in *Tra donne sole* (Pavese 1949) and the film transposition *Le amiche* (Antonioni 1955).	103

Acknowledgements

My thanks to every person and institution who brought this research to life.

Notes on the Text

This text is accompanied by a body of audiovisual interview extracts. All translations from the original Italian into English are the author's own.

Introduction

Italy is a democratic Republic founded upon work.
(Assemblea Costituente 1946)

Work empowered and regenerated the male citizen.
(Bonifazio 2011: 163)

Women's political presence, or rather the political nature of their action, is not generally recognized as such either by their peers or their historians and often not even fully by the protagonists themselves.
(Rossi-Doria 2000: 361)

If post-Second World War Italy was a Republic founded upon work, working women have been largely erased from this legacy. By that, I mean that the working woman has rarely been celebrated or studied for her identity as a labourer or a professional. This book redresses this absence: by looking at films and oral histories, it reveals and argues that working women are instrumentalized, sexualized, or problematized both in cultural materials and in their own recollections. It is not only cultural materials produced in the post-war period but also contemporary scholarly enquiry which fails to remember or study women workers. Anna Rossi-Doria points out the erasure of women's participation in the antifascist Resistance, but this is symptomatic of the erasure of women's work more generally. Historian Laura Ruberto notes how work 'ordinarily performed by women [...] (paid or unpaid) is not usually discussed in labour histories' (2008: 4). This book is not a labour history, although it draws upon and augments historical knowledge of women's work. Rather, this book provides a comparative analysis of filmic representations and oral histories of working women. Its aim is to respond to a threefold shortcoming regarding working women in this period: an absence of their representation in cultural productions, an absence of their own voices and an absence of critical scholarship on working protagonists. It is important to look at working women in this period because they both shaped and represented the post-war nation, and as such produced new and controversial models of femininity and nationhood.

This book was inspired by a search for working women in films made between 1945 and 1965. Having been struck by filmic portrayals of professional opportunities for women in post-war beauty contests (Gundle 2007: 58–80), I began to ask myself where were the other working women?[1] If, 'although actual numbers did not rise, many women were doing more visible types of work' (Willson 2010: 118) in postwar Italy, where are the cashiers, the waitresses, the secretaries, the labourers, and the teachers in films? The short answer to this question is, if anywhere, working women can be found in films' on-screen backgrounds. It is difficult to find films made in Italy between 1945 and 1965 which feature working female protagonists, and even more rare to find those where their work is a key theme of the narrative. Where they arise, filmic images of women workers 'rearticulate the social significance of female work' (Bonifazio 2011: 174) and are important because they offer citizens 'an image of how they need to see themselves in order to have access to a national identity and imagine their roles in the historical process' (Vacche 1992: 277). It is the frequent emphasis on other aspects of female characters' lives, such as their sexual or criminal behaviour, which leads me to argue throughout the book that women's work is erased, obfuscated, problematized, or diverted in narratives, and that this is symptomatic of social anxiety around the newly visible working woman.

Where are women's voices in histories of post-Second World War Italy? Of the few historical studies of women's work, most use archival and press materials to reconstruct women's professional realities. In her investigation of the role of gender in historical labour studies, Joan Scott argues that although labour historians now understand the importance of gender, they consistently discount it because, 'class, after all, is still the issue that really counts' (2018: 54). It is particularly true that oral history studies have put class before gender.[2] This book responds to the need to intersect class and gender in investigations of labour. Inspired by the developing field of scholars who triangulate filmic analysis, oral history, and archival materials, the book asks how cultural representations compare to women's own memories of their work. Historian of women's work Eloisa Betti points out that triangulating written, visual, and oral sources can redress gendered absences in historical accounts (Betti 2015: 312). The present book is a thin triangle; filmic representations and oral histories are its long sides, underpinned by its base of contextual historical and archival sources.

Finally, there is a lack of study of women's work in post-Second World War Italy. Less than a third of the Italian active female population was officially recorded as employed in 1950, 'the absolute lowest participation rates of women in the total workforce at the time' (Tomka 2013: 67). However, as historian Molly Tambor argues, including informal labour and prostitution would significantly increase this number (2014: 13). Women played a key role in running the nation and their work interacted with major currents in post-war Italy like consumerism, secularization and modernization. Tambor describes how post-war politicians tried to construct the ideal female figure as follows:

> She would be a mother, a worker, a member of political associations and trade unions. She would be a participant in building a new democracy and reconstructing a dynamic economy and society. She would have dignity and individuality, but she would also be the moral pillar of a stable, happy family and the anchor of a productive community.
>
> (Tambor 2014: 4)

This description highlights a number of contradictions which this book will underline: namely, women as the site for rehearsing (and often condemning) new social realities and old political wounds. Work was key to discussions of nation, as evidenced by its inclusion in Article 1, and the specific reference to 'the working woman' in Article 37 of the 1946 Constitution. Women's work occupied a particular place as symbolic of national, moral, and gendered change. By studying how working women are represented and how they represent themselves, we can observe the turning weathervane of Italy's social, religious, and political mores.

Women in post-Second World War Italy

In post-war Italy, women had just endured 'bombings, rapes, forced labour, retaliatory strikes by occupiers, and near starvation; often they were still alone in facing the prospect of rebuilding their lives' (Tambor 2014: 13). Before the war, women were subject to the contradictory rhetoric of Fascism, which Victoria De Grazia summarizes as 'a disconcerting experience of new opportunities and new repressions' (1992: 1). The same was true of the Fascist attitude to women's work, which it simultaneously deemed potentially dangerous, excluding women from many workplaces, while also relying on their labour in areas like agriculture and service in its quest for autarchy. In contrast to other post-First World War countries, Italy reacted to the population crisis by restricting women's rights, banning abortion and contraception, and channelling women into the domestic and maternal space through repressive means. Fascism attempted to cast feminism and women's independence as 'spinsterish' (De Grazia 1992: 11), and yet during the Second World War, the effort to confine women to the private sphere became compromised by necessity, and they flooded into munitions factories, government bureaucracies, commerce, farming, and healthcare. Between 1940 and 1943, women were progressively invited into more public jobs like waitresses and tram conductors (Willson 2010: 98).

As the war advanced, factors such as rationing from 1940 and intensive bombing in late 1942 rendered women's wartime experiences increasingly dire. Yet, during the war 'it was often women who dealt with the outside world' (Willson 2010: 110). Although the highest estimates have suggested that up to two million women participated in the Resistance, many women refrained from declaring themselves as partisans after the war's end. As well as this political erasure, it is important to acknowledge that women's everyday experiences of the war have equally been overlooked. Recognizing this crucial period of change for women, this book observes how wartime experiences shape women's representations and oral histories. One example from my sources is the nun Sister Cc, who remembers her only teacher being killed in bombing in Foggia, marking the end of her formal education.

The immediate post-Second World War period showcases some of the reasons for which the timeframe of this book is so rich. On the one hand, much of the misery of war continued in the form of poor supplies and living conditions, absent men and political disarray. There was also a push, particularly by the Church, back to traditional gender roles and the sanctity of the family (Tambor 2014: 15). On the other hand, women's wartime participation was key to their gaining the right to vote in the general election and referendum of 1946. Certainly, women's mass organizations like Unione delle Donne Italiane (Union of Italian Women) and women's branches of Azione Cattolica (Catholic Action) were extremely active during the post-war period (Dawes 2014). This book acknowledges the historical significance of women's suffrage but asks how the politicization of women translated onto the screen and into cultural and collective memory. Particularly in the light of the 1946 Constitution which, in Article 37, explicitly enshrines the equal rights of the working woman, with the qualification that 'working conditions must allow women to fulfil their essential role in the family' (Assemblea Costituente 1946), my work explores how the tension between women as politicized, workers and mothers plays out across sources.[3]

There was no tidal wall at the start of the 1950s against which prior social currents broke. Rather, they flowed and mingled into a notional decade of modernization and reconstruction. Politically speaking, the Democrazia Cristiana (Christian Democrat) party managed to rid itself of left-wing influence in 1947, and consequently pushed through changes which brought about the industrialization, liberalization, and Americanization of Italian society. Many women – 'rarely less than 60 per cent' of the DC's electorate (Pollard 2008: 116) – supported the party's embrace of modernization and free market capitalism.

These political factors influenced women's lives in a number of ways. For instance, industrialization meant many working women shifted from rural to industrial workplaces, albeit far less than men. This book examines how women

INTRODUCTION

are represented and how they identify with modernization and new gender norms. The immediate post-war period was also marked by international influence. The Allied occupation of Italy in 1943–45 was followed in 1947 by US Secretary of State George Marshall's European Recovery Programme, which invested greater sums in industrial, rather than agricultural, reconstruction and development. Ginsborg argues that, as a result of these factors, 'the myth of America acquired new and even more impressive hues' in Italy (1990: 79). The Americanization of Italian society and women's entry into mixed-sex workforces is generally held to have changed women's social and sexual behaviour, producing a generation of independent and promiscuous women (Ropa and Venturoli 2010: 199). The veracity of this discourse has been critiqued by scholars such as Penny Morris who notes the 'rigidly controlled relations between the sexes in the 1950s and the atmosphere of fear and ignorance in which many women lived' (2006a: 114). Yet, in the same edited volume, Lesley Caldwell suggests that 'traditional expectations that women's place in society and at work were subordinate to their position as mothers began to be questioned in the fifties' (2006: 225). Willson notes that 'all this change, perhaps inevitably, also made this a period of much moral anxiety' (2010: 113). This book traces the fluctuations and contradictions in discourses about gender norms and how they interacted with ideas of women's work.

Supported by the Catholic Church, American influence in Italy was determined to quash national and global communism. The Church excommunicated socialists and communists in 1949 (Pojmann 2013: 9). The fallout of this tension, or 'three-way tug-of-war' (Duggan 1995: 1–24), impacted on women, whose participation was numerically greater in left-wing political parties than in right-wing parties (Pojmann 2013: 34). After the war, many women on the Left continued their political activism and many even visited the Soviet Union (Betti, 26 May 2016). Elsewhere, women numerically dominated Catholic social action groups and Church attendance (Dawes 2014). Wider political tensions are important to this book's investigation of working women. For instance, left-wing discourse is key to understanding the working identity of the *mondine*.

The impact of post-war social change on women accelerated during Italy's 'economic miracle', which is loosely ascribed to the period between 1958 and 1963. Its features of urbanization, greater social mobility and the mechanization and restructuring of industry are of particular interest to this book. Indeed, it is the latter phenomenon that caused the decline of two of the occupations studied here, those of manual rice weeding and made-to-measure fashion. The law forbidding the firing of women workers upon marriage only came into force in 1963. Information on birth control and abortion was still illegal, the average woman had just under four children and the generally falling birth rate actually rallied in the late 1950s and early 1960s. At home, women increasingly had dishwashers, fridges, and washing machines which transformed their domestic labour, but, it has been suggested, served to isolate them from other women and the community (Willson 2010: 123). While the boom did much to modernize Italians' living conditions, it barely increased female workplace participation. On the other hand, many of those women who were employed saw vast increases in their salaries and improved working conditions, as demonstrated by contracts and salary tables held at the CGIL (Italian General Confederation of Labour) Bologna for fashion houses between 1945 and 1965.[4] In my study of collective contracts and salary scales for seamstresses in these archives, I found that the steepest increase in minimum salaries occurred between 1960 and 1963, confirming the impact of the economic boom on women workers.

Finally, the influence of Catholicism on women in post-war Italy is key to understanding social constraints and gender ideals for women. Historian John Pollard notes how 'Catholicism, in various institutional forms, played a powerful, central role in the post-war reconstruction of Italy' (2008: 109). The ideal woman envisaged by the Church at this time was first a mother, and – if necessary – a worker. Despite modernization, in the matter of Catholic gender ideals, there was a regression towards traditional models. Percy Allum describes 'the virtue of obedience' (1990: 82) for women as one of the unchanged ideological concerns of the Church. This element fits with 'the eventual reconstruction of a "normal" gender order' (Tambor 2014: 14), which appears to have animated Italian society in the post-war period. Where sexual liberation was concerned, female sexuality was still synonymous with moral corruption and disaster and was consequently often censored from cinema screens. This may have been a hangover from Fascism, whose accord with Catholicism on women's social roles has already been noted. For the Church, female sexuality and emancipation were conflated and were feared to undermine patriarchal hierarchies (Dunnett 2002: 104). This book looks for ruptures and continuities with Catholic and traditional discourse in representations and oral histories of working women.

Materials and methodology

Sources

This book examines two distinct groups of sources: films and oral histories. The films are drawn from those produced in Italy between 1945 and 1965 and were selected for the primacy that they give to women's work or working female characters. In order of appearance, the films are: representing *mondine*, *Riso amaro* (De Santis 1949) and *La risaia* (Matarazzo 1956); representing seamstresses,

Sorelle Materassi (Poggioli 1943), *Le ragazze di piazza di Spagna* (Emmer 1952) and *Le amiche* (Antonioni 1955); and representing women religious, *Anna* (Lattuada 1951), *Suor Letizia* (Camerini 1956), and *Lettere di una novizia* (Lattuada 1960). These films were available to Italian citizens through public cinemas and often also in parish cinemas. Although all films recorded decent box office figures, none, apart from *Riso amaro*, could be considered either canonical or cult. This was not a motivating factor for my choice of the films but does perhaps say something about the reception of films starring women and (what are perceived as) their issues.

The oral histories I study are all contemporary and collected from various sources. In the case of the *mondine*, I study oral histories collected by three other researchers, two of whom gave me access to their raw interview material in the form of audio recordings or typed transcriptions. I also draw on interviews recorded in three contemporary documentary films. The use of other researchers' interviews, as well as the study of oral histories contained within documentaries, presents methodological challenges and considerations which are addressed in Chapter 3. The oral histories of seamstresses in Chapter 6 and of women religious in Chapter 9 were solicited, conducted, filmed, and transcribed by myself. The theoretical considerations of this process will be touched upon in this introduction and further extrapolated in the chapters themselves.

Theoretical and methodological approaches

A highly interdisciplinary theoretical approach befits a diverse corpus. My study is broadly situated under the umbrella of cultural studies, an area which is increasingly seeing the concurrent study of films, oral histories, and social history in order to extract greater meaning from each area. An example of this is the Italian Cinema Audiences project (Treveri Gennari et al. 2013–16), which studies audiences' experiences of cinema-going between 1945 and 1960. Like Treveri Gennari's project, this book brings films and oral histories into contact, looking for crossovers and contradictions between these two groups of sources.[5] Here, this approach is pioneering, as no study like it has yet been undertaken on women's work either in Italian studies or elsewhere. The societies which I examine in this book are both contemporary and historical. For this reason, it is suitable to take a memory studies approach, asking how the identity of working women is constructed retrospectively. Memory studies and oral history are two overlapping theoretical fields. Oral history seeks out oral sources to complement other, more traditional, material sources. Memory studies only address oral sources but, like oral history, it aims to understand the meaning of past events rather than trying to reconstruct their form (Perks and Thomson 1998: 67).

Memory studies

The interdisciplinary nature of memory studies has created a number of critical overlaps. I am interested in the categories of cultural and collective memory.[6] Scholars agree that cultural and collective memory can be identified in sources which show, recount or cue memory, which are subjective, but which interact with a wider memory community and with the present. Jan Assmann describes cultural memory as a 'body of reusable texts [and] images, [...] specific to each society in each epoch, whose "cultivation" serves to stabilize and convey society's self-image' (Assmann and Czaplicka 1995: 132). In the context of this book, films and oral histories manifest these characteristics of being reusable texts in the cultural sphere which form and demonstrate socialized ideas of female workers.

Halbwachs has defined collective memory as 'the organic memory of the individual, which operates within the framework of a sociocultural environment [and] [...] the creation of shared versions of the past, which results through interaction' (Erll and Young 2011: 15). Halbwachs's insistence on the interactive nature of collective memory is immediately identifiable in the sources I study. For example, in Chapter 2 on the *mondine* of the film, interviewees meet to discuss their memories of work, later watching and commenting on the film *Riso amaro* (1949). This example perfectly manifests collective memory as 'memories that an individual shares with his contemporaries' (Erll and Nunning 2010: 112). Similarly, collective memories are permeated with cultural materials. In Chapter 5 on seamstresses in film, interviewees identify with filmic representations of the life of Coco Chanel, affirming and approving of the truthfulness of her rags-to-riches story. These examples demonstrate the importance of approaching film and oral history as co-creation between individuals and cultural products.

Memory studies is often discussed in counterpoint with history; where history has traditionally sought to ascertain narratives of the past, memory studies is a critique of what is remembered and forgotten. Writing in the 1980s, Nora suggests that in attempting to organize the past, history annihilates what really took place (1989: 9). Nowadays, however, we should acknowledge that developments in oral history and microhistory have taken great steps to address this critique. Nora's argument that 'memory is a perpetually actual phenomenon, a bond tying us to the eternal present; history is a representation of the past' (1989: 8) is key to this book, as it underlines the importance of a consideration of the contemporary context in order to extract meaning from sources. For example, in the case of women religious, with whom I conducted interviews in the more secularized context of 2017, narratives relating to travel and education were far more frequent than mentions of spirituality or doctrine, perhaps pointing to interviewees' awareness of the unpopularity of religious discourse today.

INTRODUCTION

Astrid Erll's ideas on premediation and remediation are also central to my analysis of the social construction of the female worker. Erll argues that:

> Memorable events are usually represented again and again, over decades and centuries, in different media [...]. What is known about a[n] [...] event which has been turned into a site of memory, therefore, seems to refer not so much to what one might cautiously call the 'actual events', but instead to a canon of existent medial constructions.
>
> (Erll and Rigney 2009: 392)

This statement strongly supports the value of studying oral histories in conjunction with films, as both are understood to interact and shape one another. Nora states that 'we buttress our identities upon [the] bastions' (1989: 12) of cultural memories; a key drive of this book is to address the vanishing nature of sources which recount and recall women's experiences. The women who worked during the Second World War are a rapidly vanishing demographic, and many of them have already died. One of the functions of this book is to create a corpus of sources which speak about the past and have a mnemonic function in the present.

Film

It is difficult to find films made in Italy between 1945 and 1965 which feature working female protagonists, and even more rare to find those where their work is a key theme of the narrative. To give an example, in the film *La risaia* (1956) which I analyze in Chapter 2, the drama unfolds around protagonist Elena's seduction by her second cousin, her budding romance with a local mechanic, and the discovery of her biological father. Throughout, very little is said of Elena's work as a rice weeder, although her work is the very reason she finds herself in this narrative and the characteristic by which she is defined in the film's title. I take a holistic approach to the analysis of how women are presented in these films, considering not only the features of their work but the narratives and characteristics attributed to them more generally. This is because, taking an approach inspired by reflectionist film studies (Chapman et al. 2007: 3), film can function as both informer and reflection of social ideas around the working woman. If, as Pierre Sorlin observes, 'cinema-going was the most popular national pastime in 1950s Italy' (1996: 74), this book asks what filmic representations of working women said to, and of, post-war audiences and why.

Although there have been many studies of Italian women in film, very few connect textual analysis to approaches from New Cinema History (Bilterneyst et al. 2011) and cultural memory studies. I consider films as sources of cultural memory, taking them as artefacts from which we can understand post-war and contemporary Italy. Inspired by film scholar Elizabeth Cowie's assertion that 'fantasy itself is [...] a veritable mise-en-scène of desire' (1997: 133), this book will ask what social desires we can read through representations of working women. Robert Brent Toplin has observed how 'often the depictions seen on the screen influence the public's view of historical subjects much more than books do' (1996: vii). This book looks at this interaction between filmic and historical narratives of working women. The interplay of cultural representations and personal accounts is particularly poignant in the case of women's identities, since 'it is exactly in this dialectic between reality and imagination that image plays a central role in the production of gender' (Gribaldo and Zapperi 2010: 21). Feature film and cultural memory can be the sites at which gendered identities are (re)negotiated.

I combine textual analysis with considerations inspired by New Cinema History (Biltereyst et al. 2011) and New Film History (Chapman et al. 2007). This school of study supplements narrative analysis with consideration of visual and aural elements of films. Noting the 'turn to psychoanalysis' (Chapman et al. 2007: 4) of film studies in the 1970s, this book finds theories of the gaze particularly useful to its analysis (Lacan 1981; Mulvey 1975). New Cinema History distinguishes itself from previous critical approaches by examining films' 'process and agency' (Chapman et al. 2007: 6), studying how films are shaped by practical factors like economic limitations, censorship and technology, as well as creative factors like the input of directors, stars and crew. Additionally, New Film History considers films' reception, placing 'the film text at the nexus of a complex and dynamic set of relationships between producers and consumers' (Chapman et al. 2007: 7). This approach complements a cultural and collective memory methodology, drawing out interactions between films and their spectators, of whom my interviewees were often a part. This approach also acts as a check on the excesses of the reflectionist model by critically assessing films' impact.[7] In this book, representations of working women are put into the context of their reception by triangulating textual analysis with reviews and publicity. I also address films' 'process and agency' by considering their directors, screenwriters and stars, and their economic and political contexts. Finally, this book understands that 'films that are not watched [...] may provide the most intriguing images of the past' (Erll and Nunning 2010: 395). Although none of the films studied were outright flops, films like *La risaia* (1956) were barely watched in urban areas, posing the question: if films were created 'to satisfy the desires of a mass audience' (Chapman et al. 2007: 3), what can we say about those which do not?

Oral history

It is difficult to overstate the value of an oral history approach. At its roots, oral history aimed to enrich and diversify biased historical narratives, and in Italy, it often did this by focusing on the working classes. Historian John Foot has argued that oral history research in Italy meant that 'the "silent people", finally, were being given a voice' (2008: 165) and that 'oral history has been particularly important in bringing out the personal, hidden experiences of women' (2008: 170). Within feminist circles, Passerini and others have repeatedly emphasized 'the extraordinarily oral nature of the women's movement' (1992: 676). Internationally, feminist oral historians in the late 1960s and early 1970s took up the mantra 'giving voice to the voiceless' (Gluck 2014: 35) and embraced the recording of oral sources, the reason for which was the relative absence of women from the archive.

Nonetheless, oral histories of working women in Italy remain relatively rare. Betti argues that this is a trend which is being increasingly addressed by scholars working on the twentieth century (2013: 485). Betti enumerates oral history projects with women as part of studies on working-class movements and migration and notes sector-specific enquiries on 'the history of female labour (such as *mondine*, factory, office, and domestic workers)' (Betti 2013: 485). This book not only analyzes oral histories addressing working women but also contributes a new body of sources. My choice to examine and conduct oral histories of working women is politically motivated. Oral histories are also memories and, as Jacques Derrida proposes, 'there is no political power without control of the archive, if not of memory' (1995: 4). The hope of this book is to regain a measure of control of the archive, contributing to and critiquing it. Oral history is frequently used to bring out the nuances between the histories of dominant and non-dominant subjects. For example, Sangster's point that 'managers remember history differently than workers' (1994: 8) in her study of Canadian female textile workers, informs Chapter 6's attention to the differing statuses of seamstresses, from directors of luxury fashion houses to employees in small independent outfits.

One of my prime concerns in choosing an oral history methodology was to approach sources in a holistic manner, presenting not just subjects' words, but their expressions, prosody, and body language. The importance of multimodal analysis is being increasingly recognized across disciplines (Morgenstern 2014: 123). In memory studies, Nora observes how 'true memory, […] has taken refuge in gestures and habits' (1989: 13). Multimodal analysis of oral histories deepens our understanding of what is recounted. Passerini states that 'these days, I am convinced that visual sources are at the forefront in the struggle for innovation in history and its methodology' (2011: 249). Most oral history research uses transcriptions of audio recordings, limiting the researcher's analytical potential. In her article 'A memory for interpreting women's history', Passerini expresses a commitment which this book shares, to 'over-turn; […] the traditional value of chatter, confidences, confessions, and gossip […] putting into a new context women's previous language; the creation of new forms of expression; the great importance of the body, gestures, signs of emotion, facial expressions' (1992: 677). My research responds to this commitment not only by taking women's words seriously but by recording, filming, and assessing their multimodal expression. A revealing example of this can be noted in Chapter 9 on oral histories of women religious. When discussing her decision to become a nun, Sister Pc remembers her choice in reaction to the death of her mother; crying, and almost in a whisper, she remembers telling herself, 'I must be a nun, I must become a nun' (Pc 2017). By assessing the vocal and gestural performance of this interview, we are able to observe how emotion permeates women religious' narratives of work and career choices.

Chapter 6 engages with theory on interview practice, as it is the first instance in which I present interviews conducted by myself. Here, I limit myself to pointing out Passerini's argument, that 'a life story is also a serious business, and can, if treated with due rigour, become the object of scientific enquiry' (1987: 4). I approach the 'realities' described in oral histories 'with a critical eye', as advised by oral historian Primo Levi (1989: 6). Oral history handbooks consistently alert researchers to the mutative process of the interview. The collaborative character of oral history is similarly underlined, since 'oral history […] refers [to] what the source [i.e. the narrator] and the historian [i.e. the interviewer] do together at the moment of their encounter in the interview' (Portelli 1997: 3). An example of how I consider this in the book is the recognition that my access to women religious and interviewees' oral histories in Chapter 9 might be influenced by my (female) gender.

Sociology of work

Underpinning this book are theoretical reflections about the interaction between work, the individual and society. This book is interested in mapping and expanding traditional definitions of work and labour. Karl Marx describes labour as 'a process by which man, through his own actions, mediates, regulates and controls the metabolism between himself and nature' (1976: 283). Marx's insistence on the interaction of nature and worker finds echoes in my discussion of the use of female workers as symbols of land and nation, particularly in Chapter 2 on the *mondine*. The book also considers the distinctions that have been made between labour and work. Philosopher Hannah Arendt makes a fulsome analysis of this issue, noting the linguistic persistence of these two different terms to indicate the same activity (1998: 80). Unlike other European languages, Italian has only one verb for work, *lavorare*, but various nouns *lavoro*, *mestiere*, *professione*, and *occupazione* demonstrate the nuanced meanings of what it means to 'have' work. Arendt distinguishes work as a social value which determines our worth and purpose as citizens, whereas labour encompasses the actions necessary to fulfil our needs (1998: 80).

She also outlines historical notions of labour as servile, productive, unskilled, or painful. Laurie Cohen argues that career is a conception of work that workers deploy retrospectively (2014: 18), but conceiving one's work as career is also a class-bound concept. This discussion opens up questions of which activities can be qualified as labour and which as work, and what work can be called profession, career, or occupation, a conversation with which this book consistently engages. The blurring of women's work and labour is a debate of particular relevance to Chapter 9 and its discussion of nuns' narratives of their work as vocation.

The blurred boundary between work and gendered care is also key to discussions of affective and immaterial labour (1999). Micheal Hardt understands affective labour as caring, bodily labour (1999: 96) and immaterial work as 'labour that produces an immaterial good, such as a service, knowledge, or communication' (1999: 94). Hardt underlines the gendered nature of affective and immaterial work and suggests it might be an opportunity to revalue women's work and liberate them (1999: 100), and that work creates 'communities and collective subjectivities' for women (1999: 99–100). This both crosses over and is at odds with Arlie Hochschild's study of emotional labour as work which is not recognized as such (1983). Hardt's idea that new kinds of labour produce emancipatory opportunities is contrasted by Marx and Arendt, who critique the 'theoretical glorification of labour' (Arendt 1998: 4) both in the modern and postmodern periods. The above assertions are key to this book's evaluation of whether female citizens were empowered by work in post-war Italy.

Sectors and geographical considerations

This book does not imply a homogenous Italy where working women's experiences were unaffected by their geography. The geographical scope of the films' reach is difficult to ascertain because we do not have geographical details of the films' receptions. However, it is interesting to note that all the films specify their setting and, except the *mondine* films, these settings are invariably urban centres like Rome, Turin, or Milan. This reinforces my argument in Chapters 5 and 6 that working women were strongly associated with the modern urban space.

The industries that this book examines have been largely determined by the availability of films and interviews relating to them. My methodology was consequently to first find a body of coherent filmic sources on women in a given sector, then to ascertain suitable oral history opportunities in that same sector and finally to assess the originality of any research into women working in these sectors. The sectors I examine span very different areas of work, from agricultural to artisan and into the more ambiguous area of religious work. This gives wide disciplinary interest and relevance to the research. For instance, an online article published in *The Conversation* on my research on *mondine* (Derounian 2018a) drew the interest of scientists at Cornell University working on the System of Rice Intensification as well as enquiry from journalists in food and travel writing.

The oral history case studies of this book are, for practical and industrial reasons, geographically restrained: the northern 'rice belt' towns of the *mondine*, Bologna and Rimini for seamstresses, and Rome and its environs for women religious. Despite the geographical focus of my interviews, in the case of seamstresses and particularly women religious, interviewees had come from and lived all over Italy, expanding the scope of my enquiry. Additionally, this book briefly acknowledges how geographically specific history and identity can influence representations and recollections of women's work. The geographical and sector-focused approach of this book means that it addresses a critical gap in scholarship on women's work, providing the opportunity to draw out parallels between industries and areas.

Existing scholarship

Women and work

Canonical works on post-Second World War Italian women's history have proved to be excellent contextual sources for my study of women's work.[8] In her essay in Morris's book, Rebecca West notes how in Italian post-war domestic manuals 'the new times are acknowledged, but the overwhelming impression [...] is a world that would be much more liveable if women would simply return to their traditional roles [...] and would stop creating complications for society in their desire to work outside of the home' (2006: 27). This quote is exemplary of the useful insights which historical works on women and Italy provide for this book on women's work. Francesca Bettio's study, *The Sexual Division of Labour: The Italian Case* (1988), is crucial to how I identify women working in typically 'female' sectors and the impact this had on their representation and self-image. Bettio notes that in twentieth-century Italy 'only major disruptions "external" to the labour market seemed able to break the customary resilience of sex-linked job divisions' (Bettio 1988: 37), supporting my hypothesis that there was a reflexive relationship between sociopolitics and women's choice of professional roles. Laura Ruberto's transnational study of Italian women's work in post-war Italy and America (2008) is particularly informative in its study of the *mondine* and is a key source for Chapters 1–3. Similarly, Rosella Ropa and Cinzia Venturi's *Donne e Lavoro, Un'identità Difficile* (2010) is useful for its geographical focus on *mondine* working in Emilia Romagna, and the cultural attention given to working women in the post-Second World War period. Underpinning my analysis is evidence from these texts that can be used to assess how representations and oral histories reflect or reject dominant historical narratives. For example, in Chapter 6 on oral histories with seamstresses, one interviewee told me how her father experienced her employment and financial gain as a humiliation (Torri 2016). Bearing in mind Tambor's argument that 'processes of "re-feminization" of women as serene managers of children, households, and budgets, and "re-masculinization" of men' (Tambor 2014: 15) were fundamental to the post-war period in Italy, we see how interviewees evoke such discourse.

Scholarly literature on women's work is much ampler in the periods preceding and following 1945–65, supporting Willson's observation that the post-war period, particularly after 1950, is 'perceived [by feminist historians] as a boring gap between the excitements of the Resistance and the resurgence of second-wave feminism' (2010: 118).[9] Willson's own scholarship focuses on women's work under Fascism ([1993] 2002), highlighting Fascism's contradictory attitudes to women's work and the lasting Italian anxiety over women's extradomestic work.[10] I use insights from historical texts on Fascism to assess how representations and oral histories reference and break with previous discourse on women's work. For instance, in Chapters 4–6 on seamstresses, I draw on De Grazia's observations about the fascist encouragement of women into acceptably 'feminine' roles such as 'nurses, seamstresses, or social workers' (1992: 166). This fortifies my argument that seamstresses' work after the Second World War was regarded as less transgressive than female work in emerging or traditionally 'male' sectors.

There is also a greater wealth of historical studies on women in specific industrial sectors, often because employment sectors were so gender-divided. Bettio notes that in 1901, '89 per cent of total female labour was concentrated in 22 per cent of all listed occupational entries' (1988: 39) and that this sexual division of labour continued into the latter half of the twentieth century. I discuss the sector-specific texts which inform my study in their relevant chapters. I limit myself here to drawing one representative example to the reader's attention. In March 2018, the publication of the article entitled 'Il lavoro (quasi) gratuito delle suore' ('The [almost] free work of nuns') (Kubacki 2018) in the Vatican newspaper *L'Osservatore Romano* caused a global shockwave. Journalist Marie-Lucile Kubacki used contemporary interviews with women religious to argue that their work is undervalued. Both Kubacki's methodology and argument underline the timeliness of this book, using women's own words to address the representation and valuation of their work. Throughout the book, sector-specific enquiries like Kubacki's are drawn upon to inform and inspire my analysis.

Oral histories, career narratives and women's work

In the Italian context, oral history studies of women's work are scarce. Luisa Passerini's work *Torino operaia e fascismo: Una storia orale* (1984) is particularly instructive in using oral history to study subaltern subjects and work. The urgency of Passerini's argument for studying oral histories of women's work is supported by Betti who herself has produced studies on oral histories of women's work (2015). Betti condemns 'the highly masculine narratives of the events put forward [...] both by historiography and collective memory' (2015: 311) in the post-war period, a problem that this book aims to address. Vanessa Maher's book (2007) is a formative example of an oral history project that not only presents evidence from interviews but also analyzes interviewees' lexical choices. Maher's examination of interviewees' descriptions of their work as 'dream' or 'passion' inspires a similar discussion in Chapters 6 and 9 of this book. In an Anglophone context, Sangster's investigation of the value of oral history for recording women's participation in Canadian manufacturing supports Passerini's and Betti's convictions that 'oral history offered a means of integrating women into historical scholarship' (1994: 5).

Relating to these historical oral history studies is research on women's career narratives. Laurie Cohen's work *Imagining Women's Careers* (2014) emphasizes how career narratives are constitutive of subjects' past and present identities, as well as reflections of historical and contemporary society. This evaluation of women's oral histories as both historical and contemporary artefacts is one of the fundamental goals of this book. An example of this can be found in my analysis of the *mondine*'s modern-day fame, and my contention that the current political climate is one of the reasons for their foregrounding of antifascist activity in interviews.

(Working) Women in cinema

The quest for literature on the filmic representation of Italian working women has produced few results. Ruberto (2008) investigates cultural representations of Italian migratory female workers, and Elisabetta Babini's article studies portrayals of nuns in melodrama (2012). Bonifazio looks at portrayals of work in Italian and American propaganda of the post-war reconstruction period, taking a comparative approach to representations of male and female work. Bonifazio's assertion about women's work being confined to feminized tasks (2011: 45) draws our attention to *how* work is feminized. This book considers Bonifazio's claim that female professionals are 'either overtly sexual or stereotypically frigid' (2011: 49), asking what might motivate sexualized portrayals of female professionals. Mary Wood suggests that post-war film allowed women to 'explore how to combine work and family' but that these narratives were 'experienced as profoundly disorientating' (2006: 60–61). Arguments like those of Bonifazio and Wood inspire this book's investigation of how semiotic strategies like focusing on women workers' bare legs, or showing scenes of workers having miscarriages, are ways in which films feminize and problematize female workers.

In his investigation *Le donne, la famiglia, il lavoro nel cinema* (2011), Carlo Carotti laments that his study 'was not easy [because] the three themes [of women, family, and work] follow on from and mingle with one another' (2011: 7). Carotti identifies a key point here; that working women are rarely allowed to be portrayed or understood predominantly as workers. It is perhaps for this reason that investigations of representations of women's work in this period are usually minor sections of studies on *auteurs* or female stars. Examples of these might include Gundle's critique of Silvana Mangano in *Riso amaro* which focuses closely on the actress' body (2007: 143–47), or Calisto Cosulich's analysis of *Anna* (1951) as a forebearer of Alberto Lattuada's later foray into sex films (1985: 52). However, narrower investigations of the films in this book have been useful and are discussed in the chapters that they inform. My research is unique in making an analysis of portrayals of women's work in diverse sectors its central purpose.

Although not explicitly concerned with women's work, there are several film studies texts which have made a significant contribution to this book. The first of these is Mary Wood's book (2005). Wood includes a chapter on gender representations and gender politics, in which she outlines how, in the post-war, 'the Censorship Commission and the Catholic Church caused problems for films that projected a pessimistic view of the Italian family, and therefore women's traditional role. Female power became a sign that something was amiss' (2005: 155). Wood's argument informs this book by indicating the role of national and religious institutions in setting gender norms, and the contentious nature of portrayals of female power.

Of equal importance is literature which discusses the significance of female star figures at this time. Richard Dyer's definition of 'star signification' (1998: 1) is deployed several times in this book and is valuable in drawing out the intertextual meanings which actresses brought to their portrayals of working women. For instance, by studying Anna Magnani's star signification in the context of her role as a nun in *Suor Letizia*, I argue that the character's eventual digression from religious to maternal is forecasted by her existing signification as mother of the Italian nation.

Similarly, the legacy of equating women with the nation in cinema has been fundamental to my analysis of women workers. It was Nira Yuval-Davis who first unravelled women's national symbolism in her work *Gender and Nation* (1997).

Her thesis that 'gendered bodies and sexuality play pivotal roles as territories, markers and reproducers of the narratives of nations' (Yuval-Davis 1997: 39) is echoed in the literature on the post-war Italian context. Gundle notes that the 'connection established in post-war cinema between the female body and the landscape was crucial insofar as it formed a basis for the "rebirth" that was so frequently invoked in the period of reconstruction' (2007: 145). Elsewhere, the instrumentalization of female characters, specifically female *working* characters, to bear notions of national war guilt through film has been criticized by Danielle Hipkins (2014, 2016).

Cinematic context

From my research in the Cineteca di Bologna, I found 21 films released between 1941 and 1965 which indicate female professional protagonists in their title or listing details.[11] These films span a number of genres, directors, and release dates, begging the question: how did the cinematic context influence representations of working women?

Post-Second World War Italian cinema is perhaps best known for neorealism. This genre, with its portrayals of the supposed gritty 'realities' of the post-war nation, brings a political conscience to portrayals of working women. Neorealism was decried by a number of commentators at the time, including writer and journalist Guido Piovene, whom Bonifazio cites as describing neorealist films as 'an exhausting confession of all our sores' (2011: 29). The desire to represent female workers within this canon of misery and reconstruction is discussed in Chapter 1 on *Riso amaro* (1949). In reaction to gloomy neorealism, in 1949 minister for entertainment Giulio Andreotti famously called for 'fewer rags, [and] more legs' (Franco 2008: 52) in cinema, and thus hailed a new wave of cinema in the form of pink neorealism, light comedies, and melodramas, all of which used female characters and their bodies to attract audiences.[12] Bonifazio argues that the Italian state used film to 'surveil […] desires by controlling people's social and sexual behaviours' (2011: 29–30). If we consider this in the context of a desire to return to traditional gender models, it is not difficult to see why so many post-war films struggled with the representation of female workers. Although all different in character, the book argues that neorealism, comedies, and melodramas are motivated by the desire to reassure rather than threaten the status quo, and therefore portray working women in ways that neutralize the threat they pose to social order.

The influence of censorship and Catholicism in cinema should be noted. Daniela Treveri Gennari has produced a comprehensive study of Vatican influence over post-war cinema (2009), and in this work, she notes the tension between imported

American and homegrown Italian films. Despite ideological opposition to the female models proposed by US film, the Italian film industry, 'for the sake of its own financial stability and well-being, needed to produce a popular genre cinema' (Treveri Gennari 2009: 8). This meant that during this period, Italian films often exploit decidedly un-Catholic features, like women's bodies, whilst bringing female characters back to conservative narrative conclusions. An example of this is the protagonist of *Anna* (1951) who is shown dancing provocatively and engaging in extramarital sex, before becoming a nun. Treveri Gennari summarizes the restricting grip of the Church when it came to portrayals of women, saying 'all of the female characters of the films banned by the Centro Cattolico Cinematografico are to a certain extent the image of that immorality from which the Roman Catholic Church wanted to free the cinema: *working women*, prostitutes, singers, and dancers' (2009: 130, my emphasis). This book argues for a consideration of films within their cinematic context in order to fully understand the motivating factors and effects of their portrayals of working women.

Book structure

The book is organized into three distinct sections: *mondine*, *sarte*, and *religiose*. Each section is divided into three parts, including a brief contextual introduction, a chapter on filmic representations, and another on oral histories. The first section (Chapters 1–3) presents the *mondine*, looking at how their representations and oral histories interact with post-war politics and notions of nationhood. This section is particularly inspired by Yuval-Davis's work (1997) on women as symbolic of nation and collectivity. Chapter 1 introduces the *mondine*. Chapter 2 analyzes the films *Riso amaro* (De Santis 1949) and *La risaia* (Matarazzo 1956), discussing how *mondine* in film symbolize the notions of collectivity, solidarity, and antifascism and how this marries with their instrumentalization by the political Left. Chapter 3 continues this investigation, studying how interviewees echo and internalize cinematic identities and left-wing discourse. Focusing on the assassination of Maria Margotti, the last part of the chapter investigates how the commemoration of Margotti reflects wider trends in the cultural and collective memory of the *mondine*.

The second section (Chapters 4–6) studies *sarte* or seamstresses, with particular attention to their relationship with modernity. These chapters draw on concepts from feminist geographers Gillian Rose (1993) and Doreen Massey (1994) to ask how space and place are fundamental expressions of gender relations. Chapter 4 introduces seamstresses in post-Second World War Italy. Chapter 5 studies the films *Sorelle Materassi* (Poggioli 1943), *Le ragazze di piazza di Spagna* (Emmer

1952), and *Le amiche* (Antonioni 1955), looking at the interplay between national change, modernity, and representations of women. Chapter 6 examines oral histories of seamstresses. Engaging with literature on career narratives, I argue in this chapter that seamstresses occupy a peculiar position as modern female professionals in a traditionally feminine occupation, and investigate how this manifests in their identity construction.

The final section (Chapters 7–9) addresses women religious. This section is interested in the ambiguous position of women religious as workers, assessing how they might be considered transgressive and emancipated female figures in the post-war period. Chapter 7 introduces women religious in post-war Italy. Chapter 8 studies the films *Anna* (Lattuada 1951), *Suor Letizia* (Camerini 1956), and *Lettere di una novizia* (Lattuda 1960), notes the boom in films portraying women religious in post-war Europe and offers some hypotheses for why this might be. Chapter 9 presents oral histories of women religious from three different Roman convents, observing how women religious recount their professional lives, blurring the boundary between religious, emotional, and professional work.

This book is the first to make a cross-sector analysis of women's work in the post-Second World War period by bringing filmic representations into contact with oral histories. The capacity of films and oral histories to reflect historical realities and discourse has already been elucidated, as has the neglect of studies of women as workers in this period. This research sheds light on how women felt about their work, how it affected their identities and how it related to wider social change. Similarly, the book connects cultural products and lived experiences to show that the sea change and political evolution of women's existences went far beyond their gaining the right to vote in 1946. Operating within the fields of Italian, gender, memory, film, and oral history studies, this book makes an original and important contribution to the study of women's work and its cultural value.

NOTES

1. See, for example, *Miss Italia* (Coletti 1950), the first episode of *Siamo donne* (Guarini 1953), and *Villa Borghese* (De Sica and Francolini 1953).
2. See, for example, Bosio (1996), Passerini (1984), and Gribaudi (1987).
3. Five of the 447 members of the Consulta who drew up the Constitution were women (Tambor 2014: 1).
4. These documents show the addition of insurance, working hours, statutory holidays, workplace canteens, etc. Maternity regulations were included in the collective agreements from 1948, allowing women six months' leave, as well as two-thirds of their full pay for a duration of three months and six weeks (before and after birth).

INTRODUCTION

5. Jo Labanyi (2007) has undertaken a similar project on cinema-going and oral histories in Spain in the 1940s and 1950s. See also the seminal works on cinema and memory relating to filmic stars by Annette Kuhn (2002) and Jackie Stacey (1994).
6. See, for example, Pierre Nora (1989, 1999, 2006, 2009, 2010), Aleïda and Jan Assmann (1992), Maurice Halbwachs (1925), and Astrid Erll (Erll and Nunning 2010; Erll and Rigney 2009).
7. For a critique of the reflectionist model, see Graeme Turner, *Film as Film* (1988: 129).
8. See Morris (2006b), Willson (2010), Pojmann (2013), Tambor (2014), and Ginsborg (1990).
9. On women's resistance work, see Bravo and Bruzzone (2000).
10. Victoria De Grazia also includes a chapter on women's work in her book (1992).
11. This number is probably an underestimation of the number of working women in films, as many may not have featured in films' listing descriptions. The films (not including those studied in this thesis) are: *Teresa venerdì* (De Sica 1941), *Cercasi bionda bella presenza* (Renzi 1942), *La maestrina* (Bianchi 1942), *Due lettere anonime* (Camerini 1945), *Un americano in vacanza* (Zampa 1946), *L'onorevole Angelina* (Zampa 1947), *Fiamme sulla laguna* (Scotese 1949), *Non c'è pace tra gli ulivi* (De Santis 1950), *Tre storie proibite* (Genina 1951), *I figli non si vendono* (Bonnard 1952), *I bambini ci amano* (Della Santa 1954), *La donna del fiume* (Soldati 1954), and *Le ragazze di San Frediano* (Zurlini 1955).
12. For a discussion of pink neorealism, see Peter Bondanella (2001: 74–102).

SECTION 1

AGRICULTURE – RICE WEEDERS

1

A Brief History of Rice Weeders in Italy

The *mondine* (Italian rice weeders) are a thing of the past. The mondine (Italian rice weeders) are a thing of the past. Despite there still being 3557 mondine in 1958, these were their years in which their labour was progressively replaced by the use of pesticides and mechanization (Negrello 2006: 17). Yet, though their role might have ceased to exist, the *mondine* are one of the few female workforces to have achieved and maintained visibility and renown in the public sphere. Over little more than the 50 years following the Second World War, the *mondina* has become 'the most idealized, most stereotyped, and most present figure' (Ropa and Venturoli 2010: 155) of working women in the post-Second World War period.

    These days, if you ventured towards one of the numerous rice plains spanning Italy's northern regions in the month of May you would likely be awed by the glassy surface of its flooded fields, broken only by the ripples created by a lone harvester. Travel back to the 1940s, however, and you would be met with a different scene altogether. In fact, perhaps moments before laying eyes on a *mondina*, you would hear her song with her companions in the fields. Upon squinting across the mirrored square of the rice field, you would be arrested by lines of perhaps hundreds of women, bent over and submerged to the thighs, toiling to cultivate the crop. Beyond this evocative image, the *mondine* were much more than picturesque muses for the rural nostalgic. They represented a unique all-female, working-class, and highly politicized workforce. They were one of the only labour forces to gain concessions under Fascism. They were active members in the struggle against Nazi-Fascism during the Second World War. Seasonal *mondine* travelled, sometimes hundreds of kilometres, to work for 40 days away from their homes at a time when women only left the family sphere upon marriage. Perhaps for all of these reasons the *mondine* have become both celebrated and instrumentalized in national memory. The subsequent chapters interrogate how and why these remarkable women became symbols of a nation.

Pre-Second World War

It is generally acknowledged that rice began to be cultivated in Italy in the mid-fifteenth century, and was reportedly brought to northern Italy in the form of a sack of rice gifted by the Duke of Milan to the Duke of Ferrara in 1475. Rice production was and is centred around agricultural zones in the North, including Vercelli, Novara, Milan, Pavia, and further to the East, Bologna, Reggio Emilia, Ravenna, and the Veneto. These areas are called Italy's rice belt and stretch along the irrigated land flanking the river Po (Figure 1.1). Between 1450 and 1900, the areas suitable for rice plantations increased significantly, thanks to greater irrigation from the Cavour canal, opened in 1866. Between 1870 and 1940, modernized production methods also meant that farmers were able to increase the yield of rice crops whilst maintaining the same surface area of their exploitation. At the turn of the nineteenth century, Italy was Europe's largest rice producer. By the dawn of the First World War in 1914, each *mondatura*, or rice harvest, brought about one hundred thousand *mondine* to Italy's rice belt. Between 80 and 95 per cent of those employed in the rice harvest were female (Zappi 1991: 10).

The gender division of labour in the rice fields dates from 'at least the seventeenth century' (Ruberto 2003: 5). Female rice workers were referred to as *mondariso*, *mondatrici* or *mondine*. Since the latter term is currently the most popular, it is the name I elect to use in this book. Why were women chosen to work rice? Some say

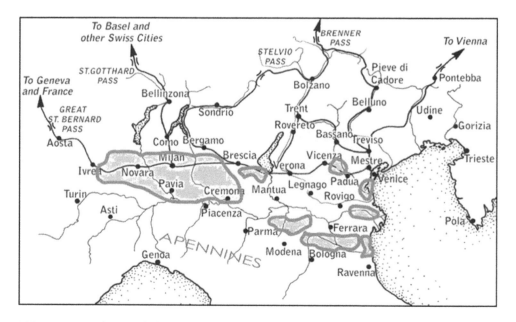

FIGURE 1.1: Italy's rice belt. Personal drawing, Flora Derounian, 1 January 2017.

that labour in the rice fields was easier than other rural jobs (Marano, *Il maggio delle mondine* ['Mondine's May'], 2011). while others conjecture that other, heavier agricultural tasks also had to be performed over the same *monda* period and thus male agricultural labour was unavailable. Others mention the efficacy of employing women, who were paid a fraction of men's wages (this may also explain why children were employed for the *monda*). Others still argue that women's bodies were better suited to the task, with supposedly nimble fingers and flexible backs. There are also those who argue that the seasonal and shift nature of rice work meant that it fit well with domestic responsibilities and childcare (Zappi 1991: 17).

While the first records of rice workers' protests date from the mid nineteenth century (Zappi 1991: 61), rice itself became politically charged with the dawn of Fascism, and the regime's push for autarchy, promoting rice as a national crop. Far from being crushed like other workers' movements, under Fascism there were 'some successful strikes carried out by women rice workers between 1927 and 1931' (Pojmann 2013: 21). The coming chapters will focus on the *mondine* living and working after Fascism. The legacy of the *mondine*'s political and industrial activism is a key focus of these chapters, revealing their links to the Second World War Resistance and their anti-state activity. The post-Second World War working woman was both controversial and essential, transgressive and modern; and nowhere is this tension more evident than in the *mondine*.

Work and conditions

'Dante was not aware of the work of the *mondine*; but if he had been, he would have included it as a punishment in one of his circles of hell' (Cortese 1953: 40429). So Senator Giuseppe Cortese described rice weeding in 1953. What exactly was the nature of the hellish work evoked by Cortese? Practically speaking, the work of the *mondine* was performed in three stages: 'in May we sowed the rice seeds and at the end of June or July we went in to weed it. Then in October, we harvested' (Zagatti et al. 1998). The most intensive period for the *mondine* was the famous *quaranta giorni di monda* ('40 days of rice harvest'). This was the period between May and July in which a large – partly migratory – workforce was required to *pulire* ('clean') or *disinfettare* ('disinfect') the rice, removing the parasitic plants which grew among it. In the sources, I study the weeds known as *erbacce* and *giavon*, although Elda Gentili Zappi alleges that there are 'numerous' species of weeds that hinder rice growth (1991: 1). The weeding process allowed the crop to flourish. Manual rice weeding was far preferable in terms of yield to the earlier and cheaper practice of sliding a wooden board over the rice plants in order to destroy weeds. It was, however, a physically demanding if not torturous occupation. Veronese Doctor Giovanni Zeviani maligned the 'lives of pain, [...] their crumbling constitutions and the fact that they are, in fact, like elderly women at just thirty years old' (Marabini in Castelli et al. 2005: 7).

As rice cultivation expanded, the necessity for larger seasonal workforces meant that from the early 1900s landowners began to bring in *forestieri*, or temporary workers. These *mondine* are those who have received the most representation and cultural memory, most notably in fiction film. Non-local workers lived on-site in accommodation provided by landowners and were often from nearby urban centres, working for families who needed the extra income to live, or occasionally, like the protagonist of Marchesa Colombi's book (*Mondine*, 1878), for a dowry. Significantly, the *forestieri* were often drafted in by landowners when local workers went on strike for better pay and conditions. This stoked the desire of local workers to form cooperatives and buy out private landowners. These tactics drew distinct lines between local and seasonal rice workers. It is perhaps unsurprising that local groups of *mondine* are more studied than seasonal workers; they are less disparate and identify more strongly as a social and political group. I agree with Laura Ruberto's statement that we should acknowledge the 'power of migratory labour as integral to national identity' (2003: 6). Certainly, the remarkable influxes of seasonal workers made a significant mark on cultural representations of *mondine*. For example, Giuseppe De santis was said to have been inspired to make *Riso amaro* (1947) after having come across floods of seasonal mondine returning from the harvest at Turin train station (Lizzani 2009).[1]

Songs

If you watch Netflix, you have likely heard one of the *mondine*'s songs, although you may not have recognized its heritage. The traditional partisan song 'Bella Ciao', sung by two characters of the Spanish Netflix drama *La Casa de Papel* (Pina 2017), is an excellent example of how the political content of the *mondine*'s songs is able to cross generations, nations, and media. The songs of the *mondine* were inspired by many sources, including folklore, military, traditional, and political songs. Songs were used in the rice fields to motivate and organize the workforce, 'just as one who is tired of walking might prop themselves up on a stick' (Viganò in Castelli et al. 2005: 13–14). Not only did their songs relieve boredom and fatigue but they served a pedagogical purpose 'transmitting the main elements of socialist propaganda and proselytism, creating a kind of group consciousness' (Castelli et al. 2005: xviii). Technically, too, a *mondina* cannot sing alone. Her songs are not simple unison chants but complex, polyphonic, and responsive. One *mondina* summarizes the power of their songs saying 'singing engaged us' (Marano 2001: n.pag.). Here, the dual sense of the word 'engagement' hints at both the motivation to work, and the political impulse to protest which interweave in the *mondine*'s songs.

Cultural representations

The *mondine* are one of the only all-female workforces to be widely commemorated across cultural materials, including literature, art, and film. While I would question Ruberto's assertion that they 'have been significantly neglected in Italian history' (2003: 4), their representation has been problematic. The *mondine* have been the subject of a considerable amount of cultural and academic enquiry, yet the nature of that enquiry has scarcely been examined. The *mondine* have been reported in newspapers, narrated in novels, described in public and political discourse, depicted on screen and reincarnated in contemporary choirs, represented in fiction films, interviewed in documentaries, and so on.

Prior to the release of *Riso amaro*, Marchesa Colombi wrote the book *In Risaia* in 1878 about a seasonal *mondina* who goes to work in the rice fields to earn a dowry for herself, and Ada Negri published a number of poems in her volume *Fatalità* (Negri 1897), which mention the *mondine*. In the late nineteenth century, Angelo Morbelli also produced several paintings – *Per ottanta centesimi* (1895) and *In risaia* (1901) – showing *mondine* wearing long skirts to perform their work. Even pre-*Riso amaro* materials conjured a highly eroticized image of the *mondine*. For example, writer Carlo Emilio Gadda recounted how the *mondine* 'came toward us, svelte, languid, bare-footed, with blouses of sky blue or such a vivid red that they would drive even a bull mad' (1937).

These artefacts alone allow us to trace the evolution of the *mondine*'s image; in cultural materials following *Riso amaro* we commonly see *mondine* wearing shorts and stockings like the film's protagonist Silvana. *Riso amaro* was a launchpad from which cultural representations of *mondine* sprung in the post-Second World War era. The release of the film was almost contemporaneous with the assassination of the agricultural worker Maria Margotti in May 1949 at a peasant protest, and Margotti's shooting interacted with the release of *Riso amaro* in the media furore which followed both events. *Riso amaro* was so controversial that it motivated politician and journalist Antonello Trombadori to write a denunciation of the film in the Communist publication *Vie Nuove*. This prompted a national debate over the film's morality that played out in the pages of *L'Unità* and saw interventions from heavyweights like Senator Francesco Leone. Following *Riso amaro* and Margotti, the *mondine* were captured in press photographs, the artist Renato Guttuso – whose partner Marta Marzotto was a *mondina* – produced the publicity brochure for *Riso amaro* and paintings showing the *mondine* at work in the fields, and in 1956 Matarazzo released copy-cat film *La risaia*.

The national left-wing newspaper *L'Unità* played an important role in rendering the *mondine* visible to the public in the period following the Second World War; writer and journalist Renata Viganò regularly published pieces on the *mondine*, most notable of which is her yearly commemorations of Maria Margotti's assassination in the official magazine of the Union of Italian Women (Unione della donna Italiana – UDI) *Noi donne*. Viganò also published her book *Mondine* in 1952. Ruberto notes that publications regarding the *mondine* were frequently funded and written by left-wing political or trade union publications (2008: 49). Ruberto's comment reinforces the argument of the coming chapters that the *mondine* have been exploited for political and industrial symbolism. The *mondine* have also become symbolic of regional and local identity. Their link to northern Italy, and more specifically to the minor towns of its rice belt, have meant that '*mondine* (and not peasant workers more generally) have had two monuments dedicated to them; of Attilio Gartmann in Novara, and of Agenore Fabbri in Vercelli, both of which can be found outside the respective city's train station' (Castelli et al. 2005: 18).

Since 1965, the *mondine* have remained part of the Italian cultural imaginary, aided by documentaries, oral history projects and musical studies such as those discussed in Chapter 3. Choirs of ex-*mondine* have flourished in recent times, making appearances on national television, touring the country, collaborating with famous contemporary musicians, and even being invited overseas.[2] For example, the choir featured in the documentary *Di madre in figlia* (Zambelli 2008) collaborated with folk band Modena City Ramblers, world music ensemble Fiamma Fumana, and were invited to perform at the Festival of Colours 2007 in Detroit. Ruberto also describes another performance by a *coro delle mondine* at the Bologna Sogna music festival in 1996 (2003: 12). The *mondine* are, therefore, an example of rich, unusual, and lasting commemoration of female labour force. To understand *why* they may have gained this status, it is apt to study *how* they have been described in memory.

Political heritage

'More than one [*mondine*] faced death not only on the battlefield, but also before the firing squad: they fell with their heads high and shouting their social and patriotic beliefs' (Imbergamo 2003–04: 220). This statement, made by ex-partisan Senator Cino Moscatelli in 1953, highlights how the *mondine* were celebrated for their participation in the Second World War Resistance. Their association with antistate and anti-Fascism has its roots in a rural working-class legacy of left-wing activism.

Even before the Second World War, the *mondine* had strong associations with the Left. Around the early 1900s, there was an effort by left-wing activists to organize the rural working classes. Socialist students, for example, went to rural areas in Lomellina in southwestern Lombardy to spread the socialist message and set up leagues that functioned much like trade unions to protect agricultural workers against capitalist farmers. Although the *mondine* were not a formalized political group, they were certainly politicized, with their own newspapers *La risaia*, *Mondariso*, and *Risaiola*. In my research, I have come across a number of *mondine* publications, not all of them consultable, such as *Mondariso* (one example of which is available at the Istituto Gramsci in Bologna), as well as *La risaia*, which is widely referenced and quoted in Imbergamo's 2014 work, and Ropa and Venturoli (2010: 73) also mention '"*La risaiola*" published in Lodi (1919)'. *Mondine* frequently belonged to political organizations like the Unione delle donne italiane (Union of Italian Women), the Partito Comunista Italiano or PCI (Italian Communist Party), the Partito Socialista Italiano or PSI (Italian Socialist Party), and other civic working-class institutions like the Case del popolo (People's Houses, which were working-class community centres). They had particular links with the Socialist party formed in the 1890s, and were a key focus of the party's generalized support of agricultural workers (Zappi 1991: 77). Socialist organization of the *mondine* was, in some regions more than others, highly sophisticated, with leagues and socialist leaders at the helm, 'none of whom were women' (Zappi 1991: 89).

Perhaps because middle or upper-class women 'had far more exposure than working-class or peasant girls and women' (Willson 2010: 64), the *mondine* were distanced from pre-war Fascist rhetoric. They undertook successful rebellions under Fascism (Pojmann 2013: 21), gaining 'numerous provisions' (Ropa and Venturoli 2010: 156). Specifically, they obtained discounted travel to the rice fields and the assurance that they would be transported in train carriages rather than animal wagons, improved accommodation and food provisions, and better pay for overtime and holiday work (Ropa and Venturoli 2010: 156). The *mondine* also actively contrasted Fascist and Nazi interests through civil resistance. The summer of 1944 saw the 'mass desertion of the rice fields' as the *mondine* refused to provide food for Fascist or Nazi occupying forces (Imbergamo 2003–04: 216).

The *mondine*'s connection to the Left is historical. In the post-Second World War context, these historical allegiances became all the more important because, as Willson notes, 'party membership was often an all-embracing social identity, shared by [...] whole communities' (2010: 130). I argue in the coming chapters that the all-embracing political identity of the *mondine* emerges clearly from my sources, where class, political and historical identities converge. The Left exploited any event which might exemplify the oppression of the working class by the state. The shooting of Maria Margotti is just such an event.

NOTES

1. Ruberto affirms that 'rice workers do not conform to standard notions about the composition of labour groups. As seasonal migrant women working outside of the home, they are by definition an unusual group' (Ruberto 2003: 6).
2. Ruberto also describes another performance by a *coro delle mondine* at the Bologna Sogna music festival in 1996 (2003: 12).

2

Earth and Rebirth: Filmic Representations of Rice Weeders

On the rice plains of northern Italy are the indelible traces of the hands of millions and millions of women. Their hands have tended these fields for 400, 500 years. Those same hands that patiently thread needles and nurse newborn babes.

Riso amaro (De Santis 1949)

This is the declaration made at the very beginning of the film *Riso amaro* (De Santis 1949). It conjures and confirms Nira Yuval-Davis's observation that 'women are often constructed as the cultural symbols of the collectivity' (1997: 67). The symbolism of women as collective, and responsible for a nation's conscience and future is the focus of this chapter, assessed here in the films *Riso amaro* (De Santis 1949) and *La risaia* (Matarazzo 1956).

The question of women as symbolic of collectivity is particularly suited to both the time period between 1945 and 1965, and to the *mondine* as a workforce. Women in Italy had proven on a large scale during the Second World War that they could support, shape and renew the national labour landscape. The idea of women bearing the nation was not abstract for those living in the aftermath of the war. Leslie Caldwell recognizes Italy's 'extensive iconographic and cultural histories' of creating 'equivalence between women, the land and the nation' (2000: 136), and Stephen Gundle notes how the 'connection established in post-war cinema between the female body and the landscape was crucial insofar as it formed a basis for the "rebirth" that was so frequently invoked in the period of reconstruction' (2007: 145). The *mondine* are these women; connected to both landscape and labour they are drawn by film into notions of nation building.

It is the earthiness of the *mondine*'s work that mirrors notions of nation and reproduction, and thus made them desirable fictional protagonists. Most female stars of the 1950s emerged in 'films that situated them in rural locations and disguised them as peasants or agricultural workers' (Gundle 2007: 142–43). The chapter considers the trends and pitfalls of using women to symbolize the nation, specifically in ways which glorify their link to nature and sexuality. As Yuval-Davis notes, identifying women with nature causes them to be seen as less civilized and less sociopolitically valuable (1997: 6). This chapter assesses the impact of portraying female workers as part of nature, rather than as real-world citizens or workers.

Mondine were arguably the first all-female working collective to truly enter the Italian imagination through film. In the recent project *Italian Cinema Audiences* (Treveri Gennari et al. 2013–16), one interviewee says of *Riso amaro*, '*mondine*? We didn't even know what they were. We discovered through this film what being a *mondina* meant' (Barberis 2015: n.pag.). Although film augmented the visibility of these particular working women in post-war Italy, the notion of 'knowing' the *mondine*, or indeed any historical subject, through a film is problematic. Prolific journalist and champion of the *mondine* Renata Viganò wrote to the women themselves in 1952 that she had seen 'portraits, literature, lyrical descriptions, non-fiction: accounts and novels and colourful articles [about the *mondine*]. But your real lives, I didn't know about them' (Viganò 1952: 10). Her statement highlights how the cultural fabrication of the *mondine*'s identities was more fantasy than reality. The two films examined here, *Riso amaro* and *La risaia*, originate from different historical moments – 1949 and 1956 – and thus different sociopolitical contexts, genres, and reception contexts. This chapter first discusses the history of representation of *mondine* and the importance of *Riso amaro* as a 'memory making fiction' (Erll and Rigney 2009: 395). It explores the political significance of the films, and how this links to notions of women as responsible for national rebirth. The chapter then goes on to examine how *mondine* are portrayed as workers and women, and how these portrayals construct womanhood as natural and sexual.

In her description of the protagonist of *Riso amaro*, Giovanna Grignaffini describes Silvana as a 'rival, accomplice, seductress, seduced, guilty, innocent, object of desire, sacrificial victim, etc.' (1982: 44). Grignaffini's notable omission is a description of Silvana as a worker. The intense publicity campaign preceding *Riso amaro* quite literally pasted Silvana Mangano onto Italy's landscape, and created a furore around Mangano's body. When the film was exported to the United States, Mangano was again foregrounded as the film's key image, and pictured alongside descriptions of 'fiery beauty' and 'Italy's Rita Hayworth' (Figure 2.1).

This reflects a wider issue with scholarly analysis of the *mondine*; their beauty and association with the Italian landscape have been explored by Stephen Gundle (2007), their symbolic links to Fascism extrapolated by Ruth Ben-Ghiat (1999),

FIGURE 2.1: US publicity poster for *Riso amaro* (1949). Posteritati, n.a., 1949.

their role as neorealist subjects investigated by Elizabeth Alsop (2014). These studies, among many others, have in common the consideration of the working woman as symbolic rather than representative. In its final sections, this chapter demonstrates how *mondine* serve as sexualized metaphors.

The corpus

Riso amaro is a film so famous that it barely needs an introduction. Directed by an already-famous neorealist Giuseppe De Santis in 1948–49, and involving some of the most brilliant minds of Italian cinema at the time, *Riso amaro* was a film much larger than the sum of its parts, even before it was released. As well as De Santis, *Riso amaro* brought together successful screenwriters like Carlo Lizzani and Gianni Puccini. Award-winning author and journalist Corrado Alvaro also contributed to the script, as did prolific screenwriter Ivo Perilli. Carlo Musso worked as a writer on the script of *Riso amaro*, as well as on *La risaia*.

The plot follows protagonists Silvana (Silvana Mangano) and Francesca (Doris Dowling), two *mondine* whose fates become intertwined as they meet on the train transporting seasonal rice workers for the *quaranta giorni di monda*. Silvana is a *mondina* with a regular contract and dreams of a romantic life like those of the heroines of the *fotoromanzi* she reads. Francesca used to be a domestic worker until she became pregnant by the thief Walter (Vittorio Gassman) and ran away. She becomes a clandestine *mondina* in an attempt to escape the police who are looking for her and Walter. Francesca and Walter are in possession of a stolen necklace, which Silvana later pilfers and wears. Once she arrives in the rice fields, Francesca collaborates with other clandestine *mondine* to obtain employment contracts. However, a fight breaks out between the clandestine and regular workers as the weeding begins. Francesca successfully leads the crusade to obtain regular contracts for the clandestine *mondine*, a negotiation which is mediated by police officer Marco (Raf Vallone). Silvana is fascinated by the perceived glamour of Francesca's life, and particularly by Walter, who has followed Francesca to the rice fields. Silvana purloins the stolen necklace from Francesca and pursues an ambiguous flirtation with Walter until he eventually rapes her in the fields. Silvana becomes in thrall to Walter, while Francesca attempts to warn her off. Meanwhile, Marco initially courts Silvana, who is uninterested. The drama reaches a climax when Walter persuades Silvana to flood the rice fields as a diversion while he steals the harvested rice. Francesca and Marco realize what is happening and give chase to Walter and Silvana, confronting them in the farm's abattoir. Inside the abattoir, Francesca explains to Silvana that she has been duped by Walter and that the stolen necklace he has given her is a fake. Silvana turns on Walter, shooting him. Shortly after, at the celebration marking the end of the rice harvest, Silvana commits suicide by throwing herself from one of the farm buildings just after having been voted 'Miss *Mondina*' by her colleagues. In the closing scene of the film, Silvana's *mondine* colleagues scatter a few grains of their rice earnings on her lifeless body. As the film ends, Francesca and Marco walk into the distance together, looking towards the future.

La risaia was released in 1956 by Raffaello Matarazzo and has largely been forgotten by audiences and critics alike. In academic study, *La risaia* is most often mentioned in enumerations of Matarazzo's melodramatic oeuvres, and barely ever studied in its own right.[1] Even in instances where scholars endeavour to analyze *La risaia*, it is usually done in relation to *Riso amaro*. This is because *La risaia* is widely regarded as 'a clear retracing of *Riso amaro* […] reworking every one of its ingredients for guaranteed success' (Uffreduzzi 2017: 74) (Figure 2.2). The plot

FIGURE 2.2: French publicity poster for *La risaia* (1956). Avoir-alire.com, n.a., 1955.

of *La risaia* sees Elena (Elsa Martinelli) leave her urban home to work in the rice fields. Little does she know that the owner of the rice fields, Pietro (Folco Lulli) is her estranged biological father. Pietro realizes Elena is his illegitimate daughter upon seeing her and goes to visit her mother, who confirms his suspicions. Meanwhile, Elena catches the eye of Pietro's playboy nephew, Mario (Michel Auclair), who attempts to seduce her by driving her into the remote countryside. Elena escapes from his clutches and runs into Gianni (Rik Battaglia), a local mechanic who agrees to drive her home. Gianni and Elena begin courting, but Pietro's interest in Elena arouses Gianni's suspicions, and he eventually accuses her of having a relationship with Pietro. The couple break up, and at the party marking the end of the *quaranta giorni di monda*, Elena decides to drown her sorrows. Mario seizes the opportunity and again attempts to rape Elena. Just in time, Gianni hears her cries for help and breaks into the barn where the two are struggling. A fight ensues and ends when Gianni accidentally kills Mario. Pietro arrives on the scene and decides to hand himself in as the guilty party in order to grant Gianni and Elena the freedom to marry. The film ends with Pietro being driven off by the police while Elena looks on at the man she has just learnt is her father.

Political significance of the films: Context, genre, reception

Both *Riso amaro* and *La risaia* are materials which contribute to the cultural and collective memory of the *mondine*. While they form a 'body of reusable texts, [and] images [...] whose "cultivation" serves to stabilize and convey society's self-image' (Assman and Czaplicka 1995: 132), they also create 'shared versions of the past' (Erll and Rigney 2009: 15). An example of this interaction can be found in the fact that real *mondine* were used as extras in *Riso amaro*, and were used to provide advice to the crew. In the documentary *Sorriso amaro* (2003), several of the ex-*mondine* recount their experience as extras, feeding back their memories into the collective and cultural sphere. Inspired by New Cinema History (Chapman et al. 2007; Maltby et al. 2011), we will now explore how the films' historical contexts, genres and receptions affect how their representations of working women entered the popular imaginary.

Carlo Lizzani, who co-wrote *Riso amaro*, acknowledges the links between the sociohistorical context of 1949 and the film, which exhibited 'all of the moments of worry, individualism, and the descent into consumerism and neocapitalism that would later be seen' (2009: 87). In his book, Lizzani mentions American influence through the Marshall Plan, the attempt on Togliatti's life and the election of the Christian Democrats in 1948 as historical features which influenced both the film and its reception. The film was produced as Antonio Gramsci's *Prison Notebooks* began to be published and widely read, another fact which intensified interest in left-wing cultural activity.

The film was also topical in terms of labour history; the late 1940s and early 1950s saw the beginnings of protective labour legislation in Italy. Yet, the deleterious effect on workers of industrialization and neoliberalism (1990: 186–87) caused the working classes to dub this period *gli anni duri* [the hard years]. Lizzani acknowledges how in *Riso amaro*,

> we confronted the social conflict head-on, it weaved through the whole story. [...] It revealed the effect of the intense exploitation of the *mondine* (their working hours and piecemeal pay) and the unrest this caused in the workforce itself, poisoning relations from within.
>
> (2009: 35)

There has been some suggestion that *Riso amaro* also put 'the problem of work and social issues at the heart of cinema' (Morreale 2011: 264), and showed 'an Italy in which women were present in the workplace and not only in the drawing rooms of old-fashioned films' (*Sorriso amaro* 2009: n.pag.). I would be critical of both of these statements. Although labour conditions are addressed, the films are more interested in women's symbolic value than their lived experiences.

Where *Riso amaro*'s immediate post-Second World War context poises it at a moment of profound national change, *La risaia* was made in 1956 in a more stable political atmosphere. Emiliano Morreale says of *La risaia*, that 'any trace of social enquiry was eliminated' (2011: 276), a reading which I would contradict. What is remarkable about the two films' political significance is that although both present class struggle, only *Riso amaro* is remembered as a political film. *La risaia*, like *Riso amaro*, is a tale of a subaltern heroine who works for her own emancipation and that of her colleagues. As honest workers, she and Gianni are oppressed by members of a dominant class (Mario and Pietro), but resist them and finally gain emancipation. Although the film does not explicitly comment on American influence in Italy, it expresses similar anxiety over changing gender norms and social structures. What makes *La risaia*'s tale less incisive is its lack of novelty or relevance to its sociohistorical context. Marcus describes the mid late 1950s as characterized by 'ideological complacency' (2000: 339). The potential for a popular revolution and the political sensitivity of capitalism and foreign influence in Italy had somewhat passed out of popular discourse by 1956. There was a stable Christian Democrat government in power, and Italy was moving towards the individualist and consumerist dynamic of its boom years. Matarazzo's altogether more peaceable *mondine* are no less reflective of ideas about nationhood than De Santis's; it is simply a more complacent nation that they are reflecting.

Another way in which *Riso amaro* was politically charged was in its genre. In an interview in 1960 with *La table ronde*, De Santis declared the aim of neorealism to be to 'redeem our guilt [by] taking a hard look at ourselves and telling ourselves the truth' (Ben-Ghiat 1999: 84). Truth is evidently a goal of *Riso amaro*, which in its opening sequence imitates newsreel footage. Neorealism's supposed truthfulness was controversial because it manifested in often gloomy portrayals of the nation, which elicited 'telegrams and missives which ordered these Italian films showing only rags and misery not to be circulated abroad' (Lizzani 2009: 89). We must ask ourselves whether the 'truthfulness' of neorealism extended to its portrayals of working women, and if not, why not? Elizabeth Alsop has argued of *Riso amaro* that 'post-war cultural production in Italy can readily be seen to have served fantasmatic and even mythopoetic ends' (2014: 28). *Riso amaro*'s portrayals of women's work play into these mythopoetic ends. In a seemingly oxymoronic move, *Riso amaro* also straddled the genre of melodrama, presenting exaggeration and excessive emotion in contrast to the supposed reality of neorealism. Rice workers lent themselves to these two contrasting genres; they were a politically active subaltern workforce ripe for bearing the symbolism of tumultuous post-war Italy. Yet, as many scholars have repeated, melodrama both addressed and featured women and was thus an apt genre for a film about female workers.[2] Both these choices of genre come at the cost of realism in portrayals of women's work.

By 1956, neorealism had been overtaken by more sunny and appealing genres. *La risaia* was the contemporary of light comedies by Dino Risi and Mario Monicelli, and light-hearted narratives by Luciano Emmer. Both *Riso amaro* and *La risaia* exhibit melodramatic features like heightened emotion, ill-fated romance and corrupting sexual desire. *La risaia*, however, had a more commercial pull, thanks to its use of cutting-edge colour and cinemascope filming techniques (Bisoni 2015: 239). These technical choices may account for the film's ample use of wide panning shots of women working in the rice fields. *La risaia* swings between an ambition for realism and Matarazzo's roots in melodrama, somewhat glossing over the gritty 'realites' that *Riso amaro* represented. These issues of genre demonstrate the subtle difference between *Riso amaro* and *La risaia*: while one film sought realism and emotion in its genre, the other deployed more commercial strategies to interest audiences.

Despite *La risaia*'s audience-grabbing full-colour aesthetic, Matarazzo's melodramas – of which he was the grand master – had begun to seem increasingly 'transparent and a bit old-fashioned' to audiences of the late 1950s (Uffreduzzi 2017: 64). Critics extended their scorn of Matarazzo's chosen genre by saying of the film, 'a [*fumetto*] comic book-style film by Raffaello Matarazzo will always be a comic book-style film by Raffaello Matarazzo' (Anon. 1957). This critique reflects a general scorn for traditionally popular female cultural materials like the '*fumetti*' and the photobook story '*fotoromanzi*' in a male-dominated critical context. Again, a disconnect between critical and popular tastes regarding genre at the time of *La risaia*'s production may account for its cool reception.

The historical context and genre of *Riso amaro* set the stage for it to become a 'memory making fiction' (Erll and Rigney 2009: 395), whereas *La risaia* continues to be deemed an outmoded remaking of the former. The reason for this, it could be posited, is that 'what is needed is a certain kind of *context*, in which [...] films are prepared and received as memory-shaping media' (Erll and Rigney 2009: 295). *Riso amaro* enjoyed the influence of 'media representations [which] prepare the ground, leads reception along certain paths, [and] opens up and channels public discussion' (Erll and Rigney 2009: 138). One such representation was the publicity poster of Mangano standing in shorts in a rice field, which was put up all over Italy before the release of the film. Consequently, and unlike *La risaia*, we could argue that *Riso amaro* has come to be what Pierre Nora describes as a *lieu de mémoire*, a 'significant entity, whether material or non-material in nature, which [...] has become a symbolic element of the memorial heritage of any community' (Nora and Kritzman 1996: XVII). This poster and its image of Silvana in the fields became the memorial heritage of the *mondine*.

Proving the canonic nature of the poster image of *Riso amaro*, *La risaia* was promoted with an almost identical picture abroad (Figure 2.2). Unsurprisingly, Matarazzo was accused by critics of creating *neorealismo d'appendice* [copycat neorealism]. Critics of *La risaia* used terms like 'a copycat story' (Casadio 1990: 111), and 'a facsimile, in melodramatic form' (Spinazzola 1974: 119) when comparing it to *Riso amaro*.

In a more general sense too, the films' box office takings attest to their varying impacts on cultural memory. Understanding film-viewing figures in post-war Italy is a complicated science, as Christopher Wagstaff (2007) explains; a film with unimpressive box office figures may in fact have been seen extensively in second or third run or parish venues, and vice versa. In the case of neorealism, there was a marked difference between critical and popular receptions. *Riso amaro* recorded 385 million Lire at the box office (Chiti and Pioppi 1991: 310) and was one of 1949s biggest box office earners. Particularly abroad, *Riso amaro* 'came out as a box office champion' (Michelone 2009: 26), with American audiences preferring it to other Italian neorealist works like Vittorio De Sica's *Ladri di biciclette* ['Bicycle Thieves'] (1948). Perhaps most striking is the longevity of *Riso amaro*'s reception. In the 1990s, the film was named among the '100 best films of all time' ['I 100 migliori film di tutti i tempi'] by *Radiocorriere TV* (Michelone 2009: 27). The film also impacted upon successive behaviours of *mondine* and media alike; one critic observes that *Riso amaro*'s portrayals of the *mondine*, 'had a strong influence both on how the *mondine* were represented – from then on they were always portrayed with their legs out and wearing short shorts "alla Mangano" – and also how they themselves behaved' (Lucia Motti in Imbergamo 2014: 155).

Inversely, *Riso amaro* was received negatively by the Left in the period directly following its release. The main objection was to De Santis's use of American-style pin-ups, eliciting the response that 'Silvana's bare legs won't teach the working classes' (Vitti 2011: 57). Exception was also taken to the '[un]realistic picture of the world of the rice weeders' (Gundle 2007: 146). For similar reasons, both *Riso amaro* and *La risaia* were received negatively by the Catholic Church, which strongly advised audiences against the former, and deemed the latter only suitable for 'adults of fully-mature morality' (Centro Cattolico Cinematografico 1956: 117).

La risaia's box office takings were 477 million Lire. However, it took most of its revenues outside of first-run cinemas (Spinazzola 1974: 116). Figures were also boosted by inflation which occurred between 1949 and 1956 and mean that higher takings in Lire do not necessarily translate to greater viewing numbers. *La risaia* was also a rural success (with only 5 per cent of its takings coming from urban centres), again suggesting that Matarazzo was neither aiming for, nor obtaining, a film of cutting-edge social or intellectual critique (Spinazzola 1974: 116). *La risaia*'s success in second or third-run cinemas suggests that it lacked the hype of *Riso amaro*, and was a film which was eventually seen, rather than a must-see. There is markedly less critical and scholarly literature on *La risaia* in comparison to *Riso amaro*, which in itself points to a lack of public interest. However, we should recall Erll's remark that films which are not watched are valuable sources through which to study cultural memory (Erll and Rigney 2009: 138). In the context of this chapter, we might conclude that *La risaia* represented working women in a way which was less remarkable for its historical context, its genre and its reception.

Working (class) women

State propaganda films of the same period as *Riso amaro* have been shown to only portray 'the type of work [which] required "female skills": "agile light fingers, a taste for trimming and decoration"' (Bonifazio 2011: 173). Echoing this trend, the Radio Torino presenter in the opening scene of *Riso amaro* underlines how 'only women can perform' the *monda*, continuing, 'the work requires delicate agile hands. Those same hands that patiently thread needles and care for newborns'. Never is the viewer allowed to forget the gender of the female worker, whether in the focus on their bodies or in the miscarriages or sexual violence which occur as the women labour. Gundle notes that Italian film stars were adored overseas because they were 'representatives of a lifestyle that rested on clearly defined gender roles' (2007: 142). The explicit feminizing of women workers means that they reassure traditional gender orders and notions of national identity, even in a supposedly radical and socially critical film like *Riso amaro*.

One of the meanings which the *mondine* symbolize is that of left-wing, working-class struggle. The presenter of Radio Torino enumerates the kind of women who come to perform the *monda* as 'rural peasants and working-class labourers' [*contadini e operaie*]. These two classes of labourers were particularly known for their left-wing affiliation. The opening scene pans from the Radio Torino presenter to the crowds of *mondine* swarming the train station, waiting to depart. We see male workers from the FIAT car manufacturing company holding placards which declare 'best wishes to the *mondine*. From FIAT, quality motors', and 'See you in forty days. From FIAT Lingotto factory'.

One of the FIAT workers carries a box of goods, telling Walter 'last year we did a whip-around, but this year we're just bringing them some things to eat'. This exchange suggests that the FIAT workers deem the *mondine* part of a unified class of manual labourers. Not only is the aesthetic of the opening scene reminiscent of workers' protests, with whistles, placards and a slowly processing crowd, but the explicit support of FIAT workers aligns the *mondine* with a workforce well known for its antifascism, resistance participation, strong trade unions, and ties to the Communist and Socialist political parties (Baldoli 2011; Amendola 1968). Mangano too signified ties to the working class, having previously been used in electoral posters for the Democrazia Cristiana (DC) in 1948 as a factory worker dressed in overalls. Dino de Laurentiis said that it was upon seeing this poster that De Santis exclaimed his conviction that Silvana was 'our *mondina*: because she is working-class, beautiful, sweet, fresh, and young' (Kezich and Levantesi 2001: 71). All of these elements suggest that Silvana, and the *mondine* more widely, symbolized a politicized working-class identity.

Not only are the *mondine* of *Riso amaro* and *La risaia* working class, but they are in *miseria*. Roughly translatable as 'hardship', *miseria* is prominent both in the films and throughout the oral histories discussed in Chapter 3. In *Riso amaro*, Silvana says to Francesca, 'at least you've done something with your life, you haven't always been surrounded by this *miseria*'. Similarly, in *Riso amaro* we are shown the interior of the *mondine*'s transportation. The contracted workers' carriage bustles with the *popolana* [female peasant] sound of singing, chatter, and Silvana's gramophone. The atmosphere surrounding these *mondine* is of a rustic and utopic working-class female universe which reflects Yuval-Davis's claim that 'women are constructed in the role of "carriers of tradition"' (1997: 61). Sarah Culhane's (2017) typology of the *popolana*, with her regional accent and loud cries, being 'of the people' (Culhane 2017: 255), can be seen in both the films studied here. Dino De Laurentiis's comment that Mangano was 'the image of the *popolana* that we need' (*Sorriso amaro* 2009: n.pag.), even calling her a 'physico-semantic unit' (Kezich and Levantesi 2001: 72), reinforces my argument that *mondine* characters were constructed and exploited as symbols of the working class.

In contrast, the film's clandestine workers are transported in gloomy graffitied wagons with no seats. The camera pans the carriage to show a woman swigging directly from a bottle, another tending a young child and another anxiously tearing at a hunk of bread. One woman is sleeping on the floor of the train, and two more are hunched over with their faces to the wall, conveying an image of destitution and desperation. Similarly, in *La risaia*, one *mondina* remarks to Elena, 'it's obvious you really need some work, who have you left behind at home?', inferring that her work must be motivated by some personal or domestic hardship. In his analysis, Antonio Vitti describes the clandestine characters as the 'true *mondine*' (2011: 64), suggesting that film accurately represents the desperation of working women. Representing female workforces as either stereotypical traditional female peasants or desperate migrants might suggest an anxiety around women's labour participation in post-war Italy.

Work and the collective

Although there were few visible female leaders in the post-war period, those that existed were 'constructed as the cultural symbols of the collectivity' (Yuval-Davis 1997: 67). Notions of female interconnectedness and plurality tally with essentialist ideas of femininity. In the films, the *mondine*'s work is transformed into a symbolic fight for collective justice. Lizzani commented on De Santis's interest in the *mondine* that they represent 'the subordination of women, but at the same time from an archaic point of view, woman as creator of life, and woman as creator of conflict too' (2014: n.pag.). In an early scene in *Riso amaro*, a dispute is depicted between contracted and non-contracted workers. It is Francesca who acts as a creator, taking the initiative (and defying the male rule of the squad commanders), 'to integrate the clandestine workers into the legal workforce. Francesca is 'regenerated in the rice fields' (Ben-Ghiat 1999: 96), thanks to her 'assimilation of the hard work of the *mondine*' (Vitti 2011: 66). Her action, however, creates conflict between the different groups of women and is only resolved with the revisiting of a previously mentioned concept: necessity. When mediating between the two groups of *mondine*, Marco observes of Francesca, 'perhaps she has more need of work than you', and another *crumira* [scab worker] emphasizes, 'can you not see how wretched we are?' An almost identical scene in *La risaia* shows Elena taking the initiative and risking her individual gain for the collective good. The message of these scenes is one concerning forgiveness and clemency, and is perhaps a nod to the post-war pardoning of collaborators and Fascists in Italy (Ben-Ghiat 1999). This policy and the 1945 general amnesty that released most Fascists from prison was a policy supported by left-wing figures like Togliatti (Millar 1989: 18). Films discuss national polemics through the figure of the *mondina*.

The concept of collaboration in any form was politically charged in the post-Second World War period, and Francesca and Elena's solidarity with their own subaltern class rather than with a ruling elite render them left-wing heroines perfectly suited to what Silvana Patriarca (2010) describes as the myth of *Italiani brava gente* ['Italians, good people'], according to which Italians were 'a good, humane people, basically untainted by Fascism' (2010: 189). Marcus argues that instances of collaboration in post-Second World War films connote 'the ephemerality of the regional and class unity achieved by the CLN [Comitato di liberazione nazionale – National Liberation Committee]' (2000: 337). Here, Marcus evokes the cross-spectrum political consensus of the antifascist organization that temporarily governed Italy from 1944 to 1946. Both of these comparisons explain how portrayals of rice weeders as cohesive collectives chimed with the national post-war context and its need for characters who could provide unity.

The particular type of unity demonstrated in the films is left-wing in nature. For women, these ring rather essentialist, summoning ideas of women's supposedly innate propensity for nurturing, creating and sustaining. However, in both cases of conflict in the films, the solution is proposed by a masculine presence (Marco in *Riso amaro* and owner Pietro in *La risaia*). Combined with the films' emphasis on the *mondine*'s desperation and necessity, this could be read as symptomatic of anxiety around the figures of working women and their power as a collective. Danielle Hipkins observes the 'nervousness engendered by many women's ability to cope without their menfolk during the war, and the notorious attempt to re-establish the post-war status quo' (2014: 45) in film. The same could be argued for representations of the *mondine*'s work: although they gain symbolic value as a successful industrial force, a collaboration between them is made contingent on male intervention in a way that speaks of squeamishness over depicting female agency. Such portrayals suggest that although keen to present women as symbolic of nation through conservative gender models, the films still imagine women's 'nature' to be subordinate to male 'culture' (Yuval-Davis 1997: 6).

The *mondine* in the films are also linked to the iconic left-wing figure of the organic intellectual. In his work on hegemony, Gramsci argues that unlike traditional intellectuals, organic intellectuals arise 'from within and [...] [are] passionately connected to, the subaltern class' (Meek 2015: 1181). Like Francesca and Elena, organic intellectuals demonstrate 'active participation in practical life, as constructor, organiser, permanent persuader and not just a simple orator' (Gramsci 1978: 10), catalyzing their comrades into collective action. Like the film *L'onorevole Angelina* ['The Right Honorable Angelina'] (Zampa 1947), the tale of a working-class Roman woman who is elected to be a member of parliament, *Riso amaro* and *La risaia* show female workers successfully gaining class rights. Such portrayals repeat tropes of women caring for and nourishing the collective.

Impegno

The Italian word, *impegno*, means commitment, political activism, hard work, and occupation. It is a term particularly suited to the films' construction of the *mondine*'s work as blurring labour, politicization and activism. The *mondine* were recognized not only as a workforce but as a strikeforce. Historians conjure images of *mondine* 'violently coming up against the carabiniers and fascist police while crying out the names of arrested and condemned activists Gramsci, Terrani, Scorcimano, Romeda, Flecchia, Negarville, etc.' (De Lacroix 1971: 72). Wholly accurate in this sense, the films show political activism to be part and parcel of *mondine*'s work.

In *Riso amaro*, the trajectory of the two female protagonists demonstrates Marxist doctrine on the redemptive power of industrial collaboration, and the destructive path of individualism. Considering Richard Dyer's theory of star signification and the paratextual meanings of actors, even Francesca's relationship with Marco connotes and promotes the Left. Marco is played by Raf Vallone, an ex-partisan and journalist with left-wing newspapers *La gazzetta del popolo* and *L'Unità* in Piedmont. Dyer's argument (1998: 1) that stars had a 'signification' which went beyond the specific character they were portraying would support Louis Bayman's assertion that Vallone's character represents the left-wing hope 'that after the Partisan Resistance the Italian army might become a popular militia' (2011: 63).

Silvana, on the other hand, is seduced by liberalism and Americanization, manifested in the film through boogie-woogie and chewing gum. She desires individual intrigue rather than collective survival. She betrays her comrades and is transformed from a popular darling into a lifeless heap, estranged from her community. Of her character, Lizzani tells us, 'it is precisely in the character of Silvana that all of the moments of worry, individualism, and the descent into consumerism and neocapitalism [were manifested]' (2009: 87). Silvana and the burden of class and nation she bears demonstrate how women workers are used as symbols rather than representatives.

A final observation to be made of the portrayal of *mondine*'s work is their association with the military. Comparisons between the *mondine* and soldiers appear in both (pre-Second World War) historiography and film. Castelli observes 'the temporary uprooting of *mondine* during the harvest brought them close to the figure of the soldier or the conscript and also introduced into their lives elements of solidarity and class consciousness' (Castelli et al. 2005: xvii). The link between *mondine* and military is also present in the vocabulary used to describe their organization in the rice fields, with the use of titles such as *caporale* [squad leader] and *squadra* [squad] taken directly from military parlance. Military imagery also permeates oral histories of the *mondine*, with an ex-squad leader describing the workforce organization in the rice fields as 'a strategic maneuver' in the documentary *Sorriso amaro* (2003). In the films, the *mondine* are divided and named according to their local area, as in army regiments. Visually, these squads are represented in long shots marching in lines to the rice fields or linking arms to cross the treacherous ground. There are frequent references to the military in the choice of music and song in both films. In *La risaia*, the opening scene features a song which appears to make direct reference to the alpine military song '*Mamma mia vienimi incontro*'. The lyrics replace the phrase '*la mia vita militare*' ['my army life'] with '*la mia vita di risaia*' ['my life in the rice fields']. Similarly, in the scene showing *mondina* Gabriella's miscarriage, her colleagues adapt the famous '*Testamento del capitano*', an alpine military song which became widely known during the First World War for its antiwar message. Throughout the film, long shots of the women working in the rice fields are accompanied by the extradiegetic marching beat of a drum.

In *Riso amaro*, the *mondine*'s link to the army is even more explicit. The *mondine* physically replace an army unit which has been lodging in the farm buildings. Once the *mondine* take up residence in the *cascina*, the soldiers' slogans painted on the walls become the *mondine*'s own. Marco's philosophical graffiti is modified by the *mondine* to read, '*vivo morendo in ~~caserma~~ risaia, non in tempo di guerra ma in tempo di vita*' ['I live dying in the ~~barracks~~ rice fields, not in wartime but in lifetime'].

It is interesting that a group of working women should be portrayed as soldiers, arguably the symbol of traditional masculinity *par excellence*. Yet 'militaries and warfare have never been just a "male zone"' Yuval-Davis argues (1997: 93); the militarized portrayal of the *mondine* supports this. The militarization of working women supports the idea of female characters bearing Italian collective and national symbolism following the Second World War.

Solidarity

Solidarity '(*solidarismo*), charity, associationism [...] were constant themes' (Ginsborg 1990: 153) in post-Second World War Italian discourse. These notions were also essential to the popular doctrines of Marx and Gramsci, and were a key feature of working-class consciousness and struggle. In Chapter 3's oral histories with *mondine*, solidarity is a point of pride for interviewees, and this is mirrored in these films. The clearest filmic examples of solidarity can be found in instances where a *mondina* is in peril. In *Riso amaro*, the *mondina* Gabriella miscarries while at work in the rice fields. The other *mondine* instantly respond, picking Gabriella up and lying her on the bank. Their bodies form a tableau which physically and emotionally shields Gabriella.

Eventually, Francesca lifts Gabriella and carries her to the farmhouse, consolidating Francesca's transformation, 'to become a leader and, quite literally, a carrier of women' (Pierson 2008: 275). Francesca's behaviour demonstrates what Gramsci describes as the second stage of the *rapporto di forze politiche* [political power relations] and *autocoscienza* [class consciousness]; when all members of a social class recognize the need for solidarity between them (2014: XXX). The other *mondine* similarly lend their symbolic support to Gabriella by singing, in what De Santis (1987) calls a demonstration 'of secular protest opposing the brutal and infamous working conditions of women'. This episode and the 'choral peasant sharing of pain' (Vitti 2011: 71) are essentially feminine in nature and politically charged in substance. In an almost identical scene in *La risaia*, the *mondina* Angela faints and is carried off by her colleagues, whilst the remaining *mondine* intone a song of solidarity. Beyond a portrayal of unity, this incident gives space to the expression of distinctly counter-hegemonic discourse; following her departure, one *mondina* comments, 'if she hasn't come back to work in an hour she'll lose the whole day's pay', soliciting the sarcastic retort, 'of course! It's her fault if she's fainted!' Here, the women are united in their contempt for the ruling elite who dictate unfair terms of employment. In both films, representations of solidarity are feminized, revolving around fertility and physical fragility. Women's solidarity is articulated through their bodies, maternity and the earth. This is problematic because it glosses over the reality of the *mondine*'s coordinated, committed, and sometimes violent industrial action.

On the other hand, Silvana of *Riso amaro* is understood to represent the antithesis of solidarity. Although represented in opposition to Francesca's journey from individualism to collaboration, Silvana's betrayal of her gender and class is more ambiguous than it may first appear. Despite being coerced and abused by Walter, Silvana still protests at his scheme to steal the harvest, saying 'this rice was supposed to be given out to my companions, and it's not much as it is'. Silvana also gives away her rice earnings to Gabriella's sister, to compensate for the loss of income which Gabriella's miscarriage and incapacitation caused. Despite her wish for individual escape, Silvana still attempts to soften the blow of the theft for her companions. Of this act, another *mondina* says 'she might be a little crazy, but she's not bad'. This observation is important to understand Silvana's character, and recalls the character of Padron 'Ntoni from *I Malavoglia* (Verga 1881) who was apparently De Santis's inspiration for Silvana. Padron 'Ntoni 'is a tragic figure, who is plagued by misfortune' (Pierson 2008: 278) in his struggle for economic and social advancement. The alignment of Silvana's story with this cult novel underlines the film's core questions around economic morality and attributes Silvana's moral decay and betrayal to the hardship of her life, rather than any innate evil. Silvana herself confirms this when Marco asks her, 'boogie woogie, romantic novels, Grand Hôtel magazines, can't you think of anything else?', responding 'that's just it, it's all I think of from dawn 'til dusk while I'm to my knees in water'. This statement reinforces the notion that Silvana's sin is motivated by the misery of her daily life. Her betrayal is to be pitied and read as a critique of the false promises of neoliberalism, rather than a condemnation of her character.

In their moments of collaboration, *mondine* in film express left-wing critiques which would not have been out of place in the mouth of Togliatti; criticisms of the ruling classes, and assertions that crime is motivated by poverty. This echoes historiography which observes that the *mondine* found ideological and practical solutions to their hardship through Socialism (Castelli et al. 2005: 4). As I will argue in Chapter 3, it is important to recognize the political nature of representations of the *mondine*, because it reflects the under-exposed political character of women's work (Rossi-Doria 2000: 361). Yet, the use of women to articulate wider political and national concerns diverts attention from their professional identities, often in ways which draw focus to their bodies. Women workers in film are trapped in the metaphor of their bodies, and the *mondine* are no exception.

A final example of the *mondine*'s purported solidarity is in their songs. The songs of the *mondine* are unique in their polyphony, connoting and necessitating collaboration. In her analysis of chorality in neorealist film, Alsop defines chorality as 'a device used by directors […] to project or enact an imaginary [group], acting to evoke amplitude and solidarity; to convert individual affects or experiences into collective ones' (2014: 28). These features are important to this section, to argue that portrayals of *mondine* reflect a fantasy, glorifying the left-wing concept of solidarity.

The first instances of chorality in both *Riso amaro* and *La risaia* are the grand sequences showing the *mondine*'s departure to the rice fields. These moments are marked by the merging of individuals into one collective force. In *Riso amaro*, the commentator for Radio Torino tells listeners, 'they come from all over Italy. The rice harvest mobilises women of all ages and from all professions'. We are then told we will hear 'the word of a *mondina*, one among many'. However, instead of hearing the voice of one *mondina*, the interview is drowned out in the collective song of the women as they depart. Here, the film demonstrates the primacy of representing the *mondine* as collective rather than individuals. This scene uses a crane shot to follow the women mingling together like the tracks of a train. Similarly, the opening scene of *La risaia* shows wagon-loads of *mondine* arriving at the farmhouse, singing and chatting in a way which mingles diegetic and extra-diegetic sound. Upon arrival at the farmhouse, the noise increases as the *mondine* jump from the wagons and run towards their dormitories, shouting and thronging. The audiovisuals of both these opening sequences reflect the convergence of many women into one collective, 'powerfully dramatiz[ing] the kind of collectivity that becomes a central theme of the film' (Alsop 2014: 31).

Chorality is also deployed in the scenes showing the *mondine* beginning their work. In *Riso amaro*, they sing and shout as wide-brimmed hats are distributed. Again, both the visuals and audio serve to collectivize the women; the hats lend them a homogenous group identity – particularly when shown from above – reflecting the chorality of the sound, to generate the impression of amplitude and solidarity. In *La risaia*, the women are similarly shot in wide panning shots, showing them linking arms, with crooning diegetic singing. Again, visual and audio effects mirror one another to portray the *mondine* as a cohesive group.

Bodies and sexuality

Silvana's thighs, clad in shorts and ripped stockings, have become the symbol *par excellence* of female work and the *mondine* in the post-war period. Why, though, such an intense focus on the bodies of the rice workers? Marcus observes that sexualized female figures provide a canvas 'on which post-war filmmakers will base their critique of the national self' (2000: 330). A similar assertion could be made of filmic *mondine*. The work and the identities of *mondine* are reduced to sexualized bodies both by films and later by scholars and critics. This historical focus on the sexualized bodies of female workers makes me loath to contribute to it; and yet it must first be described in order to then critique it.

Promiscuity has become associated with the *mondine* as a labour force, and film has played a primary role in this, particularly spreading this reputation beyond the narrow lands of the rice belt. Historically, the *mondine* were migratory workers, existing temporarily away from the moral anchors of the family, Church, and local community. These conditions have meant that commentators have often sought and found evidence of promiscuity among *mondine*. Historians of the *mondine* have noted a 'moral depravation [...] fed by promiscuity between men and women' (Crainz 1994: 4). The inclined position in which the *mondine* toiled, and the atmospheric conditions of heat and humidity which influenced their dress, may also have contributed to a sexualization of their work. De Santis himself described the rice fields as, 'an explosion of female sexuality exposed to the sun all day long, of detonating bodies, boiling breasts, inviting laps, […] naked thighs, […] vigorous calves, inflamed and juicy mouths' (1987: 122). Sexualizing the *mondine* objectifies them for a fantasized spectator, diverting their identity as workers. It also expresses the implicit threat of female work, highlighted by De Santis's violent vocabulary, more reminiscent of battle than of agriculture.

The way that *Riso amaro* and *La risaia* were marketed meant that women's work was eclipsed by their sexuality. American publicity for *La risaia* bore the tagline 'Men are animals … I'm here to work – nothing more!' (Betz 2013: 501) (Figure 2.3).

This summarizes the impossibility for the *mondine* of maintaining a professional identity when so many phantom male eyes look on. Both *Riso amaro* and *La risaia* support Mark Betz's claim that the films betray 'a frequent concentration on […] female sexuality, as iconic markers of the films' purported content' (2013: 501). The sexualization of the *mondine*'s work is important because it reflects a discomfort or disinterest in working women, diverting their identity. Such discomfort is manifest in the films' receptions. *Riso amaro* passed the censors, but it did not measure up to the 'intransigent standards of Vatican censors, who, in order to preserve the public from the tempting sensuality of Silvana, included the film in their list of prohibited works' (Vitti 2011: 54). Similarly, critics of *La risaia* commented on the 'complacency with which the film needlessly displayed numerous girls in skimpy costumes' (Casadio 1990: 112). However, the box office

FIGURE 2.3: US publicity for *La risaia* (1956). Cinematerial, n.a., 1955.

earnings of both films should not be ignored. We should be aware of a discrepancy between the theoretical moral reception of female sexuality by some critical and religious institutions, and the reception of these female characters by the public and industry. We might hypothesize that while for critics and religious authorities working women and their promiscuity were condemnable, for the public, they were experienced as perhaps more appealing and less of a threat to their quotidian.

If Catholic and left-wing organizations hoped for innocent, rustic portrayals of the *mondine*, the films do little to serve this end. In both films, the protagonists and supporting characters display problematized sexual behaviour in a way which eclipses their working and political identities. To cite just one example in *Riso amaro*, protagonist Silvana flirts suggestively with Marco and Walter, sneaking off with both to deserted outbuildings. Even before this, we are aware of her sexual knowledge as she negotiates with the squad leaders, using coquettish glances and drawing their attention to her body to manipulate them, only to slap away their hands, with a curt 'hands off' when she obtains her wish. Silvana's rape itself is also framed as proof of the danger of female sexuality. Silvana is quite literally beaten with the stick of her own sexuality; originally used to keep him at a distance, the stick is snatched by Walter and ultimately used against Silvana. Whilst capitalizing on women's sexuality, the films simultaneously demonstrate its danger, leaving women vulnerable to exploitation. Ruberto reads Silvana's rape as signifying 'not only a defilement of her body but of all *mondine*' (Ruberto 2008: 46). This conclusion is supported by Marcus' analysis of female characters in De Sica's *La Ciociara* (1960), who, she claims, 'become texts onto which history inscribes its most atrocious incursions' (2000: 335). The message is clear: women who use their bodies as sexual capital risk not only their own personal downfall, but that of their class, gender, and nation.

Dance is a key way for female sexuality to be exploited and therefore punishable. Dance scenes allow for *mondine*'s bodies to be gazed upon and sexualized, while credibly maintaining them in their folkloric, working-class setting. The nature of dance means that women's bodies become the focus of the gaze of both intra- and extra-diegetic spectators. Laura Mulvey (1975) theorized the use of the cinematic apparatus to create a sexualizing heterosexual male viewpoint. In other words, the spectator is made to view films' content through the eyes of a straight male. Mulvey calls this the male gaze and argues that it is objectifying, and diverts the meaning of female subjects into objects of sexual pleasure without agency.

In *Riso amaro*, Silvana is introduced to spectators through boogie-woogie. Here, the camera pans from Francesca and Walter who openly stare, across the marvelling faces of onlookers, to pan slowly up Mangano's body. This technique demonstrates that 'in their traditional exhibitionist role women are simultaneously looked at and displayed, with their appearance coded for strong visual and erotic impact' (Mulvey 1999: 837–38). This scene of women preparing to migrate for work becomes a perversion of their purpose; the *mondine* are not there as workers but as bodies to be gazed upon. All dance scenes in the film are moments of suspense and corruption articulated through the female body. Mulvey reminds us that the male gaze acts to 'freeze the flow of action in moments of erotic contemplation' (1999: 837–38). It is this erotic contemplation which causes disaster in the films. Walter's attraction to Silvana catalyzes a chain of events which lead to her downfall, and her boogie-woogie is the impetus for their first meeting. It is also the direct precursor to violence in the form of an armed police chase. In a later scene showing the *mondine* climbing over the wall of the farm to consort with men, Silvana dances a boogie-woogie. This scene is the first time we see her directly participating in criminality, as she wears the necklace she knows to be stolen. Silvana's dance aptly demonstrates the problems of displaying and sexualizing the female body by linking it to exploitation and corruption.

Moreover, we are shown that Silvana's sexual behaviour is in fact commonplace among the *mondine*; in a long shot panning the length of a high wall, we see the *mondine* receiving messages from and consorting with men who have congregated around their lodgings. One of the men declares in a message, 'I've been thinking about you for twelve months', and another 'we danced together last year', suggesting that these women engage in brief seasonal relationships with local men. Later, we see the same scene at night. If we are in any doubt of the sexual nature of these encounters, one man suggests to his partner, 'I've found a little spot under the poplars that's a marvel, tall grass up to here!' In this way, the promiscuity of the *mondine* in *Riso amaro* is portrayed as endemic.

In *La risaia* too, promiscuity is repeatedly referenced and condemned. The *mondina* who proposes to Mario that he should remedy his initial preference for Elena and court her is ultimately jilted in a scene where he violently twists her arm. In *La risaia*, *mondine* who use their bodies to gain a fast pass to social promotion are also condemned by Gianni, who says 'you let yourselves be enchanted by fast cars and then [...] they leave you high and dry'. He seamlessly elides this observation with a story about a *mondina* who was found 'strangled in a ditch'. At the end of *La risaia* another *mondina* recounts how, when she asked her sweetheart if he would marry her, he responded, 'why would I buy a cow when milk is so cheap?' These statements follow a legacy of holding women responsible for male sexual violence. If women's sexual transgressions are supposed to mirror the moral wartime transgressions of the nation, these examples make it clear that women bear the burden of the collectivity and its honour. Bearing such meanings subsumes the *mondine*'s identity as workers.

Similarly to *Riso amaro*, in *La risaia* disaster follows moments of dance. In a scene showing Elena dancing with a female companion at a local *fête*, Mario

FIGURE 2.4: Elena (Elsa Martinelli) dances in *La risaia*. Still from *La risaia*, Matarazzo, 1955. Italy. © Minerva.

notices her and attempts to break in on the dance, but is rejected. Mechanic Gianni arrives on the scene and starts a jealous fight to protect Elena's honour. Again, dance catalyzes male violence. Later, the film climaxes in a scene where Elena becomes drunk, shows her legs, and dances closely with several men. Mario arrives, and this time the threat of his gaze is apparent in a close-up. This scene presents striking aesthetic similarities with *Riso amaro*, including an exact copy of a shot of Silvana where Elena lifts her hands to her face, exposing her armpits and chest to the camera's gaze. This scene sets in motion an attempted rape and the consequent murder of Elena's attacker. We can observe in these filmic examples that dance equals an opportunity to express female sexuality but that sexuality is the catalyst for corruption, moral transgression, and violence.

Bodies and landscape

The films are full of tableaus of women springing like poplars from the surface of the rice paddies, and rolling in the very earth from which the rice sprouted. There is a particular insistence on the connection between female bodies and the elements, whether when Silvana is whipped and raped against a poplar under the driving rain, or when in both films different squads wrestle in the mud of the paddies. The historical tendency to equate women with the national landscape is one identified by scholars (Caldwell 2000: 136), and in post-war Italy was invested with ideas about potential and rebirth of a damaged nation (Gundle 2007: 145).

It is said that neorealist films were preoccupied with the face (Dalle Vacche 1996: 53). Yet, more than the face, *Riso amaro* is interested in the female body. The first words of the film insist that 'on these plains can be found the indelible traces of the hands of millions and millions of women', and Mangano was 'presented as a creature of the earth' (Gundle 2007: 145). *Riso amaro* marked the beginning of an international obsession with Mangano's body. Her body type was known as *maggiorata fisica* and connoted voluptuousness. Mangano's case draws our attention to a special feature of Italian identity: a nation so assimilated with natural bounty could only find lasting sex symbols in women whose bodies reflected this. Mangano, like Sofia Loren, only became truly iconic because of her début in rural film. The popularity of *popolana* figures like Loren and Anna Magnani and their '*naturalezza*' and '*autenticità*' (Gundle 2017: 254) corroborates this. Other actresses whose bodies lacked such associations – like Lucia Bosè – did not reach the same symbolic status. Yet, Mangano herself grew to hate her association with the *maggiorata* body type as 'an image which she seemingly wanted to erase' (*Sorriso amaro* 2009: n.pag.). The contradiction between Mangano's celebrated and hated body recalls Marcus's arguments that Silvana's death was symbolic of 'the doubleness of the sexualized body politic' (2000: 337). On one hand, women's bodies are celebrated as representative of nation and rebirth. On another, the sexualized female body is corrupting and must be destroyed, preferably by the woman herself. This dynamic means that women are disempowered by the metaphorical meanings they are made to bear.

Although Elsa Martinelli and *La risaia* reached nothing like the same level of stardom as Mangano, we can observe some effort to make the same connection between her body and the landscape. *La risaia*'s colour filming in CinemaScope showed 'landscape and womanhood as connected, each an instrument of nature's bounty' (Betz 2013: 501). If, as Gundle asserts, the post-war context and need for rebirth were the keys to Silvana's symbolism and *Riso amaro*'s immediate cultural canonization, it is mobility and modernity which Martinelli's body represents. Her waif-like frame and sharp features reflected the new American-style models of femininity to arrive in Italy. Her body is gazed upon in a similar way to Mangano's. Yet, 'she has shaved armpits' (Morreale 2011: 278), a fact which differentiates her both in aesthetic and sociohistorical context from Mangano. Martinelli was eventually labelled as a *ragazza yé-yé*, meaning a '60s pop-girl' (Uffreduzzi 2017: 75). Her esthetic is easily assimilable with the dynamic, outward-looking 'bounce-back Italy' (Morreale 2011: 277) that 1960s Italy so wished to be. Yet as Mangano's case previously showed, the exploitation of the female body for national symbolism is problematic. Lizzani described Mangano like 'a beautiful animal or a beautiful tree' (Gundle 2007: 147), betraying how representing mondine dehumanized those who did so as fleshy metaphors rather than real representatives.

Conclusion

Riso amaro and *La risaia* are unique in presenting not only female working protagonists but also collectives of female workers. Their characters show women as influential and engaged. *Riso amaro* is particularly responsible for the renown of the *mondine* in Italian society. However, the films' portrayals of women's work are problematic. *Riso amaro* features a scene in which Silvana poses for a photojournalist and is joined by Marco, to the disgust of the photographer who cries 'it was better before, men ruin art'. One can't help feeling that both De Santis and Matarazzo shared this view, and used women's bodies to carry the symbolism of their art or politics. Silvana's death in *Riso amaro* – suicide being, 'above all, a woman's solution' (Loraux 1991: 8) – showcases the intense symbolism of the female body. Her corpse is left on the soil of the rice field and is covered with handfuls of rice from her co-workers, reabsorbing her into her class and collective. But Silvana was doomed from the beginning; because of her female body, she could not be anything other than sexualized and subsequently corrupted. Just as Silvana's body manifests 'rival meanings she cannot reconcile' (Marcus 2000: 339), in the period following the Second World War, the *mondine* could not be anything other than symbolic of the nation. In the next chapter, we will see how the *mondine* reproduce discourse around their role in national rebirth in oral histories. The two films studied here exhibit how the bodies of the *mondine* were used to assimilate women with national identity, landscape, and (re)production. Filmic portrayals heighten the idea of women as 'fertile ground' and displace labour onto the fertile female body. The concept is conservative, refiguring the female worker as bearer and mother of the nation.

NOTES

1. Morreale studies *La risaia* as a melodrama (2011), as does Bisoni (2015). Uffreduzzi makes a comparison between dance in *La risaia* and *Riso amaro*, among other films (2017).
2. That melodrama was a female genre – in the sense that it had a female audience and was female-centred – has been repeated by many scholars like Bayman (2014b), Cardone (2012: 9), and Morreale (2011).

3

Martyrs Without Medals: Oral Histories of Rice Weeders

Descend the stairs at the Confederazione Generale Italiano del Lavoro (CGIL) archive in Bologna and you will find yourself standing before a framed image of Maria Margotti, a woman who was assassinated at an agricultural protest and has become synonymous with Italian rice weeders' political activism. Yet, although Margotti was only an occasional *mondina* and like the *mondine* as a wider group, her memory has been instrumentalized over time to symbolize a fantasized peasant class, an antifascist nation, and an idyllic left-wing legacy. As already discussed, the *mondine* served this post-war purpose for 'the formation of newly cleansed collective identities' (Ben-Ghiat 1999: 83). Speaking to Micaela Gavioli, archivist and researcher at the Unione delle donne italiane (UDI) in Ferrara, she said, 'personally I don't think that there is one collective national memory of the *mondine*. The figure of the *mondina* has been exploited in some way by all parties […] stuffed with stereotypes and rhetoric' (2015). This rhetoric has been particularly politicized, and in the 1950s, it became common 'to identify [the *mondine*] as shorthand for female combatants, activists, who were left-wing and antifascist' (Imbergamo 2003–04: 219). This chapter analyzes oral histories from a number of different sources, including two corpuses of interviews generously shared with me by Gavioli (1999) and Cristina Ghirardini and Sussana Venturi (2011). The chapter also takes interviews from three documentaries, *Il maggio delle mondine* (Marano 2001), *Sorriso amaro* (Bellizzi 2003), and *Di madre in figlia* (Zambelli 2008). As well as providing contemporary evidence for the instrumentalization of the figure of the *mondina*, this chapter asks why recollections of the *mondine* are so prevalent in cultural and collective memory. The chapter also, within its limits, aims to fill in aspects of the *mondine*'s identities which have been sacrificed to political symbolism. Research on the *mondine* is important because it both reveals women's contributions to post-war Italy and asks why and how society remembers working women.

To explain the *mondine*'s legacy, we should look to both historical and gender discourses in post-Second World War Italy. Particularly, in the context of the Cold War and the anticommunism which dominated the West, it became important for left-wing parties to reclaim and recall '"ideal" categories of workers' (Imbergamo 2003–04: 220) and their struggles. Perhaps even more than filmic representations, oral histories of *mondine* portray women as symbols of the collective, with a distinct left-wing twist which suits both contemporary and post-Second World War sensibilities. This chapter first addresses the unique value of an oral history and memory studies approach to the *mondine*, then examines how the *mondine* inscribe themselves within left-wing discourse, touching on their memories of political engagement and solidarity. The chapter concludes with a close analysis of the commemoration of Maria Margotti, suggesting how it exemplifies the contours and problems of the *mondine*'s symbolism.

The corpus

All the interviewees included here worked as *mondine* in the period between 1945 and 1965. The most substantial body of eleven interviews was collected with *mondine* from Filo, a historic rice-growing area in the province of Ferrara. The interviews were conducted in 1999 by Gavioli for her chapter in the book *Le donne, le lotte, la memoria 1949–1999; a cinquant'anni della morte di Maria Margotti* ['Women, Struggle, and Memory 1949–99; Fifty Years after the Death of Maria Margotti'] (Zagagnoni 1999). The original transcripts of these interviews were given to me by Gavioli herself at the UDI office in Ferrara. The interviews are conducted either with individuals or groups, most of whom sing in the 'Coro delle mondine di Filo "Maria Margotti"' [Maria Margotti Filo *mondine* choir]. Similarly, the music scholar Cristina Ghirardini gave me access to her recorded group interviews with *mondine*, collected in 2009 as part of her research on two *mondine* choirs in Medicina (Bologna) and Lavezzola (Ravenna). Those interviews were captured in situ in the rice fields, with the *mondine* describing their surroundings and memories of their work. Both of these collections present the challenge of not having conducted the interviews myself. This being the case, I cannot assert with authority how much interviewees knew of interviewers' specific research interests, and thus how much they modified their testimonies to suit the project. Particularly in the case of Gavioli, it seems likely that interviewees were aware of the project's focus on Margotti. I also include excerpts from some interviews with *mondine* conducted by Angela Verzelli and Paola Zappaterra for their book *La vita, il lavoro, le lotte: Le mondine di Medicina negli anni Cinquanta* (2001).

Providing both oral history and evidence of cultural memory are the recent documentaries I study. These are *Il maggio delle mondine* (2001), *Sorriso amaro*

(2003), and *Di madre in figlia* (2008).[1] Like the oral history projects of Gavioli and Ghirardini, these documentaries give a contemporary perspective on the *mondine*'s lives. I chose to include documentaries in my corpus because they act as a bridge between oral testimony and film, combining spontaneous production from interviewees and curation from filmmakers. I analyze the documentaries predominantly for their oral histories but am mindful of the filming and editing processes which differentiate documentaries from my other interviews. All three documentarists declare a common goal in their studies to 'retrieve the past' (Bellizzi 2005), expressing an explicit desire to commemorate. The filming methods employed reflect the desire to simulate natural conversations sometimes by silently observing the interaction between documentees. More often in the documentaries, there is a 'pseudomonologue' (Nichols 1992: 54), in which the interviewer and their questions are masked and the interviewee almost directly addresses the camera. If it is true that 'pseudomonologue appears to deliver the thoughts, impressions, feelings, and memories of the individual witness directly to the viewer' (Nichols 1992: 54), then I would argue that the documentaries seek to create the illusion that what they show are authentic and spontaneous instances of historical

TABLE 3.1: List of the documentaries' sponsors and affiliations. Flora Derounian, 2017.

Film	Date	Sponsors/affiliations
Sorriso amaro	2003	CGIL Marche, Programma Media Unione Europea, Film Commission Torino, Regione Piemonte Comune di Nonantola, Comune di Vercelli
Le acque dell'anima	2005	Regione Emilia Romagna, Fondazione Cassa di Risparmio di Bologna, Provincia di Bologna
Di madre in figlia	2008	Piemonte Doc Film Fund, Programma Media Unione Europea, Fondazione Cassa di Risparmio Modena (50,000 euros), Provincia di Modena
Il maggio delle mondine	2011	None stated – 'I self-financed the film, I wasn't paid and I have never made a penny from it' (Marano 2018)

recollection. Ultimately, however, the intrusion and transformative process of documentary are undeniable. In his collaboration with Ghirardini and Venturi, filmmaker Francesco Marano highlights how even the best-defined ethnographic intentions cannot erase the 'impossibility of making [oneself] invisible' (Ghirardini and Venturi 2011: 151). This is further reason to approach testimony in the documentaries as cultural memory, rather than historical reality.

It is interesting to note the sponsorships and affiliations of the documentaries. All of them (except *Il maggio delle mondine*) received support from local or regional organizations, underlining the geographical specificity of the *mondine* and their local identity and importance (Table 3.1).

Mondine, *memory and oral history*

What makes collective memory? Maurice Halbwachs emphasizes interaction in collective memory, saying 'it is individuals as group members who remember' (1980: 46). In all the sources presented here, the *mondine* provide evidence of being an interactive social group that shares and discusses memories. Indeed, Ghirardini told me that should I want to interview the *mondine* of Ravenna, only need go to a certain café on a certain day and I would find them reminiscing, as they do weekly. Such anecdotal evidence is supported by the documentary *Sorriso amaro*, which shows a group of ex-*mondine* gathered in someone's home to watch *Riso amaro* and discuss their comments and memories. Individual and group memories also interact with cultural materials in what Astrid Erll calls premediation and remediation. Erll notes that 'memorable events are usually represented again and again, over decades and centuries, in different media' and that this 'mediation' means what is understood as the 'actual event' is actually a collective patchwork of memories and representations (Erll and Rigney 2009: 392).

The interaction between real-world behaviour and cultural representations has already been noted in Chapter 1 in relation to the *mondine*'s increased wearing of shorts 'alla Mangano' (Lucia Motti in Imbergamo 2014: 155) after the release of *Riso amaro*. But, the interaction between individual, collective, and cultural memory is not one-directional; in Matteo Bellizzi's documentary, one *mondina* recounts how she was an extra in *Riso amaro*. She recalls that when she showed Silvana Mangano how to perform rice weeding, Mangano exclaimed, 'like this over and over for eight hours? I wouldn't do this backbreaking work even for a million Lire a day!' (*Sorriso amaro* 2003). This evidence highlights how individual memories create cultural memories and vice versa. The commemoration process of re-/premediation reinforces the value of my sources as an opportunity to analyze how memory builds and shapes the figure of the *mondina* over time and across different media.

The interviews I analyze here are not my own, and as such are treated especially critically. This is supported by work on interview theory that underlines how the interview process transforms the production of memory and historical reality. The underlying philosophy of this project is that interviews allow an understanding of how memory and identity are constructed, rather than giving us access to unmediated historical reality.

As stated in the introduction to this book, my choice to examine cultural and collective memory and oral histories of working women is politically motivated. The last *mondine* were young in the 1940s; we can expect the opportunity to gather their memories to expire within the next few decades. Oral histories have made the creation of the archive accessible to subaltern classes and brought out their voices. The *mondine* span a number of 'silenced' groups: (many) illiterate, working class, and female.

Women of the Left

The strongest currents of memory, both in these sources and in wider Italian society, evoke the left-wing identity of the *mondine*. This is hardly surprising: Laura Ruberto notes that when materials concerning the *mondine* appeared in the period between 1900 and 1965, they were often sponsored by political or trade union organizations (2008: 49). Their role in the Second World War Resistance movement to liberate Italy from Nazi occupation and Fascism has already been described. In oral histories, we can observe how subaltern, peasant, and left-wing identities intermingle.

What had left-wing parties done to win the support of women? Although both Democrazia Cristiana (DC) and PCI 'embraced female suffrage and created mass women's organisations' (Willson 2010: 129), it was the PCI that publically pronounced the importance of women's rights. Palmiro Togliatti saw female suffrage as an integral part of the modernization and renewal of Italy, stating, in 1945, that 'Italian democracy needs women and women need democracy' (Willson 2010: 134), a fact which is supported by famous partisan and later PCI deputy Teresa Noce's reminiscences of Togliatti doing the washing up when he came for dinner (1977). In the 1946 elections, out of a total of 226 female candidates for the Constituent Assembly, the PCI had the greatest number at 68 (the closest party to this being the DC at just 29 female candidates). Beyond the Italian party system, it is useful to remember the global scene upon which Soviet communism was unfolding. Italian left-wing women's organization UDI 'tended to view communist states, especially the Soviet Union, as open to women's emancipation' (Pojmann 2013: 4). We can see then that left-wing discourse about female participation and emancipation was not only stronger than that of other parties but evidently had an impact on female political engagement. The *mondine* were unique even amongst the women of the Left, making up the entirety of female party participation in some areas (Negrello 2000: 92–93).

The *mondine* are a group that has adhered to and internalized left-wing allegiance. The first indication of left-wing consciousness in the interviews can be found in the *mondine*'s identification with a subaltern class. Their descriptions of class are shot through with left-wing discourse which, through figures like Karl Marx, Antonio Gramsci, and Palmiro Togliatti, referenced social stratification, cultural hegemony, and revolution. It is useful to note here the vocabulary referring to class in Italian. Italian frequently uses the terms *operai* and *proletariato* to describe what we might broadly equate to 'manual labourers', 'proletariat', or 'working class'. The *mondine* often self-describe using terms like *braccianti* and *contadine*, which although they strictly refer to a rural, agricultural class of worker carry equal weight as descriptors of a proletariat. In interviews, the *mondine* seem to achieve a specific status by describing themselves most frequently as *mondine* rather than *braccianti*. Considering that the role of *mondina* is seasonal, and probably accounted for no more than a hundred total days of work per year, it would be more accurate for these women to describe themselves as part of a wider working or agricultural class. Yet, in her interviews with *mondine* Ghirardini observes that 'if they had worked in the rice fields, even for a few seasons, they would continue to define themselves as "*mondine*"' (Ghirardini and Venturi 2011: 24–25). Post-war *mondine* may have maintained an independent identity because of how they had already been commemorated. Public discourse which identified the *mondine* as shorthand for antifascist, and cultural representations of the *mondine* like *Riso amaro* (1949) may have contributed to interviewees' recourse to the identifier *mondina*. If this is the case, it exemplifies how subjects remediate their own memories and identities.

Interviewees identify more explicitly with the political Left, frequently referencing left-wing leaders or martyrs. Exemplifying this left-wing name-dropping, one interviewee recalls her mother negotiating with police officers as part of a reverse strike. When she successfully saw the police off, she said to her colleagues, 'did you see that? You never want to listen to me but I am Togliatti's sister, what Togliatti's got in mind I've got in mind too, so listen up!' (Verzelli and Zappaterra 2001: 23). In one documentary, an interviewee visiting an old barn where *mondine* had been housed begins singing, '*e con De Gasperi non si va, non si va*' ['it doesn't work with De Gasperi, it doesn't work']. At this point, her companions specifically request the refrain which she subsequently sings: '*perché è amico dei preti e dei signori, che gli venisse un cancro / vogliamo Togli-*

atti, capo del lavoro' ['because he's the friend of priests and nobles, we hope he gets cancer / we want Togliatti, workers' champion'] (*Di madre in figlia* 2008). The refrain is evidently popular with interviewees, testifying to their left-wing identity. The song makes clear their dissociation from the state, forces of order, the DC, the Church, and the upper classes. Togliatti – 'workers' champion' – is symbolic of subaltern and peasant victory. We should not forget that, as Millicent Marcus notes, in the postwar period 'a national victory for the Left [was] something not totally unthinkable' (2000: 337), and the power of the Left was reinforced by the 'intellectual magnetism' (Broghi 2011: 13) of leaders like Gramsci and Togliatti.

Interviewees in Gavioli's project also make reference to left-wing figures, producing striking examples of memories which have been distorted over time. In these interviews, participants incorrectly recall that after Margotti's assassination, her orphaned children were adopted by left-wing leaders. In one group interview, several *mondine* confidently assert, 'they wanted to sort out her daughters for life, Togliatti took one and [Giuliana] Nenni took the other' (Zagatti et al. 1998). Margotti's daughter herself says, 'there are many people who think that one of us went to live with Togliatti' (Baldini and Siroli 1998). Five of Gavioli's eleven interviews make reference to Togliatti and socialist deputy Giuliana Nenni, and several also mention the communist Rita Montagnana in relation to Margotti's funeral. This may be another inaccuracy of memory, as there is evidence of these figures attending a commemoration event for Margotti, but only anecdotal evidence that they attended the funeral itself (Figure 3.1).

Another interviewee expresses the excitement that the alleged presence of famous left-wing figures caused at the funeral, exclaiming 'there was Giuliana Nenni, Nenni's daughter, and Rita Montagnana, who was Togliatti's wife at that time. And I remember that they came down, and it was a marvellous thing, we even took photos with them' (Biavati and Biavati 1999). These statements show the important symbolic value left-wing figures such as these had for the *mondine* and the desire to foreground this in memory, sometimes at the cost of accuracy or sensitivity.

Miseria

One *mondina* tells of how she was 'married on a Saturday, and on the Monday I was in the rice fields' (Beccari et al. 2009). Another states, 'If I die for work I'll die happy' (Zagatti et al. 1998). These comments highlight the interviewees' emphasis on *miseria* (hardship) as a way to express dedication to work and a sense of class belonging. Like much rural nostalgia, references to *miseria* evoke

FIGURE 3.1: Rita Montagnana, Giuliana Nenni, and Palmiro Togliatti at unnamed event in commemoration of Margotti. Europeana.eu, n.d. Accessed 14 February 2018.

ideas of the good peasant and an 'agrarian sentimentality and moral stoicism in the face of hard times' (Ellis 1998: 27). Paola Bonifazio contends that 'the imperative of work [...] was represented as a conversion from warfare to workfare' (2011: 32), suggesting that to be an assiduous and resilient worker represented distance from Fascism and a commitment to rebuilding the post-war nation. If this is true, the *mondine* narrate themselves as idealized post-war characters, echoing the post-war representations of women workers already discussed in Chapter 1 that 'served fantasmatic and even mythopoetic ends' (Alsop 2014: 28). The other face of *miseria* is its strong connections with the land, the rural and the agricultural. The *mondine* frequently reference their dependence on the land, saying 'there was nothing, no resources: harvesting and rice work, rice work, rice work, and harvesting' (*Sorriso amaro* 2003). Others comment, 'we were peasants, workers, in the valley and the fields' (Trombetti and Fortini 1999). During Fascism, women were given symbolic responsibility for the future of the nation through the figure of the rural *massaia*. In the post-war period, the *mondine*'s associations with the land continue a discourse of restoration of the nation through rural female labour.

The work to which these women were expressing such commitment was extremely physically demanding. Yet, recollections of physical hardship or illness among the *mondine* are notably scarce in the sources. Apart from the obvious effort of pulling weeds out of flooded fields under the sun for eight hours a day, the severity and variety of the maladies suffered by the *mondine* were extensive, from malnutrition to malaria to miscarriage. Senator Giuseppe Cortese stated of rice weeding in 1953, 'Dante did not know the work of the *mondine*; if he had, he would have described it as a punishment in one of the circles of hell for farmers' (Cortese 1953: 40429). Other sources, such as the leaflet '*Mondine, difendetevi dai pericoli!*' ['*Mondine*, protect yourselves from danger!'], produced by Ente Nazionale Prevenzione Infortuni [National Body for the Prevention of Injury] (1959) also attest to the ailments of the *mondine*, one of which was even called 'the rice malady'. The *mondine*'s health has also been historically overlooked; whether concerning laws to curb malaria, or providing adequate shelter for seasonal *mondine*, profit triumphed over welfare. Farmers were generally too mean to dispense money and influential rice producers lobbied ministers and blamed peasants' immoral lifestyles. Not only are references to illness rare in the interviews in my corpus, I argue that they are absorbed and reclaimed into the *miseria* which is so central to the *mondine*'s identities.

In the entire body of interviews, there are only two quotes referencing illness. One *mondina* reflects, 'there was illness, yes. There was tuberculosis [...] but you know ...' (Beccari et al. 2009), and another says, 'we were from the area, we had the rice fields outside our front doors [...] but these poor women who came from Modena, Piacenza, Ferrara, these girls got really sick' (*Sorriso amaro* 2003). There may be some scientific accuracy to this statement, as citizens who lived in proximity to the rice fields were likely to have developed greater resistance to malaria, to name but one illness which prospered in the rice fields. The physical toll of the work is downplayed by interviewees who say, 'when I think of it now I suppose it was tiring, but remembering it is lovely too. [...] Yes, it was tiring, but it wasn't like being in the fields hoeing' (Beccari et al. 2009). Others normalize the physical price of labour, stating, 'yes, working is tiring. They say today that they work a lot [...]. We worked really hard. Today they complain, it's become a habit' (Zagatti et al. 1998). Hardship and resilience in work are reclaimed by interviewees in a sense of geographical, historical or generational belonging, consolidating their group identities. When we compare the *mondine*'s lack of acknowledgement of work-related illness to the graphic and frequent descriptions of physical pain inflicted by police during their industrial action the difference is striking. The above accounts of hardship romanticize or dismiss certain elements of working-class existence. *Miseria* is reframed as an acceptable part of the effort for post-war rebirth.

The *mondine*'s class-bound identity can also be found in accounts of conflict with their wider communities. One *mondina* remembers the reaction of a farmer's wife to one of their strikes, recalling 'the wife came outside, she was *a teacher*, she was all riled up and started to insult us; "you bunch of whores, it's not our problem if you've got children to provide for"' (Verzelli and Zappaterra 2001: 46, my emphasis). Another interviewee recounts an incident from a protest, saying 'there was a lady next to me, a *lady from the big house*, [...] and I could see she was bleeding from her arm [...]. The lady, she started insulting me, saying all sorts of things' (Biavati and Biavati 1999, my emphasis). These recollections describe the *mondine* as being at odds with members of their communities from higher social classes. These descriptions echo Gramsci's subversive practise, where 'the "people" feel that they have enemies and identify them as the so-called nobles' (1975: 17). By describing conflict with individuals of superior class or education the *mondine* consolidate their difference as working-class women resisting an unfair and oppressive bourgeoisie and its associated values.

Solidarity

External conflict with those outside the *mondine*'s social group is recounted against a background of internal solidarity. Statements such as 'we were all like sisters' (Trombetti and Fortini 1999), and 'life wasn't easy, but we were happy together, we loved one another' (Zagatti et al. 1998) are typical. One of the most endearing accounts of solidarity recalls how a certain *mondina* at the age of fifteen stashed her money in a box in the farmhouse while she worked:

> When I arrived back from the rice fields at midday, my first thought was to look inside it because I knew I had 26 Lire. I opened up, looked in the box, and discovered that someone had stolen 25 Lire [...]. But the nice thing was this [...] I was sitting there on the bed, and [the other *mondine*] went past and put in a few coins – I almost made back all of the money that had been stolen. Eh, there was solidarity, there was, there was.
> (*Di madre in figlia* 2008)

Gavioli notes that among the *mondine*, 'the links between memories are evident in the simultaneous use of the first person singular "io" ["I"], and the use of the plural "noi" ["we"]' (Gavioli 1999: 104). These testimonies show how the *mondine* blend their individual identities and memories with the collective, advocating for it as empowering. Their solidarity is also characterized by a sense of local geographical belonging made explicit in observations like, 'in places like this [...] we really like each other, because we've got a town [...] that's pretty united' (Zagatti et al. 1998).

As in Chapter 1, representations and recollections of the *mondine*'s solidarity reinforce ideas of women as embodiments of collectivity.

When asked how women behaved during strikes, several *mondine* reply 'they were all united. […] [In comparison with the men] the women were always more united' (Ghirardini and Zagatti 1998). Interviewees stipulate that 'even when Maria Margotti died we all came out [to protest]' (Trombetti and Fortini 1999). A closer reading of these citations reveals the insistence on the feminine plural forms, again reinforcing the idea of uniquely female collective action and determination even in the face of murder. It is suggested that protests provided an opportunity for a kind of solidarity which gave space to – momentarily – overturn gender norms. Interviewees highlight that, 'in strikes, the men were immediately put in prison. But they tolerated women a little more […] it's the only time they put women in front' (Trombetti and Fortini 1999). Interviewees highlighted that men are women had the same political ideals, 'of family, and always of having a few more pennies' (Trombetti and Fortini 1999), echoing the notion that 'Communists still saw emancipation as essentially an economic question' (Morris 2006b: 131) which transcended gender. The political engagement of the *mondine* is evident in testimony and historical literature, and confirmed by evidence such as the 28 June 1951 Piedmontese edition of the newspaper *L'Unità*, interviewing *mondine* about the election. The *mondina* interviewed describes how 'they promised us special trains to go and vote, but they didn't give us anything. […] They knew who we would have voted for, us *mondine*, so they made us travel miles and miles by foot' (Anon. 28 June 1951). Such statements suggest the collective identity which *mondine* felt as a political body and electorate.

A final example of solidarity which the *mondine* frequently evoke can be found in the cooperatives. These cooperative organizations were areas of farmland purchased by local agricultural workers themselves (in this case in the early 1950s) and made into businesses which managed and divided work and profit between the peasant stakeholders. One *mondina* explains how they ran the cooperatives as a form of social justice. After Margotti's daughters married, her cooperative 'paid for their furniture, it paid for everything, because they had been left destitute' (Biavati and Biavati 1999). She also explains that 'as a union we gave more days of work to those who had more need, and to all widows' (Biavati and Biavati 1999). Another interviewee describes the acquisition of the cooperative as a triumph over the ruling classes, saying 'those lands all belonged to our cooperative. The last owner to flee was Tamba, and it was a good fight to get rid of him too' (Ghirardini and Zagatti 1998). Here we can see evidence of Gramscian subversive action. The Gramscian philosophy of class consciousness and collaboration is also shown to underpin the acquisition of the cooperatives in the interviewees' assertion that 'we laid down hours of work and tonnes of grain in order to help our organisation [...] and we saw the fruits of our labour' (Ghirardini and Zagatti 1998). The cooperatives provide a concrete example of how the *mondine*'s memories align them with the collective territory and collective identity.

Impegno

The *mondine*'s activism was not simply a struggle for better pay or conditions. It had historical ties to left-wing politics, class identity, resistance legacies, antistate and anti-Church sentiment. An anecdote that Negrello includes in her history of women from the Veneto includes one priest's recollection,

> I was there in my cassock, riding a bicycle and sweating under the beating sun. A *mondina* saw me coming up [...] and exclaimed loudly 'Go and die, priest!' and I [replied] 'Ah my dear, I'm not far off ...'. [...] There was a strong organised communist presence around there.
>
> (Jori 1990: 73)

This recollection is an example of the *mondine*'s combative anti-establishment identity in memory.

Testimonies of the *mondine*'s *impegno* draw on left-wing discourse and ideals. It was only after 1947 and the breakdown of the 'wartime Grand Alliance' that Communist anti-Americanism became more strident. Concurrently, before 1947 'there are few references to the *mondine* in newspapers and, in those few instances, they are not particularly credited with contributing to the fall of Fascism' (Imbergamo 2003–04: 218). However, after 1947, the exclusion of the Left from the government meant that Communist antistate rhetoric was stepped up, and with it rose the star of the *mondine* in cultural memory. To what extent are left-wing struggles and the 'political battle with no holds barred' (Mammarella 1966: 147) between the centre (DC) and the Left (PCI/PSI) from 1947 onwards reflected in the *mondine*'s testimonies? I note Imbergamo's argument that sometimes in left-wing discourse 'claims are made about the struggles that socialism undertook *for them* [the *mondine*] and not *with them*' (2014: 151), and I deem it important to also use this section to reveal the political character of the *mondine*'s activism (Rossi-Doria 2000: 361).

As previously noted, the *mondine* have gained a legacy as key figures in the antifascist Resistance through interventions like those made in the Senate discussion of the 1953 draft law *Provvidenze a favore delle mondariso e dei loro bambini* [Provisions for *mondine* and their children]. Senator Moscatelli recalled how, during the Resistance, the *mondine* sacrificed themselves for their political ideals (Imbergamo 2003–04: 220). Moscatelli's intervention also features the false memory that the *mondine* protested arrests made of Communist leaders in 1927 by the Fascist Tribunale Speciale which was a key legal body in the development of the totalitarian regime. Yet there is no evidence that the *mondine* did protest these arrests. Moscatelli's evocation of this false memory exemplifies the intensity of rhetoric around the *mondine* as antifascists. The interviews support this. I do not wish to discredit the *mondine*'s activism here, but to show how it has become framed within a wider left-wing discourse and the myth of Patriarca's *Italiani, brava gente* (2010).

Interviewees highlight that Resistance participation was not just a struggle against a foreign invader, but a matter of class warfare:

> We felt that the struggle for Liberation was on one hand against the Germans and the Fascists but, on another, the partisans brought with them *a great hope for us as an exploited and impoverished people: the hope of redemption*.
>
> (Verzelli 2000: 241, my emphasis)

This testimony supports the idea that the *mondine*'s activism was existential first and political second (Baldoli 2011: 187). Many of Gavioli's interviewees remember belonging to partisan groups, saying, for example,

> I had five [partisans] hidden in the area around my house, and in the morning I would pretend to be going to work in the fields with a pitchfork and a rucksack, when I was actually going to give them food.
>
> (Zagatti et al. 1998)

Interviewees often align themselves with left-wing politics through their families, stating, 'my grandma explained everything to me, because she had been a league leader at 16 years old', and 'they killed my uncle, he was a partisan lieutenant' (Biavati and Biavati 1999). This sense of belonging to Resistance communities is about more than simple political views, but rather a communal identity. Interviewees Alves and Fernanda make a statement which exemplifies the crossover of politics, heritage and class identity for the *mondine*:

> Our grandmas or mothers taught us [...] party political and partisan songs [...]. Our mothers knew the songs because our grandmothers had taught them, and then there were new songs because of the war, there were the partisans, [...] and *we took the songs forward because our work was suited to them*.
>
> (Zagatti et al. 1998, my emphasis)

Alves and Fernanda highlight how the work of the *mondine* lent itself to the spirit of rebellion and resistance of the partisan identity, expressed in their song. The *mondine*'s linkage of their Resistance activity and their families could be argued to displace partisan identity from the individual to the collective. Verzelli includes the testimony of one *mondina* whose husband was given the partisan badge, but when they went to give it to her, he said 'one in the house is enough', commenting, 'I didn't have the strength to say: "I want it too"' (2000: 244). Memories in the sources underline that sometimes women's individual identities were subsumed into communal narratives of Resistance participation, attributing it more to a class or a (male) community, than to women themselves. This trend speaks to the wider 'serious omission […] of women partisans [from] conventional histories of the Resistance' (Birnbaum 1986: 49).

Supporting my thesis that the *mondine*'s foregrounding of Resistance activism was about more than just the war, they continue to cite antistate activity after the war's end. Military and police forces may no longer have been under fascist control, but there is some suggestion that fascists were recycled or maintained in the forces of order after the Liberation (Dunnage 1999: 33). Minister of the Interior Mario Scelba more than doubled the number of police forces between 1946 and 1947 and reinforced the militarized mobile battalions known as the *Celere* (Ginsborg 2001: 148). The *Celere* were known for providing rapid-response discipline in potentially violent situations such as strikes or protests and were famous for arriving on the scene in Nazi-Fascist-style Jeeps. As a result, even in the late 1940s and 1950s, forces of order were still strongly associated by many – including the *mondine* – with Nazi-Fascism and its violence. One *mondina* elides the *Celere* and the SS in her memory of a protest, remembering, 'this is something I can never forget […] even fifty years later, I must explain to you – there was the SS, that is, the *Celere*' (Bertuzzi et al. 1999). This interviewee demonstrates an elision in memory between republican and Nazi-Fascist forces of order.

In the interviews, the *mondine* express their hatred and mistrust of forces of order. One interviewee recounts, 'the *Celere* arrived and beat us up […]. I wished a plague on them!' (Trombetti and Fortini 1999). Another advises, 'never turn your back to a *celerotti*, always look him in the face to check he's not about to hit you' (Ghirardini and Zagatti 1998). This interviewee also highlighted her mistrust of the police by recounting how, after being arrested at a protest, 'at Molinella a police captain […] offered us a drink, but I refused to drink until I'd seen him take some first' (Ghirardini and Zagatti 1998). Such sentiment and vocabulary (particularly the pejorative '*celerotti*') betray a deeply negative memory of relations with the police. This is hardly surprising when we consider the weight of testimony of police violence. Recollections such as 'we took some beatings' (Trombetti and Fortini 1999) evoke police brutality. One particularly shocking testimony reads:

There was a protest, we were on our way home, and the *Celere* picked me up, and I wasn't anything to do with it that time [...]. They gave me such a beating that I thought I would lose the child, because I was pregnant.

(*Di madre in figlia* 2008)

Testimonies of police violence and the *mondine*'s antistate activism, mingled with statements of left-wing and partisan identity, support Broghi's argument that left-wing parties 'could work as magnets for all sorts of discontent' (2011: 8).

Another way in which the *mondine* demonstrate close ties to left-wing ideology is through their intellectual activism – rarely celebrated in cultural memory and scholarly enquiry of the *mondine*. The fact of being female, working class and young during wartime were all barriers to the *mondine*'s education in early twentieth-century Italy where 'post-primary female education was considered [...] problematic' (Willson 2010: 79). Beyond basic literacy, intellectual activity was not the norm for women, particularly those from the working classes, for whose families schooling removed one salary from the domestic economy. The example of the interviewee and *mondina* Paola Brandolini, who 'went to school until the *terza elementare* [8–9 years old] and although she was a good student [...] had to interrupt her schooling to "look after her brothers and the home"' (Archivio Storico UDI di Ferrara 2014: 23), is typical of many female workers at this time. In their research on women's work, Ropa and Venturoli describe the author of an anonymous letter written to Mussolini, saying 'she wasn't [...] a *mondina*, since they certainly wouldn't have had the education to write in such a way' (2010: 138). Moreover, education was badly disrupted by the Second World War and access to schooling was often impossible. Yet, not only do the oral histories show that the *mondine* were intellectually active but they also portray the *mondine* as fitting Gramsci's model of organic intellectuals, who 'arise from within and are passionately connected to, the subaltern class' (Meek 2015: 1181).

Interviewees often acknowledge the unlikelihood of their intellectual activism. For example, Giuseppina remarks, 'even though we were almost illiterate, I always had the fighting spirit' (Trombetti and Fortini 1999). Interviewees particularly link their activism with left-wing newspapers, saying 'we always gave out *L'Unità*, *Vie Nuove*, *Rinascita*, our newspapers [...]. In the morning I would go and give out the newspaper, then I would go to protest' (Trombetti and Fortini 1999). Not only do the *mondine* remember giving out political literature, but they also remember reading it, saying, 'I read the newspaper every day' (Zagatti et al. 1998). The *mondine* remember being expected to become not only practical but also intellectual participants in their class struggle. One woman recounts an exchange with her comrade that demonstrates this, asking him

'Why do you want me to be interested in these meetings? You just need to tell me what to do with these leaflets and where to take them.' [...] But he said, 'No, to truly understand you need to be informed'.

(Verzelli and Zappaterra 2001: 50)

The understanding to which this interviewee refers is evocative of Gramsci's own class consciousness, and the 'critical consciousness of the world' (Landy 1994: 30) that organic intellectuals must possess.

The portrayal of *mondine* as organic intellectuals evokes a left-wing identity, bound to notions of class solidarity and collective emancipation. These memories of the *mondine*'s *impegno* are particularly powerful in a historical canon which has not recognized the political character of women's activism (Rossi-Doria 2000: 361). Oral histories also break down gendered ideas of *mondine* as uneducated, non-violent, tied to the domestic sphere, and fulfilling segregated or marginal roles in political organizations.

**Margotti Martire del lavoro / Madre di due bambine /
Compagna di tutti gli oppressi / In lotta per il proprio riscatto / Qui cadde /
MARIA MARGOTTI**

[Margotti Workers' martyr / Mother of two daughters /
Comrade of the oppressed / Fighting for emancipation / Here fell /
MARIA MARGOTTI]

Thus reads the plaque erected in memory of Maria Margotti, *mondina* and resident of Filo d'Argenta, assassinated by a member of the *Celere* police force at an agricultural workers' protest on 17 May 1949. Margotti was shot at Ponte Stoppino, in the area between Argenta and Marmorta, Bologna, as part of a police reaction to a large-scale protest about the use of illegal agricultural labour. I have created a detailed interactive map integrating the events and oral histories surrounding the shooting of Margotti.[2] This event is the focus of a research project by Gavioli (1999), to whom I am grateful for making the transcripts of her interviews with ex-*mondine* available to me. Gavioli's project collects testimonies in nine interviews with *mondine* who participated in the strike which led to Margotti's death, and one with Margotti's orphaned daughter, Giuseppina Baldini. I supplement the memories included in these interviews with archival material, including photographs, letters and newspaper articles, held by the national trade union CGIL and the central archive of UDI. The cultural and collective memories produced around the figure of Margotti are of importance to this chapter as a whole. By comparing interview testimonies from Margotti's contemporaries and historical sources we can make conjectures about the mnemonic construction process which has produced the figure of Margotti which we see today. This final section presents how Margotti has been commemorated, uncovering the false memories and instrumentalization of her death by the Left.

I will begin with a discussion of how Margotti has become a figurehead of cultural memory of the *mondine*. Margotti's fame is largely a result of commemoration by left-wing organizations, such as the UDI, and left-wing newspapers. For example, following Margotti's death, UDI's publication *Noi donne* published a special pamphlet dedicated to her in May 1949. Renata Viganò also commemorated Margotti's death every year in *Noi donne*, effectively writing 'Margotti-as-historical-figure into existence' (Ruberto 2008: 41). The formation of the Coro Maria Margotti has also garnered national and international recognition. A number of monuments have been erected for Margotti and her image has been included in large-scale protests (Figure 3.2) alongside figures such as Fernando Ercolei who was shot by the *Celere* at a protest in late 1948 (see Figure 3.3). Ruberto also suggests that Silvana of *Riso amaro*, released so shortly after Margotti's death, functioned as a kind of 'cinematic afterlife for Margotti' (Ruberto 2008: 45). In 1982, a road near where Margotti was shot, between Molinella and Argenta, was named after her.

Why has Margotti's death been so important to the *mondine* and to the political Left? Gavioli posits that 'the women see themselves in Maria, they put themselves in her shoes, [...] they imagine her coming back to life for a moment through their words, their songs allow her image to be evoked' (1999: 123–24). Ruberto remarks that commemoration of Margotti's death is one of the ways in which the Left has sought to reinforce 'Gramsci's emphasis on the need to build alliances and subaltern representation in order to achieve political change' (2008: 41). Elsewhere, commemoration of Margotti is described as 'a landmark' (*La Voce di Molinella* 1949: n.pag.) for the recognition of peasant struggle.

In order for Margotti to become this symbolic figure, selections and inventions regarding her identity have been made. Few of the women interviewed had actually known Margotti, yet in their choral performances Gavioli's interviewees announce 'our choir bears her name, and if you don't know us look in our eyes, we are the comrades of Maria Margotti' (Gavioli 1999: 115). This adoption of Margotti as a comrade could therefore be read as political rather than sentimental. In her article of 18 May 1950 in *L'Unità* Viganò said of Margotti, 'she died as any other woman from Mulino di Filo could have done, because they are all agricultural workers and comrades, they all go on strike [...] she [Margotti] became a symbol' (1950: n.pag.). It is precisely this representation of Margotti as a peasant everywoman that renders her a figure ripe for commemoration.

FIGURE 3.2: Margotti's image used at unnamed protest. Europeana.eu, n.d. Accessed 2 July 2018.

Statements like Viganò's may also have motivated Margotti's remediation as a *mondina*. Ropa and Venturoli note how Margotti was 'remembered as a *mondina*, when in reality she was a worker at the bakery in Argenta and an agricultural hand' (2010: 183). This is perhaps too categorical; in UDI's pamphlet, Margotti is said to have gone 'every year to the rice fields' (Anghel 1949: 10), suggesting that Margotti may have worked seasonally as a *mondina*, and her identity has been subsumed into this community. Confronting this very issue, one interviewee remembers,

> a group of youngsters came by and asked us: 'Those of you who remember Maria Margotti, was she a factory worker?', 'No, she wasn't a factory worker, she was a *mondina* – we said *mondina* – who died in our town, at a strike'.
>
> (Gavioli 1999: 115)

This contemporary memory may be the result of the remediation of Margotti's identity which happened much closer to the event itself. There is evidence from as early as 20 May 1949 that Margotti was identified as a *mondina* by the Associazione Nazionale dei Partigiani Italiani [National Association of Italian Partisans] (ANPI) in a letter proposing to take charge of Margotti's orphaned children (further discussed below), as well as in local newspapers (*La Voce di Molinella* 1949), and in the UDI pamphlet on her death.

As well as a *mondina*, Margotti is most frequently described as a mother and a *donna seria* [serious woman] in the sources. Interviewees describe her as 'a woman of few words, but sincere' (Bertuzzi et al. 1999) and 'a reserved woman […] that I didn't even know at all well' (Brandolini et al. 1998). We could hypothesize here that the *mondine* transform their scarce personal knowledge of Margotti, describing her in a way which echoes the qualities of the ideal working-class activist. Qualities like being unsophisticated yet moral, trustworthy and quiet could be said to embody certain Gramscian ideals of organic intellectuals. Unlike 'traditional' intellectuals who were full of fine words and inaction (according to Togliatti 1973: 492), memory of Margotti portrays her as reserved in word but not in deed, committed to what the *Voce di Molinella* proclaimed as 'ideals of freedom and justice […] [for which] she laid down her life' (1949: n.pag.).

Margotti's political engagement appears to have been similarly exaggerated. The May 1949 front cover of CGIL's magazine *Lavoro*, features a photograph of Margotti's daughters crying at her funeral and a caption stating: 'She was killed because she was defending her family's town' (CGIL 1949: n.pag.). Neither was the protest about defending the town nor was Margotti's family originally from Molinella. This caption could convincingly have been in a wartime article about the occupation of Italy, so reminiscent is it of Resistance rhetoric. Contemporary sources too, such as Wikipedia and *Enciclopedia della donna*, show evidence of divided or false memory.[3] Wikipedia states that Margotti 'participated in union struggles for a seven-hour working day' (Wikipedia 2017), but the website of *Enciclopedia della donna* contradicts this, saying 'she was a woman who had never been to a protest' (Borgato 2015). Other attempts are made to link Margotti's death to the success of the strike, describing it as 'heroically dramatic' (Borgato 2015), and a 'victorious peasant strike in a climate of united struggle, to which Maria Margotti's sacrifice contributed' (*La Voce di Molinella* 1949: n.pag.).

The most marked example of equating Margotti with left-wing activism can be found in allusions to her as a partisan. One author in the *Voce di Molinella* describes how she only recognized Margotti in reports of a death when referred to by her nickname, because 'everyone has a nickname, like battle names […] like we had as partisans' (*La Voce di Molinella* 1949: n.pag.). The letter sent to Margotti's family by the ANPI serves a similar function. This letter, in which the ANPI offers to care for Margotti's daughters in the 'Boarding School for Orphans of Partisans', does so 'interpreting the partisan spirit of fraternity and solidarity towards all workers who gave so much of themselves in Resistance struggles' (ANPI 1949). Margotti's Resistance participation is ambiguous: even the UDI publication on her death states only 'all of Filo [was] on the side of the Resistance' (Anghel 1949: 10). Here again we can observe a desire to render Margotti a figure of the left-wing Resistance.

These sources conflate Margotti's death with wider social and political struggles which may have in fact featured minimally for Margotti during her lifetime.

This section concludes with a reflection on the politics of commemoration read through Margotti. On one hand, many interviewees express the importance of keeping Margotti's memory alive, saying 'they should learn it at school, they should write her into history' (Zagatti et al. 1998). Other interviewees echo this lament, saying 'some say these things aren't true [...] they're not interested in knowing about local history, the struggles theirs mothers undertook [...] but that's terrible, because you should know these things' (Biavati and Biavati 1999). We are reminded of Yuval-Davis's argument that women are used as 'cultural symbols of the collectivity, [...] and as its intergenerational reproducers of culture' (1997: 67). This conflict between remembering and forgetting is just one tension in the remembrance process. The case of Margotti raises questions not simply about the politics of changing or remediating history, but about removing it from the cultural sphere altogether. If 'remembering and forgetting are two sides – or different processes – of the same coin' (Erll and Nunning 2010: 8), there is much to be asked about the society which would wilfully forget a figure like Margotti. The issue marks a point of tension between the generation of *mondine* who actively commemorate Margotti and the generations following them, perhaps reflecting that in a new national context, the relevance of Margotti's symbolism has declined.

In contrast to the desire of some *mondine*'s enthusiasm for remembering Margotti, her daughter Giuseppina provides a sobering example of the impact of the attention her mother's death received. When asked how she felt about the formation of the *Coro di Maria Margotti*, she replied 'they asked me before if I agreed, but ... how could I say no? It means she will be remembered' (Baldini and Siroli 1998). A friend of Baldini's, Ansalda, who was present at the interview goes on to explain: 'Giuseppina's family [...] didn't like them [Margotti's daughters] to go out and about a lot, because [...] they thought they were being instrumentalised [...] it was the Left at that time, that was doing that' (Baldini and Siroli 1998). These statements speak of the conflict between the perceived political duty to commemorate and the personal right to private grief.

Supporting the thesis that Margotti's death was unethically exploited, the CGIL holds a number of photographs which, by today's standards, would be judged at best insensitive and at worst unethical. These photographs include one taken through the window of the car transporting Margotti's body from the scene of the crime (Figure 3.3) and another close-up shot of Margotti's daughter crying at her funeral (see Figures 3.4 and 3.5).

The latter photo was used on the May 1949 front cover of the workers' magazine *Lavoro* (CGIL 1949). Giuseppina also refers to a photo of Margotti as a young woman which became 'in vogue' (Baldini and Siroli 1998) in the Italian

FIGURE 3.3: Margotti's body being transported from the crime scene. Europeana.eu, n.d. Accessed 2 July 2018.

press after her death. Recognizing the psychological damage of the commemoration of Margotti by the left, Ansalda comments:

> *I'm proud of my party*, but I understand now that young people today, well they would say 'If you cared so much why did you go up on stage!' My mother had just died [...]. *But, back then, it was our history. There was the Cold War, they had killed your family and you were trying to remind people of the injustices.*
>
> (Baldini and Siroli 1998: n.pag., my emphasis)

This testimony powerfully connects the sense of duty on the Left to exploit the political importance of Margotti's death and the personal trauma which it caused. Gavioli's interview with Margotti's daughter Giuseppina is marked by reticence, shown in minimal or evasive answers. When I enquired about this, Gavioli confirmed,

> it was difficult to get her to talk. I think she and her sister had suffered a lot because of the whole affair [...] because they were – we would say today – very exposed in the media. I believe they would have preferred to live out their grief in a more private way.
>
> (Gavioli 2015: n.pag.)

FIGURE 3.4: Margotti's daughters at her funeral. Europeana.eu, n.d. Accessed 2 July 2018.

The commemoration of Margotti is rearticulated here as a loss rather than a gain. This problematizes commemoration, suggesting that the female subject is instrumentalized, and her truth is lost. This is even more problematic for memory studies which seek to give voice to subaltern subjects. In Margotti's memory, the personal is sacrificed for the collective and women become, unwillingly, 'embodiments of the collectivity' (Yuval-Davis 1997: 23).

Conclusion

This chapter has evidenced the link between left-wing discourse and the collective and cultural memories of the *mondine*. The *mondine* are presented, and present themselves, as idealized working-class, rural labourers, able to symbolize Italy's rebirth. Both their pre-Second World War history and their participation in the

Resistance made them ripe for symbolic exploitation by left-wing organizations. The oral histories studied here exemplify the Italian Left's nostalgia for agriculturalism, associationism, solidarity, and Resistance during the years between 1945 and 1965. Although the *mondine* foreground their political, industrial, and intellectual activism, there is an argument to be made that their wartime Resistance was as much motivated by the potential emancipation of an exploited subaltern class as it was by a specific opposition to Nazi-Fascism. Yet, as the case of Margotti proves, the transformation of the *mondine* into political figureheads is not without complication. As in the case of filmic *mondine*, the symbolic burden of the nation may come at personal cost. Certainly, the *mondine* are remembered and commemorated more for their symbolism as heroines and martyrs than for their work.

NOTES

1. *Il maggio delle mondine* was filmed by Francesco Marano at the request of Cristina Ghirardini and Susanna Venturi as part of their aforementioned project (2011).
2. See http://www.scribblemaps.com/maps/view/Uccisione_di_Maria_Margotti/MariaMargotti.
3. These are the top two search results on Google: https://www.google.fr/search?q=maria+margotti&oq=Maria&aqs=chrome.0.69i59j69i57j69i65l2j69i60j0.947j0j7&sourceid=chrome&es_sm=93&ie=UTF-8 (accessed 24 June 2015), excluding an article on 'i-Italy' by Laura E. Ruberto (2009), which paraphrases much of her excellent section on the rice workers in her book *Gramsci, Migration, and the Representation of Women's Work in Italy and the U.S.* (2008: 40–50).

SECTION 2

TEXTILES – SEAMSTRESSES

4

A Brief History of Seamstresses in Post-war Italy

The *sarta*, or seamstress, walked the streets of post-Second World War Italy in the early morning or late evening, passing through urban centres, catching the train or tram, and mingling with a very different class of people to that of her clients. She might stop at a café on her way to work, paying with a few coins from her modest salary. Yet inside the city she is hidden in the sanctum of the atelier. Although she bathes in the ultra-feminine world of fashion, surrounded by female colleagues around her own age and with similar concerns to hers, she might be accompanied home by a young suitor from the city. She will be a seamstress for life, although she may work from home once married, and she will take a sense of pride from her profession. She will both provide for her family, and yet occupy a traditionally submissive role within it. She dreams of career progression, community, luxury, and romance.

Such are the narratives and images we find in both film and oral histories of seamstresses in the post-war period. The character of the seamstress embodies many of the major social preoccupations of this time. Seamstresses' work poised them at the convergence point of practicality and luxury, of artisanal production and industrialization, of the domestic and the professional. In other words, their lives and work exemplified post-Second World War Italy's crossroads: tradition or modernity? The next two chapters on seamstresses look at how *sarte* interacted with ideas of modernity and new spaces. Paying particular attention to the urban context of *sarte*'s work, the chapters address Laura Ruberto's criticism that 'even within the city, work ordinarily performed by women […] is not usually discussed in labour histories' (2008: 4). Chapter 5 examines filmic portrayals of *sarte* in the films *Sorelle Materassi* (Poggioli 1943), *Le ragazze di piazza di Spagna* (Emmer 1952), and *Le amiche* (Antonioni 1955). In Chapter 6, a comparison is made with oral histories from a body of seven original interviews with seamstresses who worked between 1945 and 1965. Research into the work of seamstresses is important not only because *sarte* have been neglected in historical scholarly enquiry but also because their work is so closely tied to social and economic change in post-war Italy.

Fashion and nation

Fashion and its employees navigate the dialectic between tradition and modernity. In post-war Italy, fashion was associated with glamour, film, Hollywood, America, and consumerism. *Sarte* worked outside the home, often in urban environments, opening them up to all the good and bad that an urban reality might present. They earned wages, which, although systematically lower than those of their male counterparts, gave them a degree of financial independence and agency. *Sarte* had greater social mobility than most women; often from *ceti popolari* [working classes], they nonetheless became known and appreciated by their upper-class clients, sometimes forming romantic relationships with them (Maher 2007: 286).

Yet, the *sarte*'s work also fits into conventional notions of female employment. Needlework, and cultivation of appearance, have traditionally been women's work. During Fascism, women were forced out of certain professional sectors and encouraged into other, more acceptably 'feminine', ones, including that of the seamstress (De Grazia 1992: 166). In post-war Italy, women's bodies were a site where concerns about morality, politics, and nationhood were negotiated. There is a direct interplay with fashion here; the way in which women dressed their bodies was socially, politically, and even religiously charged. In 1941, Pope Pius XII 'exhort[ed] women to dress modestly and with dignity in the face of the unbridled hedonism of cinema' (Bossaglia 1984: 42). As influential players in vestiary practices, *sarte* participated in the construction of women's bodies, and by that merit, the nation. In terms of gender norms, seamstresses' work positioned them at an ideological faultline between domesticity and emancipation.

The role of fashion as a symbol of a nation has long been identified by historians and reinforces the idea that the *sarte*, as creators of style, wielded more influence over society than we might first assume. In her introduction to a special edition of the *Journal of Modern Italian Studies* on fashion, Eugenia Paulicelli has explained the link between fashion, modernity and nation (2015), pointing to the period between 1950 and 1960 when fashion began to play a key part in creating an international identity for Italy. She highlights the rise of 'Made in Italy' as symbolic of an embrace of America and, in a Cold War context, of capitalist values (Paulicelli 2015: 5). In this way, fashion was a form of diplomacy, populated and, to some extent, spearheaded by women. Fashion is also a form of embodied cultural capital, as defined by Pierre Bourdieu (1985). The coming chapters discuss how this capital becomes currency, and how *sarte* were facilitators and managers of this.

Sarto, sarta, sartina, caterinetta

The label *sarta* covers many different roles and ranks of women working within made-to-measure fashion. In post-war *sartorie* [made-to-measure boutiques] there remained a strict gender division of labour; employees in men's clothing were mixed, but only women could work in women's clothing (unless men were high-level designers). This fact is confirmed by collective contracts and salary tables held at the Confederazione Generale Italiano del Lavoro (CGIL) Bologna, where provisions are made according to the gender of workers. In documents for women's clothing, *fattorini* [delivery boys] or *magazzinieri* [stockroom workers] are the only male workers cited. It appears that there were a few, high-ranking men working in women's clothing shops as fabric cutters or the like. Often the clear distinction between a designer, seamstress and so on was blurred. At the highest levels, in the famous Roman *sartoria* Sorelle Fontana for example, the women who designed the garment also cut and constructed it. In my interviews, it became apparent that designs were often bought in the form of paper patterns from France, and then shared and adapted by *sarte* and their clients. Commonly, several *sarte* clubbed together to purchase and share amongst themselves a handful of costly Parisian designs.

The *sartoria*'s employment structure between the 1940s and 1970s was complex, as shown by collective contracts and salary tables in the CGIL archive in Bologna. These archival documents ranging from 1945 to 1963 show that employees were subdivided into multiple categories (in descending order): *Maestra, 1' categoria, 2' categoria, 3' categoria, aiutanti, apprendiste. Apprendisti* [Director, 1st, 2nd, 3rd Category Worker, Assistant, Apprentice]. Apprentices were also known in northern dialects as *cite* or *piscinine*, and were at the bottom of the pile; usually employed between fourteen and twenty years old, they had to undergo two to four years of training. Models were also included in the collective agreements and were used to show the designs to clients, who would then order them to be made to their measurements. Notably, most categories and salaries were determined by seniority. Even among employees of the same level, there were further specificities: women who only sewed hems, women who embroidered and so on.

The terminology for seamstresses varied and to some extent reflected their hierarchical positions. Fiorella Imprenti describes how women working as women's seamstresses were referred to with the diminutive *sartine* 'in reference to their low average age, but also to the idea that producing women's clothes required less professionalism' (2007: 147). There were also the *caterinette*, the provenance of whose name appears to be related to their associations with high fashion. The etymology of the word *caterinetta*, with its link to Catherine of Alexandria, patron saint of girls of marriageable age, suggests that it was used for younger seamstresses in search of a label which distanced them from the more staid *sarte*. Some suggest that the term *sarte* sounded 'too pompous' (Rossi and Pilotto 2014).

The category of *sarte* comprehends a wide variety of professional experiences. Their work varied from domestic piece-work to working in rural workshops with a handful of women (often relatives), to working in large ateliers with scores of colleagues. Works such as that by Vanessa Maher (2007) engage with the history of domestic *sarte* and contribute to the important recognition of domestic work as work. In this book, I have elected to focus on seamstresses in public workplaces, because of the associations with modernity, urbanity, and new ideas of womanhood that this implied.

The ateliers of the post-war period were rigidly structured, whether large or small. They were hierarchical, and climbing the professional ladder was perilous. Vanessa Maher suggests that apprentices were neither encouraged nor trained because they represented a potential threat to the women working above them and a greater financial burden to owners as they became more skilled. Conversely, if a seamstress married, she could no longer work in the atelier and was henceforth given piece-work to do at home, or, if she was enterprising, would seize the opportunity to set up on her own [*mettersi in proprio*]. The law forbidding the dismissal of *sarte* upon marriage was only established in 1963 (Maher 2007: 87). Oral histories collected for this project do not suggest that *sarte* were competitive amongst themselves, but that the working environment was simply too pressurized for training or nurturing less-skilled workers. Close contact with designs, or even one *sarta* undertaking a whole project, was regarded by directors of fashion houses as risky because it meant the workers might be able to reproduce or steal designs. Even before being able to set up their own businesses, seamstresses posed the threat of changing employer, taking with them an atelier's training, knowledge and possibly its designs. This led fashion houses to take a division of labour approach, with each *sarta* completing a fraction of a project.

Poor treatment of workers is an issue raised in a number of the historical works, yet this does not tally either with the interviews I collected, or with the contractual documentation from CGIL Bologna. Maher raises the issue of excessive working hours, as well as back pain and eye problems as a result of poor light and strain (2007: 86). Maher also notes that women worked with the ebb and flow of the fashion seasons, and so at peak times could be working twenty-hour days, whereas during the *stagione morta* [off-peak season], they might be sent home without pay (2007: 75–76). Vicenza Maugeri, who studied the *sartoria* Maria Venturi in Bologna in the 1950s, states that 'at the end of each season the workers were fired to then be re-hired when the new season began' (2012: 20). The testimonies I collected do not support the above statements, possibly because the women I spoke with worked mainly in the post-Second World War period, during which protective legislation was put into force. Both stability and pay were unpredictable until the mid 1940s, after which point contracts ensured fundamental rights like an eight-hour working day, statutory holidays and paid maternity leave (although to a large extent only in larger urban ateliers) (Maher 2007: 103). Salaries increased, in some cases by as much as 1400 per cent between 1945 and 1963.

Existing literature on sarte

Literature on seamstresses in this period is not ample. Vanessa Maher's work (1987, 2007) on oral histories with seamstresses in Turin between 1860 and 1960 is the most similar enquiry to my own. Eugenia Paulicelli also produced an article and special edition *Journal of Modern Italian Studies* (2015: 20:1) which is useful for understanding the fashion industry in Italy between 1920 and 1960, and particularly the 'link between fashion and [...] rapid industrialization and social change' (Maher 1987: 134). These studies lead me to scrutinize *sarte* as symbols of modernity and national development; this link between fashion and nation has been bolstered by theoretical works by fashion sociologists (see, for example, Crane 2001 and Kawamura 2004). Most scholarly works have focused on the late nineteenth century, addressing seamstresses' working conditions (Imprenti 2007). Elsewhere, more focused studies of particular localities (Tolsi Brandi 2009) or designers (Maugeri 2012; Fontana 1991) are available. More recently, the Victoria & Albert Museum in London held the exhibition 'The Glamour of Italian Fashion, 1945–2014' (2014). This exhibition's curator, Sonnet Stanfill, underlines the 'little-studied area of fashion production, that of Italy's regional, small-scale dressmakers' (2014: 84), underscoring the critical gap to which this book responds.

The lack of interest in Italian fashion of the post-Second World War period may be explained by the moments between which it occurs; following Fascism's fashion autarchy in the 1920s and preceding the rise of *prêt-à-porter* in the 1960s and 1970s. The post-Second World War period marks a rise in the importance of the creators of garments, particularly thanks to cinema. Before the war, 'tailors and seamstresses were often faceless workers, only known by their names, beneath their clients', but 'in the post-war this narrative was turned inside-out: and they were filmed, photographed, offered up to the public in the press' (Bossaglia 1984: 45). The coming chapters augment the currently scant historical material available on the subject of post-war *sarte* and ask how representations and oral histories interact with social change in Italy.

5

Modern Women: Filmic Representations of Seamstresses

> *[The* sartoria *is a space for women] to transgress class boundaries, to evade the domestic and private norms considered proper to their sex, [...] to avoid male control of relations among women.*
> (Maher 1987: 145)

Seamstresses were, in spatial terms, a privileged class of women in post-Second World War Italy. Their mobility concerned not just the physical act of going to the workplace, but the ideological and social implications of their work. Feminist geographer Doreen Massey asserts that 'spaces and places are not only in themselves gendered but, in their being so, they both reflect and affect the ways in which gender is constructed and understood' (1994: 179). This chapter examines the spaces and places accorded to *sarte* in post-Second World War Italian films, asking how and why they are gendered. Post-war cinematic narratives which explored female mobility were 'experienced as profoundly disorientating' (Wood 2006: 60–61), according with the wider observation that 'the attempt to confine women to the domestic sphere was both a specifically spatial control and, through that, a social control on identity' (Massey 1994: 179). This chapter asks how spatial control of female working characters expresses attempts to manage emerging female identities. With particular attention to the urban space, it explores how working women in the city represent disorder, and how in the context of 1950s Italy this disorder was manifested as a threat to patriarchal control. Fashion has already been noted as exemplifying national identity and modernity (Paulicelli 2015: 3). The present chapter looks at how the *sarte* interact with and exemplify modernity, and how this reflects wider social and political debate. In doing so, this section finds continuity with the previous chapters on the *mondine* and the interplay of women, modernity, and nation.

The films studied in this chapter are *Le ragazze di piazza di Spagna* (Emmer 1952) and *Le amiche* (Antonioni 1955). The chapter also provides an analysis of

Sorelle Materassi (Poggioli 1943), as a wartime counterpoint to these representations of seamstresses. These films span the liberation of Italy to what scholars have called the 'restoration' period of the early 1950s and into the increasingly affluent context of the late 1950s. We should recall the presence of the Christian Democrat government, and its embrace of modernization, Americanism, consumerism, and individualism. It is also pertinent that these films are set in Rome, Turin, and Florence, respectively, cities which saw extensive damage during the Second World War, and which (certainly in the cases of Rome and Turin) saw rapid rebuilding and modernization between 1945 and 1960 (Avveduto 2012: 18). These rebuilt locations strengthen associations between modernity and *sarte*.

The *sarte* studied here worked in more visible public positions at a time when 'many commentators [...] spoke of women's increasing presence on the labour market' (Willson 2010: 207). The films analyzed in this chapter demonstrate the new interest and concern over women in the public sphere. If political scientist Carole Pateman's statement is true that 'the dichotomy between the private and the public is central to almost two centuries of feminist struggle' (1989: 118), seamstresses are at a faultline in that terrain. This chapter reveals how concerns about women's entry into the public sphere are articulated in film, and how this reflects wider concerns over national change.

The last few decades have produced a number of television and film materials looking back at *sarte* in the post-war. These include the television series *Atelier Fontana: Le Sorelle della Moda* (2011), *Velvet* (2013), *Le ragazze di piazza di Spagna* (1998), and the film *Coco Before Chanel* (2008). These productions may speak of a growing contemporary realization of the role seamstresses played in modernization and change. There is, however, an evident lack of scholarly analysis of *sarte* in film, highlighting the unique value of the present chapter within the wider context of representations of working women.

The corpus

The earliest film I study, *Sorelle Materassi*, was filmed and released in the later stages of the Second World War and is a comedy film claimed by Marcia Landy to 'hover between melodrama and satire' (1992: 320). The film is based on a 1934 novel of the same name by Aldo Palazzeschi and tells the tale of two late-middle-aged sisters, Teresa and Carolina (Emma and Irma Gramatica) who fall prey to their charming but exploitative nephew, Remo (Massimo Serato). The two women have reached financial and social success through hard work as rural *sarte*, and own their own business. An impoverished past, caused by a wayward father, is hinted at. The sisters' financial success is threatened by their blind love for Remo, who appears in their lives only to begin borrowing money and eventually coercing the sisters into paying his debts. The two sisters live with their married (but abandoned or widowed) sister Giselda, their housemaid Niobe (Dina Romano), and apprentice Laurina (Anna Mari) who is also Remo's lover.[1] The film is loosely divided into two parts; in the first part, Remo swindles his aunts and is generally portrayed as a cad. In the second part, Remo has a moral epiphany and becomes a car salesman, where he meets the rich Argentinian heiress Peggy who persistently seduces him. Initially, her advances provoke his rage, but later, after she tricks him into staying in a rural hotel overnight with her, she procures a marriage proposal. Remo's marriage leads him to move out of his aunts' home, leaving them bereft. There has been very little study of *Sorelle Materassi*, perhaps because of its awkward historical position between Italian Fascism and Liberation. While Marcia Landy reads critiques of Fascism in *Sorelle Materassi*, it is 'the sexual politics of power […] [and] the fictions of masculinity and femininity' (2002: 268) which are of particular interest to this chapter.

Le ragazze di piazza di Spagna is a 1952 film by Luciano Emmer, known for his light-hearted comedies such as *Domenica d'Agosto* (1950). Emmer was one of the founding fathers of 'pink' neorealism, 'comedies [produced] in response to the critical post-war years' (Carmini 2013: 467). Pink neorealism was a reaction to the bleakness of the first neorealist oeuvres, articulating its narratives through laughter and sentimentality. The film follows the intertwining lives of three young *sarte*, Marisa, Lucia, and Elena (Lucia Bosè, Liliana Bonfatti, and Cosette Greco). It traces the passage of the three friends as they court boyfriends who eventually become fiancés. Marisa faces turbulence in her relationship when she gets a promotion from *sarta* to fashion model. Lucia's love interest evades her because, as a professional jockey, he is initially too short to interest her. Elena's boyfriend, unofficially engaged to the daughter of his boss, gives Elena the run-around until she discovers his deceit and unsuccessfully attempts suicide. After Elena's crisis, the three women draw together in traditional and reassuring conclusions; Marisa gets engaged to her childhood sweetheart and gives up modelling, Lucia renounces her romantic explorations and settles on the vertically challenged jockey, and Elena finds love with an ultra-traditional taxi driver (Marcello Mastroianni). With box office takings of 400,000,000 Lire (Chiti and Pioppi 1991: 303), the film had the most positive popular reception of those studied in this chapter. The film's genre blends elements of comedy into the narrative, reminding us of Danielle Hipkins's observation that 'comedy, with its inherent optimistic beat, pulls in the direction of resolving anxiety about gender roles' (2016: 16). This is one of the ways in which *Le ragazze di piazza di Spagna* differs from *Le amiche*, which tends towards more ambiguous conclusions. The film was described as 'lively and entertaining' (Meccoli 1952) by *Epoca* magazine. Its use of popular actors such as Marcello

Mastroianni, Eduardo De Filippo, and Renato Salvatori, as well as the traditionalist and reassuring narrative of Emmer's film, may go some way to explaining its popularity.

Our final seamstress film, *Le amiche* is an adaptation by Michelangelo Antonioni of Cesare Pavese's 1949 novel *Tra donne sole* [*Among Women Only*] and recounts the return of protagonist and Roman fashion house supervisor Clelia (Eleonora Rossi Drago) to her native Turin. Co-written by Suso Cecchi d'Amico and Alba de Cespedès, the film shows Clelia's entry into high society after discovering the wealthy Rosetta in critical condition in the hotel room next to hers, having attempted suicide. The acquaintances Clelia makes from this incident introduce her to a set of upper-class, but ultimately morally corrupt and purposeless, characters. Simultaneously, Clelia begins to fall for the assistant architect Carlo (Ettore Manni) who she meets at the construction site of the new *sartoria*. After an ambiguous flirtation, Carlo proposes marriage, but after some prevarication Clelia rejects the proposal, citing too great a difference in lifestyles and expectations. Both Pavese's novel and Antonioni's film are supposed to reveal the myth of a homogeneous post-war Italy, elucidating class differences and the fallacy of attributing war guilt to members of other classes (Binetti 2003: 202). *Le amiche* was a critical success, winning the *Leone d'argento* [Silver Lion] at the 1955 Venice Film Festival. Popular reception was more muted, recording box office takings of 256,740,000 (Chiti and Pioppi 1991: 31), perhaps because of what Antonioni came to later call its *freddezza morale* [moral coldness], shot through with ambiguous characters and conclusions.

As a note on the films' genres and spectatorships, it is interesting to observe Paulicelli's assertion that films were, for 'Italian working-class women, particularly dress-makers, traditionally [...] a "source of inspiration"' (cited in Hipkins 2016: 63), begging the question, who were these films for? Post-war audiences were predominantly female and the films studied here could be qualified as 'woman's film[s]', with female protagonists and revolving 'around the traditional realm of women's experience: the familial, the domestic, the romantic' (Hipkins 2016: 32). The fact that these films may actually have been consciously speaking to women – if not working women – reminds us of the interaction between cultural materials and individual and collective identities.

Physical space

Space is political; how and by whom it is occupied, how it is organized and divided. To take but one example of this, we might look to current debates over gendered toilets. Feminist geographers Doreen Massey and Gillian Rose have studied women's access to and occupation of space, particularly noting the divisions between private and public. Portrayals of working women in specific spaces and places illustrate 'dimensions along which run relations of power and control, or dominance and subordination' (Massey 1994: 88). If we can assert that women's visibility in new spaces caused anxiety, examining portrayals of working women occupying these new spaces helps us understand the contours of this anxiety. What specifically is threatening about the working woman? What behaviours are most equated with change and rupture? Portrayals of the physical space occupied by *sarte* are important because they provide the canvas upon which new notions of nation and norms are depicted.

The *sarte* represented in these films are remarkable because they work in professional urban spaces rather than in the domestic space. As noted in the introduction to these chapters, the structures in which the *sarte* worked were often divided between workroom (private), salon (semi-public), and exterior (public). The *sarte* moved between these public and private spaces in a way which would have been impossible without their professional status. This provides a counterpoint to the work of domestic *sarte* which was '"invisible" and not "memorable" for most of society because it was described as domestic, private, home work' (Maher 2007: 83–84). Recalling that women's occupation of the public sphere has been the core concern of feminism, we can assert that the professional *sarte* of these films occupy public spaces, challenging patriarchal gender norms.

In *Sorelle Materassi*, the sisters are *sarte* and own their own business. Their model of *sartoria* is what Imprenti describes as a 'very small workroom', employing fewer than five workers and therefore also qualifying as 'artigianato' [artisan] (Imprenti 2007). The *Sorelle Materassi* business is structured like a classic rural atelier; the sisters live in a small town on the outskirts of Florence and the atelier is a part of their home. Their workroom is also where clients are received and measured, blurring the line between private and public. Similarly, the sisters' roles as owners and workers converge and we see them both measuring clients, cutting material, and handing out tasks to their young employee Laurina. Such tasks would, in a larger or more industrialized model, have been divided between different grades of employee. This spatial location of the sisters as domestic workers tallies with the reassuring gender stereotypes found in this film; professional identity is downplayed, and the 'association of feminine with the home' (Rose 1993: 60) is foregrounded. Recalling the 1943 release date of this film, we might argue that in the context of increased visibility for female professionals, this film provides a reassuringly domesticized vision of women's work.

Conversely, the *sarte* in *Le ragazze di piazza di Spagna* are unmistakably urban. In fact, the setting for the *sarte*'s workspace was borrowed from the Sorelle Fontana. The atelier *Sorelle Fontana* was one of Rome's most successful and celebrated fashion houses in the 1950s and fashion historian Rossana Bossaglia describes how 'while the film [...] was shot, one of the Fontana sisters (Micol, probably) was constantly on set' (1984: 69). Many features of the set indicate a strict spatial division between private (*laboratorio* [workroom]) and public (salon, exterior). The atelier environment is ordered and hospitable, with women grouped around long tables in a small, minimally furnished space.

The environment of the *laboratorio* is not only a safe space where women collaborate, but there are elements of the space which actually suggest gender role reversal. Whereas the *mondine* are commanded by a male squad leader surveilling them with a long wooden stick, the *sarte*'s *laboratorio* is managed by a diminutive but assertive young woman. Pictures of male celebrities are pasted on the walls, not only increasing our impression of a female-gendered space but one where women reverse an objectifying male gaze. Maher notes that the atelier was a 'social space that was anomalous and interstitial with respect to social structure' (1987: 138). Filmic portrayals that imply a transfer of power to women in their workspaces support Maher's statement.

However, outside the atelier is a busy urban street with thick passing traffic and pedestrians. The threat of the outside space is made evident; at the entrance of the atelier the girls stick close together, and when they are left alone they are immediately subjected to invasive male gazes and catcalls. We see this trope of sexualizing and harassing women in the public space repeated in a later scene in Villa Borghese when the protagonists are pursued by dozens of men (Figure 5.1).

The *laboratorio* and cloakroom are elevated above street level with a window whence the women look down, watching for the arrival of suitors. Like nuns gazing from convent towers, the women are concealed but able to observe the scene below, underlining their reluctance to enter (or be seen in) the urban space alone. The contrast between public space and workspace creates a dichotomy between the utopian female universe of the workroom and the implicit threat of the public urban space. If it is true that 'unequal class relations do not, as the saying goes, exist on the head of a pin [but] are organised spatially' (Massey 1994: 87), the spatial organization of the *sarte*'s workplaces suggests that men still rule the public urban space and pose a threat to women working within them.

Le amiche also presents seamstresses in environments which are clearly divided between private workspaces and public urban spaces. When she first arrives, the *sartoria* is still under construction, and the barrier between public and private is a flimsy layer of scaffolding. This pressing-in of the male public sphere is made explicit by the construction workers who objectify and patronize Clelia. She has to fight for dominance in this space, resisting being gendered by Cesare who comments on her physical appearance and youth and asks if she has children. Within this space, Clelia states 'I prefer to count on my own abilities', instating an

FIGURE 5.1: Men pursue the female protagonists of *Le ragazze di piazza di Spagna* in Villa Borghese. *Le ragazze di piazza di Spagna*, Emmer, 1952. Italy. © Cine Produzione Astoria.

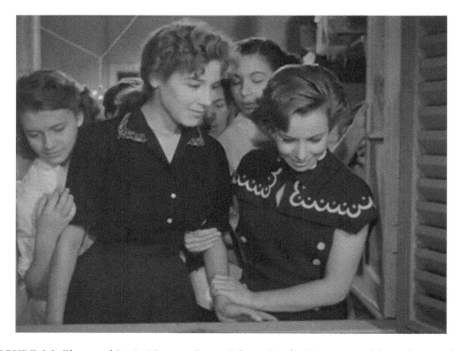

FIGURE 5.2: Elena and Lucia (Cosette Greco, Liliana Bonfatti) gaze out of the atelier window in *Le ragazze di piazza di Spagna*. *Le ragazze di piazza di Spagna*, Emmer, 1952. Italy. © Cine Produzione Astoria.

independence and autonomy in her professional role. As in *Le ragazze di piazza di Spagna*, the workplace is portrayed as a cossetted female universe, and it is Clelia who has to consciously feminize the workplace. Much is made of the necessity for the *sartoria* to reflect the aesthetic elegance of its female occupants. Clelia states that 'ours is only an office by name, it must have character', emphasizing the impossibility of women's workspaces being purely professional. When Clelia later returns to the *sartoria* after a trying day with the suicidal Rosetta she tells Carlo 'I needed to come home'. Once the space is fashioned into femininity it becomes somewhere women can have emotional conversations (such as that between Nene and Rosetta about their mutual love for Lorenzo). Only female characters move between the public and private spaces of salon and workroom uninhibited. Again, the *sartoria* is rendered a feminine space where women can occupy dominant roles and find a sense of identity and intimacy. Yet, there is also an implicit threat in the portrayal of exclusively female spaces: Mariella comments of Momina's home, 'in a house inhabited by a single woman [...] you always have the impression of doing something you shouldn't', highlighting the anxiety-inducing potential of female-only spaces. When the architect Cesare transgresses the boundaries of this female-only space and enters the *sartoria*'s workroom he causes immediate disarray and implied sexual threat, asking 'have you never seen a man fully-dressed?' This scene recalls Hipkins's analysis of *Noi vivi* (Alessandrini 1942) where she observes that entering a woman's space 'can permit access to her interiority, as well as her absent naked body' (2016: 58).

The urban settings of these films are also fundamental to articulating ideas of national change and concerns over women's new professional visibility. The 1950s marked the rise of the city space in Italy. Particularly from 1955, there was mass population movement from rural to urban areas, transforming Italy's major cities (Ginsborg 1990: 220). While this shift represented opportunity and affluence for many, it also caused significant social angst. Women in the city space are key to this symbolism and are used, as Vincenzo Binetti argues of Pavese's writing, to articulate 'a more credible national identity' (2003: 202). The link between 'new' womanhood and the urban space is principally due to the increased mobility which cities gave women, including wider economic, professional, social, sexual, cultural, and spatial opportunities. *Sarte*'s professions enabled them to inhabit such public spaces, but Wilson cautions that women in the city 'symbolised the promise of sexual adventure. This promise was converted into a more general moral and political threat' (1991: 6). The rest of this section assesses how the films present the links between working women in the city space and modernity, sexuality, opportunity, and threat.

Even in the most rural of our examples, *Sorelle Materassi*, the sisters have increased physical mobility. In contrast, the sisters' non-*sarta* sister, Giselda, has no mobility whatsoever; she is only shown within the house, either gazing out from behind shuttered windows or languishing in bed. Giselda provides a counterpoint to the sisters, suggesting the greater degree of mobility that the sisters' profession affords them. The sisters' greatest moments of mobility occur in urban spaces, the most important of which is their visit to Rome to meet the Pope. In a later scene, the sisters are taken to dinner in Florence by Remo. Both of these occasions mark moments of joy and honour for the sisters. However, just before we are able to glimpse the sisters being received by the Pope, the scene is cross-cut with an upshot of a speeding train containing Remo, a symbol of urbanity, threat, and corruption. In the case of their visit to Florence, the sisters are intimidated and mocked by the urbane Florentine customers. These scenes mimic a longstanding exclusion of the rural from modernity; the rural sisters are comically outmoded and ill-fated in the urban space. Both of these examples suggest an incongruity of women in the urban space which ties in with the fascist idealization of rural femininity.

Le ragazze di piazza di Spagna is set in Rome, 'at the core of all [...] dreams of rebirth in Western culture' (Jeannet 2003: 99). This is even truer for Rome of the 1950s, the capital of a nation in (re)construction. As well as in its title, the mise-en-scène underlines the women's urban environment, picturing them in urban locations like Villa Borghese, Termini station, and at dances, bicycle races, and the zoo. The link between the urban environment and the mobility of the characters is shown by their respective journeys from work to their homes; Lucia and Elena walk alone or accompanied by male suitors through recognizably urban settings, and Marisa travels in a motorcar with her boyfriend Augusto. The women gain not only spatial independence in this journey through their urban setting but also, we are shown, greater social and sexual freedom. As Chiara Saraceno (1988) explains, in modern urban environments, privacy was only possible in public spaces; this is exactly the case in *Le ragazze di piazza di Spagna*, in which each of the women is able to engage in unsupervised contact with male suitors in the very public setting of their daily commute. These portrayals equate shifting sexual and gender behaviours with the city space.

Their urban setting allows the *sarte* a mobility, which is not only spatial and sexual but specifically modern. Frames such as the one picturing Lucia being carried off by a boyfriend on a bicycle under the shadow of a departing aeroplane make semiotic associations between women, modernity, leisure, and the urban space. Similarly, there are detailed references to geographically modern features of urban Rome. The film specifies the train which Lucia takes to get home – 'the *Littorina* train departing at seven thirty-five from Termini Station', and makes reference to locations such as Capannelle and Garbatella. These are all recognizably modern features of the city: the *Littorina* was a new kind of train introduced to Rome in 1933 which could travel at speeds of up to 100 kilometres per hour, and Capanelle and Garbatella were both constructed in the 1920s to the South and South-East of Rome, respectively.

The equation of city, women and modernity is problematized. Elena is shown to be coerced by her boyfriend Alberto, who leads her off the urban and moral map and into illicit spaces and sexual behaviours. She pleads with him, 'mother always waits for me so po-faced [...] promise me we won't be late', highlighting the digression from sexual and moral norms and the generational split of modernity. Using dramatic irony, the audience is aware before Elena that Alberto is not a good guy, and that he is only interested in Elena if he can acquire her mother's flat as their marital home. Elena eventually discovers his duplicity in the ultra-urban setting of the central train station. When she subsequently attempts suicide, it is in the warehouse of the *sartoria*, linking her peril to the urban setting. We can observe how portrayals of women in the city are linked to their greater sexual liberty in these films, and how this liberty is converted to threat and disaster, as Wilson predicts (1991: 6). Angela Jeannet argues of women's fiction of Rome that location is used to underline a 'solidly present, slowly changing [...] city' (2003: 102). The same is true of these filmic portrayals of working women in Rome; their presence and mobility in the city draw spectators' attention to the changing social dynamics of the modern city and thus to the post-war nation.

Le amiche's representation of women in the urban space is more ambiguous. The film was made using real locations in Turin, 'a city in itself rife with internal contradictions' (Binetti 2003: 201) between a politicized working class and a powerful bourgeoisie. These contradictions are embodied by the originally working-class Clelia and the bored aristocratic characters of Momina (Yvonne Furneaux) and her entourage. The city setting highlights Clelia's social mobility within the urban space. When she visits the working-class neighbourhood where she grew up, Carlo tells her (and the audience) 'you don't live in places like these any more', underlining the social and spatial transition she has made, thanks to her profession. Clelia is often pictured in her urban surroundings: in cafés, restaurants and walking through Turin's streets. Like *Le ragazze di piazza di Spagna*, *Le amiche* also associates women's urban setting with greater freedom and modernity. For example, the urbane Momina emerges into the narrative from the urban environment outside Clelia's hotel. She leads Clelia from the private space of the hotel and into the city outside. The urban space is again linked to modernity when Momina indicates her motor car waiting outside at the same time as she reveals her unconventional marriage arrangement saying 'I live alone, it's better for him and for me'. The women travel through the city alone, not only moving but driving themselves through the narrative, recalling Binetti's argument that women in the city space are offered alternative narrative paths (2003: 207). The city space also provides the opportunity to portray characters moving across diverse class spaces. Clelia not only attends soirées in the atelier and art galleries but contrastingly visits a reclaimed furniture yard and a shabby *rosticceria* eatery with Carlo. Of this occurrence Carlo exclaims, 'I didn't think you came to places like this', alluding to what Binetti calls the 'impossibility of [Clelia] establishing a harmonic relationship either with "her" city, this being the poor proletarian quarter she came from, or with the empty and false aristocratic community of Turin' (2003: 205). Clelia's ultimate estrangement from both old and new Turin problematizes the social mobility available to women in the urban space.

Recalling Elizabeth Wilson's observation that women in the urban space represent sexual adventure and moral threat (1991: 6), we can observe how the city and its inhabitants are linked to sexual liberty and corruption in *Le amiche*. Most of the characters' significant moments of sexual transgression occur in the public space: Rosetta and Lorenzo begin their affair on the city's outskirts along the banks of the River Po, Mariella seduces Cesare on the beach, and Clelia leaves Carlo on a train station platform. Even when Momina and Cesare become lovers we are shown the scene from the outside looking in, through the window in an up-shot from street level. The perspective is that of an anonymous suitor who, at street

FIGURE 5.3: Rosetta's (Madeleine Fischer) body is collected in the hyper-public city space in *Le amiche*. *Le amiche*, Antonioni, 1959. Italy. © Trionfalcine.

level, emerges from the city space to seduce Momina's maid while Momina is occupied with Cesare. It seems that the city space represents the opportunity for transgression, but only in hyper-public settings. Momina draws our attention to the precarious nature of public displays of female sexuality, saying 'if you ask me, when a man kisses you in public it means he feels nothing'. In a latter scene, the group arrives at an urban restaurant where Lorenzo observes the proximity of a brothel. Binetti notes of the novel *Tra donne sole* that the city is 'reduced to an almost infernal landscape [...] within which the community of women becomes emblematically equated [...] to the level of prostitutes' (Binetti 2003: 206). To return to Wood's work on portrayals of women in the 1940s and 1950s, we see how cinema shows women's entry into new spaces and places 'as profoundly disorientating' (2006: 60–61). Nowhere is this more evident than in the hyper-public urban setting of Rosetta's suicide. She is first pictured running down a dark urban alleyway to her death, and finally framed in a high-angle shot where a crowd gathers to watch her body being collected.

The physical spaces and mobility that the *sarte* enjoy emerge as both emancipatory and transgressive in these films, offering a degree of problematized sexual, social, and spatial freedom.

Sexual and economic ideological spaces

Space is not just about physical setting; it 'reflect[s] back [...] and reinforce[s] [...] other characteristics of social relations, among them those of gender' (Massey 1994: 183). This chapter now examines the ideological spaces of *sarte* in film, looking at the moral, sexual, and economic attitudes that are attributed to seamstresses, and how these reflect their modern character. Maher notes that 'seamstresses were first in line to enthusiastically embrace new lifestyles' (2007: 17–18). This embrace of novelty was a serious point of contention in post-Second World War Italy where new 'ideas of the development of the economy and society clashed with those of Catholic integralism, which emphasized the need for society to correspond to and reflect Catholic values' (Ginsborg 1990: 154). Images of the working woman are a site where this tension between Catholic morality and social and economic modernity is extrapolated. Catholic ideals of femininity remained decidedly traditional in the post-war. Exemplifying this, Maher explains how even in post-Second World War Italy 'all factions – socialists, the Catholic Church, and the Fascist regime – agreed [...] on their condemnation of seamstresses', particularly in their own way of dressing and their love of dance (Maher 2007: 18). This chapter looks for expressions of the clash of modernity and traditionalism in the representation of filmic *sarte*.

In *Sorelle Materassi*, the two sisters are shown to have led exemplary moral lives, having worked themselves out of debt and never having been tempted into supposedly immoral behaviour. Indeed, when their apprentice Laurina becomes pregnant with Remo's child out of wedlock and confesses this to the sisters, their initial reaction is astonishment rather than outrage. Carolina expresses her incomprehension saying, 'we are maidens too. We were twenty once, but we never gave anyone anything to say against our characters, nothing', with Teresa adding 'and we never got *pregnant*, goodness!' Their naivety is further demonstrated by their clichéd ideas as to whom the father of Laurina's baby might be; Teresa speculates, 'the milkman? The postman?'

Other examples of their piousness are manifested in their religious behaviour. The sisters are shown to be pious, proudly and obsequiously making garments for the local priest and even being invited to Rome to be received by the Pope for their services. Historical materials suggest that religion was indeed an important part of life for real *sarte*; *Sorelle Materassi* actually foreshadows the Pope's invitation to the Sorelle Fontana in 1957 where they were gifted one of his skullcaps. Maugeri states that at the Bolognese *sartoria* of Maria Venturi 'before cutting, we always made the sign of the cross' (2012: 18). Despite religion apparently being a staple of *sarte*'s lives, and one that was socially and morally 'correct', the films present a rather disparaging vision of their religiousness. Rather than being portrayed as moral heroines, the sisters' virginal states and monastic behaviour are ridiculed throughout the film. Their sister Giselda says of them 'you don't know what it is to be in the arms of a man [...]. You might breathe, but you aren't alive. Balls, theatre visits, art, travel, love, what do you know of these things?', suggesting that their traditional values have robbed them of the stuff of life. They are similarly mocked for being virgins by their housemaid Niobe, who, when the sisters remark upon the fact that they can wear orange blossom – a traditional symbol of the virginal bride – on Remo's wedding day, says 'at your age you could wear fully-grown oranges'. Indeed the climax of the film, Remo's marriage, is a moment of hyperbolic ridicule of the sisters, in which they arrive at the ceremony also dressed as brides, to the hilarity and scorn of the local population.

Although we might anticipate some tension in a film made during Fascism around the figure of the unmarried woman, such explicit ridicule of the celibate woman is surprising. Indeed, if we transposed the sisters into nuns, it seems unlikely that their behaviour would elicit such humour. We might hypothesize that although the sisters' choice to remain chaste and single was theoretically moral, for an audience of that time, it would be a mark of alterity and was perhaps just as destabilizing to gender norms as the women who transgress them completely. It may also be that 'each character – especially Teresa and Carolina [...] – is drawn in caricature to the straining point of credibility' (Landy 1992: 290) and that this caricaturing allows us to observe a gap between theoretical moral ideologies and those which were responded to by audiences in 1940s Italy. Although Catholicism was a powerful influence in Fascist Italy, Fascist ideology expounded the ideal of the productive and reproductive woman above that of the morally intact *zitella* [spinster]. De Grazia quotes Mussolini as saying of the working woman, 'in the general scheme of things her work is a source of political and moral bitterness' (1992: 168), and discusses how work for women was seen as secondary to the full-time 'employment' of motherhood. Mussolini stated 'work, where it is not a direct impediment, distracts from conception. It forms an independence and consequent physical and moral habits contrary to child bearing' (Mussolini, 'Macchina e donna', *Opera omnia*, XXI: 311, cited in Alexander De Grand 2000: 957–58). To a wartime audience, the Materassi sisters transgressed on two counts; as childless, working, women.

The *sarte* were particularly infamous for dancing and fraternizing with men, and *Le ragazze di piazza di Spagna* includes three dance scenes, all of which suggest a threat to the social order. As in Chapters 2 and 3, dance is a vehicle for discussions of female sexuality, morality and modernity. Lucia is shown at a Sunday open-air dance with a man she meets on her journey home. Her suitor fails to buy the correct tickets and is expelled, immediately after which Lucia is grabbed by a strange man and embroiled in a fight. The context of the dance is imbued with references to modernity, including the Coca Cola signs on the walls and the intra-diegetic American-style rockabilly music. At the very moment the band switches from an Italian to an American song the crisis breaks. This fits with the argument that American boogie-woogie is imagined to have a corrupting influence on Italian youth (Forgacs and Gundle 2008: 64). The scene closes with Lucia departing through a landscape marked by ruined buildings and new electricity pylons.

This scene mirrors the dissonances between old and new moralities and landscapes. It recalls a nation marked by the disaster of war and the invasion of modernity. The next dance scene shows Marisa in the luxurious setting of a fashion show dancing with an unknown man. In the next shot, she stumbles drunkenly out of the venue and is whisked away in his convertible. The threat of this situation is underlined by Lucia, who immediately hails a taxi and gives chase to the couple, anxiously asking the unwitting driver (Mastroianni), 'but don't you read the papers? Every day there are crimes, killings, robberies, blackmailings'. Again, dance is associated with unchecked female sexual liberty, which in turn leads to danger and disaster. In the final dance scene, Elena and good-guy traditionalist Marcello (previously Lucia's taxi driver) dance together, employing a conspicuously traditional style against the background of other dancers doing the boogie-woogie to fast-paced music. Marcello observes, 'I'm not very suited to this kind of dance', marking him out as traditional and – by merit of his precipitous marriage proposal – virtuous. Dance scenes represent moments of moral panic over female sexuality and modernity.

Le amiche's Clelia also transgresses Catholic sexual morality. Antonioni's Clelia is less sexually transgressive than that of Pavese's novel, who has been said to

FIGURE 5.4: Lucia (Liliana Bonfatti) cycles through a landscape of ruined buildings and new electricity pylons in *Le ragazze di piazza di Spagna*. *Le ragazze di piazza di Spagna*, Emmer, 1952. Italy. © Cine Produzione Astoria.

FIGURE 5.5: The atelier space in *Le ragazze di piazza di Spagna*. *Le ragazze di piazza di Spagna*, Emmer, 1952. Italy. © Cine Produzione Astoria.

present the 'profound conflicts of "modernity"' (Binetti 2003: 209). The table below compares the sexual transgression of the two portrayals of Clelia.

Although Antonioni's Clelia hints at sexuality, she does not push it to definitively transgressive conclusions, unlike Pavese's protagonist. In film, Clelia's sexual choices are intrinsically linked to her professional choices, presenting romantic and professional fulfilment as mutually exclusive. Clelia argues 'working is my way of being a woman, of participating in life', and the narrative allows her to return to Rome to continue her personally and economically rewarding work. Yet Clelia's choice of work over romance is suggested to be a cause of regret or resignation to her, having wrongly passed up the chance to exist in the conventional sexual space of marriage. The film was only allowed to be shown to over-sixteens in 1955, and the scene showing Cesare and Mariella embracing on the beach was cut from the televised version released in 1978, as was the scene in the train where Rosetta and Clelia discuss the pointlessness of life (Italia Taglia 2018). This censorship points to an Italy still beholden to Catholic values.

Like representations of the *sarte*'s sexual behaviours, their economic independence could similarly be read as a source of tension in the films. Female financial independence was uncommon in this period, and even where women worked Perry Willson notes that 'their wages (too low to permit them to live independently) were

TABLE 5.1: Comparison between Clelia's character in *Tra donne sole* (Pavese 1949) and the film transposition *Le amiche* (Antonioni 1955).

Clelia – *Tra donne sole* (novel, Pavese 1949)	Clelia – *Le amiche* (film, Antonioni 1955)
Has sex with the architect (Febo) and his assistant	Kisses architect's assistant (Carlo)
Goes out alone with a variety of men	Socializes in female or mixed groups
Refers to previous sexual relationships, insinuates a lesbian relationship between Momina and Rosetta	Does not mention sex at any point
Chooses to stay single, rejects the idea of motherhood	Chooses to stay single, but says that she should have married younger

often essential to maintain dependants' (2010: 73) and so would be channelled back into the family space. In *Le ragazze di piazza di Spagna*, there are recurrent references to women's earnings. We see both Elena and Marisa handing over their pay to their mothers, and Elena explicitly discusses with Alberto how much money she has saved. Clelia's affluence is similarly drawn to audiences' attention in *Le amiche* by other characters' admiration of her fine clothing. Yet, Elena and Clelia's economic independence is tempered with disastrous narrative outcomes. Elena's financial resources attract the exploitative Alberto who only wishes to marry Elena for her comfortable situation, and Clelia's wealth is shown to rob her of the possibility of a traditional destiny as 'a serene wife in a modest home'.

Women's financial gain is also elided with the sale of their sexuality. Particularly in Marisa's case, her promotion to model causes her boyfriend Augusto to characterize her as a prostitute. Mirroring this, Marisa's mother tells the story of how – against her husband's wishes – she modelled nude for a painter in her youth, using the money to buy herself a sewing machine. This episode highlights women as canny and treacherous, with Marisa's mother saying 'I knew your father would never step foot in a museum!' Their exchange of the body for financial profit is shown as disrupting the patriarchal hierarchy. This incident also serves to destabilize traditional masculinity. Marisa's father could be likened to the 'melomale' identified by Claudio Bisoni, with his 'low levels of familial authoritarianism' (2015: 241), a fact which is underlined by his exclamation about his role in the domestic space, saying 'Do you really think that I'm the boss in this house?' These portrayals link women's financial endeavour to deceit and destruction and encroachment on traditional masculine hegemony.

Social spaces and capital in film

Pierre Bourdieu first theorized social capital as 'the aggregate of the actual or potential resources which are linked to possession of a durable network of more or less institutionalized relationships' (1985: 248). The transfer of power through social relationships is visible in portrayals of seamstresses. Seamstresses' workspaces were organized so that they often came into contact with individuals of other classes, particularly if they were in the upper echelons of seamstresses who designed, measured or modelled. Even junior *sarte* could expect to make deliveries or assist superiors, bringing them into contact with people of different classes. In addition, Maher observes that post-Second World War Italy had strict vestiary class codes, and that through their work, *sarte* had the advantage of being 'experts on the question of status, which they translated into dress codes' (2007: 25).[2] This penultimate section examines how and why social mobility is key to cultural memory of seamstresses.

Post-war seamstresses in Italy had a powerful role in class negotiation. Lois Banner, scholar of American women's history, notes that:

> the obsession with fashion among American women in the nineteenth century has been attributed to the high level of 'status competition' engendered by 'the fluidity of American society, the universal striving after success, and the lack of a titled aristocracy'.
>
> (Banner in Crane 2001: 5)

It is not hard to transpose this situation to post-Second World War Italy in the years of the new Republic and the lead-up to the economic boom. Banner's sentiment is almost exactly echoed by one of the *sarte* interviewed in Chapter 6 who observes of clients in the 60s, 'it was the boom. Everyone wanted to climb to who knows what social status [...] so people spent money, experimented, and wanted novelty' (Coppola 2016). As a result of socio-economic circumstances, I argue that seamstresses aided and propounded a new social system, in which fashion was one form of currency. As Maher observes, 'not only were seamstresses able to identify a client in the social hierarchy, but, unlike many others of their class, they knew how different vestiary symbols should be used in different situations, and what behaviour went with what outfit' (2007: 26).

The clearest representation of fashion increasing the social mobility of its employees is to be found in *Le amiche*. It is plainly stated that Clelia left Turin as a working-class young woman and returned (thanks to her professional success) as the equal of characters 'from excellent families' like Rosetta Savoni, or the wealthy Momina Di Stefani, both of whose surnames connote noble heritage. Clelia's social ascent is marked by Momina's observation of her elegance, saying 'seamstresses usually dress like tramps'. It is interesting to note the 'star signification' of Eleonora Rossi Drago (Dyer 1998: 1). Like Clelia, Rossi Drago had undergone a similar social transformation in her personal life. Rossi Drago was a single mother who was disqualified from a Miss Italia competition for being too old, began her career as a salesclerk and shop model and ended up a rich and successful actress (Masi and Lancia 1998: 78). Rossi Drago's star signification reinforces Clelia's social mobility. Tonino Cervi is quoted as saying of Rossi Drago that 'she frequented the wealthy because she thought that, by doing so, she could gain their trust' (Masi and Lancia 1998: 78), her personal behaviour thus mirroring Clelia's. Ultimately, Clelia's access to Turin's bourgeoisie is a deception; unable to return to her original class, she is disillusioned and alienated by her new upper-class milieu. Clelia's portrayal reminds us of Bourdieu's theory of habitus where subjects produce an *'avoir devenu être'* ['having come to be'] (1979: 4) of their social class, embodying the codes and comportment appropriate to it. Bourdieu notes that habitus is only a guise, rather than an assimilation. Confirming this, Clelia is unable to fully internalize the habitus of her new milieu and is thus forever marked as an intruder.

Similarly, Marisa is shown to struggle to adopt the habitus of her new class in *Le ragazze di piazza di Spagna*. She comments that her role as a model is not simply a matter of *being*, but of *becoming*. She repeats the owner of the *sartoria*'s assertion that 'having the body is not enough: you must cultivate y'self, educate y'self, read, try 'n speak properly'. This statement almost precisely echoes Bourdieu's argument that 'the acquisition of social capital requires a deliberate investment of both economic and cultural resources' (Portes 1998: 4). Marisa delivers this affirmation in her strong Roman accent, underlining the contradiction and instability of her original and new social identities. Her social ascent is made to seem ridiculous in scenes where she barters with a bookseller, asking 'what are these made of, gold?' In the scene when Marisa goes dancing after a fashion show, she is loaned a dress, suggesting the temporary nature of her new status. When she returns home drunk after her night in high society, we note the incongruity of her expensive dress and the working-class setting of Garbatella (Figure 5.6). Hipkins reads this technique as 'connoting the wearer's dislocation with their origins' (2016: 62). These scenes suggest that Marisa's new identity and social mobility is a fallacy.

FIGURE 5.6: Marisa (Lucia Bosè) returns to Garbatella after a ball in *Le ragazze di piazza di Spagna*. *Le ragazze di piazza di Spagna*, Emmer, 1952. Italy. © Cine Produzione Astoria.

FIGURE 5.7: Lucia (Liliana Bonfatti) gazes at Marisa (Lucia Bosè) as she models at a ball in *Le ragazze di piazza di Spagna*. *Le ragazze di piazza di Spagna*, Emmer, 1952. Italy. © Cine Produzione Astoria.

Social capital in the films is shown to be a part of *sarte*'s professions, but one which is fraught with danger. 'Bourdieu uses the term "fatal attraction" to refer to the physical beauty which inspires cross-class relationships and disrupts mechanisms of social class closure' (Shilling 2012: 124). We see a similar fatalism in representations of *sarte*'s social mobility. Binetti invites us to read *Tra donne sole* as a parody of post-war Italy, in crisis between old identities and attractive but ultimately empty modern prospects. The same could be argued for the protagonists of *Le amiche* and *Le ragazze di piazza di Spagna*, where new social spaces for women are suggested to be vapid and treacherous.

Social mobility is also expressed in the films through the use of the camera's gaze. As both Jacques Lacan and Michel Foucault observe, there is a power dynamic in the act of gazing. Not only does the gaze 'look, it also shows' (Lacan 1981: 75), articulating spatio-social inequalities. Lacan describes an incident of gazing at a sardine can in the ocean and being asked by a fisherman, 'You see that can? [...] Well it doesn't see you!' (1981: 95). Lacan describes this incident as evidence of the discomfort of occupying the superior, more knowledgeable, position of the subject of the gaze. Similarly, Foucault described the Panopticon (1977) where individuals assimilate the knowledge of being constantly watched and therefore inferior to the watcher. Both of these theoreticians assert the unequal power relations which are expressed and reinforced by the gaze. Maher notes that the *sarte* are educated in a gaze, and that 'attention to clothing is part of a system of knowledge, judgement, and values, which creates and structures social relations' (2007: 28). In *Le amiche*, Clelia underlines her knowledge of strict social dress codes, explaining to Madame, 'in Rome ladies want to spend little and seem rich, here it's the opposite, they spend a lot but want to seem demure and simple'. When asked why she says simply, 'social diplomacy'. Statements such as this portray the *sarte* as knowing subjects of gaze dynamics.

In *Le ragazze di piazza di Spagna*, there are key moments of gaze which underline social inequalities. The first instance we see of characters gazing into different social spaces comes in the figure of Augusto. Emerging from the working-class space of the upstairs workroom, Augusto descends the staircase to the *sartoria*'s salon. He is arrested, however, by the visual spectacle of Marisa modelling for clients and as he looks on the fracture in their social spaces is revealed. The effect is intensified by a mirror behind Augusto reflecting not him, but the scene below. Similarly, there are two occasions in which Marisa is gazed upon by her fellow seamstresses. Elena wears an ambiguous expression as she watches Marisa model new designs, and the rupture in class unity between the two friends is intensified by Madame's dismissal of Elena, asking her 'are you still here?' When Marisa makes her public modelling debut, Lucia is pictured with two other women gazing down at her and serving as her dresser when she returns.

These scenes use the gaze to highlight the social alienation between subjects and objects of the gaze. Maher argues that 'perhaps in Italy in general, part of the skill of self-presentation lies in trapping the glance of the passer-by and compelling respectful notice' (Maher 1987: 139), by commanding a gaze, its object is shown to be empowered to new social standing.

Embodied capital

Like contemporary social media influencers, seamstresses are shown to possess and cultivate what Bourdieu calls embodied cultural capital. This refers to the process by which the body becomes 'a [...] possessor of power, status and distinctive symbolic forms which is integral to the accumulation of various resources and capital' (Shilling 2012: 111–2). I argue that this form of power is associated with modernity, because 'it must be personally invested by the investor themself [...]. This "personal" capital cannot be transferred by donation or inheritance, by selling or exchanging' (Bourdieu 1979: 3–4). In a post-war context of increasing market liberalization and the loosening of social and patriarchal hierarchies, embodied cultural capital allowed conventionally disempowered parties to find opportunities for agency. 1950s Italy was also a time when the idea of beauty was being displaced from moral virtue to physical attractiveness. *Sarte*, whose very business is the elaboration of vestiary identity and value, demonstrably manage the embodiment of capital not only for their clients but for themselves. Maher points out, 'in seamstresses' accounts many allude to the social advantages of beauty, the physical capital of the poorer classes' (2007: 180). However, such manipulation of embodied capital is shown to be transgressive, confirmed by the magazine *Il Sarto* describing how *sarte* 'enjoy a certain esteem, which is a general disesteem' (Imprenti 2007: 169). It is important to acknowledge the opportunities and limits inherent in embodying capital, and the films studied here do just this.

Réka Buckley (2013, 2008) has written about the social ascent of Italian female stars of the 1940s and 1950s who used fashion and bodily transformation both on and offscreen. Buckley (2008) underlines that gaining social mobility as a female star was not only about being attractive but about being fashioned; she uses the examples of Lucia Bosè and Silvana Mangano and their transitions from *popolana* figures in the 1940s to aristocratic characters during the 1950s and beyond. Buckley particularly emphasizes how important it was for social transformation to be embodied, using the example of Mangano who subjected herself to a punitive diet in order to shrink to a more fashionable frame during the 1950s and 1960s. Eleonora Rossi Drago who plays Clelia in *Le amiche* underwent a similar embodied process as an actress. The story goes that director Carlo Ponti 'wooed her intensively and convinced her to have her nose done' (Giacobini 2010: 23). Over the course of her career, she underwent three rhinoplasties, going on 'to star in urban dramas where awareness shifted to an emphasis on fashion and clothes [...] her role [in *Le amiche*] [...] demonstrated once again how fashion and grooming [...] were an essential part of the glamorising procedure' (Buckley 2008: 276). The offscreen transformations of both Mangano and Rossi Drago highlight Bourdieu's insistence on the 'fungibility of symbolic, social, and economic capital, and how nonmonetary forms can hold just as much power as their paper equivalent' (Portes 1998: 2). Yet, the embodied transformations of these women also imply the problematic nature of women embodying capital for social mobility, as it forces them into oppressive and ephemeral standards.

In the films, the two clearest examples of women increasing their economic and social mobility through embodied capital come from Marisa in *Le ragazze di piazza di Spagna* and Clelia in *Le amiche*. Marisa's use of her body as a fashion model gains her access to the upper classes, travel and glamour, as well as the promise of 'a safe career path' from the owner of the *sartoria*. In *Le amiche*, Clelia's trajectory from working-class girl to successful and glamourous woman is made visually credible to an audience which understands her new identity through her appearance – expensive, luxurious and fashionable. As Hipkins argues, women's 'struggle over how they dress marks the limits of their self-determination, and of their ability to control how others read them' (2016: 60). Of her success, Clelia states 'I prefer to count on my own abilities', highlighting the fact that embodied capital 'perishes and dies with its possessor' (Bourdieu 1979: 4). Women's cultivation of embodied capital is implicitly liberal and individualistic and therefore manifests the most contentious aspects of the modernity dawning on post-war Italy (Ginsborg 1990: 153).

Perhaps because of this tension, the social ascents of both Marisa and Clelia are shown as incurring penalties and problems. The anxiety that Marisa's promotion causes is highlighted in a number of ways: not only does it provoke Augusto to beat her for changing her appearance, but he elides embodied capital with prostitution, saying 'she showed up with red painted nails, hair done up [...] she looked like a street walker'. The blurring of embodied capital with sex work recalls Peter Brook's observation that the 'sold body' becomes a 'deviant' body (1984: 130). For Augusto, Marisa not only sells a product, but she herself becomes the product. Characters' manipulation of embodied capital produces anxiety because it disrupts and transgresses established social hierarchies. Hipkins tells us that 'the deceit that dressing-up entails is intimately connected with [...] the "unknowability" of the prostitute, and woman herself' (2016: 62). The woman who dresses up is a duplicitous shapeshifter, not to be trusted. Recalling Bourdieu's description of embodied capital disrupting class hierarchies as 'fatal attraction' (Shilling 2012: 124), it is precisely this threat which seamstresses embody. Reducing these mobile women to prostitutes is a way of containing and condemning their social and professional ascent. Mary Wood notes that 'the figure of the woman who uses her sexuality to move up a class echoes the position of a nation which is losing its integrity in subscribing to economic prosperity' (2006: 57), underlining the anxiety around women's changing roles and the national embrace of modernity in post-Second World War Italy.

Conclusion

In *Le amiche*, Clelia's work gives her the ability to embody another class, occupy new spaces, take control of her destiny and adopt modern behaviours. Yet, these choices estrange her from her working-class identity and the possibility of a conventional female destiny. The timelessness of this paradox is reinforced by her boss, who tells her 'I too went through a difficult time, I had to make my choice. And now I like what I do'. The double-bind of the working woman is repeated by several characters in the film: Nene is a talented artist but pays the price of her husband's professional jealousy. Rosetta only dreams of being Lorenzo's lover, but without work in her life to give her value and distract her, an aborted love affair is enough to drive her to suicide. I would modify Seymore Chatman's analysis of *Le amiche* thus: 'the implication is that for a woman without a man [or alternatively, a job] life is not worth living' (1985: 33). The starkness of women's choice between work, public space and modernity and domesticity, love and narrative fulfilment is echoed at the beginning of *Le ragazze di piazza di Spagna*. The male narrator tells audiences 'Marisa is getting married. Perhaps Elena and Lucia will also marry soon, and they won't come down here to sit on the Spanish Steps anymore', underlining the film's portrayal of the impossibility for women of simultaneously occupying new urban spaces, behaviours, and ideologies, as well as traditional female roles. Let us return to Maher's statement that *sarte* transgress social, spatial and gender norms, and thus avoid patriarchal control (1987: 145). The films exemplify the contradictory possibilities which work presents to women; at once opening new paths, but simultaneously imposing strict borders, boundaries and binary choices. If we consider that these films were speaking to supposedly female audiences, in the rapidly modernizing context of the 1950s, we see how these bordered choices presented to women reflect social and political anxiety over modernization. *Sorelle Materassi* is perhaps unsurprisingly the most conservative of the films, but it is far from alone in presenting traditional ideals of femininity for the untraditional figure of the seamstress.

NOTES

1. Landy (1992: 291) suggests that Giselda has been abandoned, but I would argue that this is left ambiguous.
2. Elsewhere, Ellen Scott (2013) discusses representations of black seamstresses in 1930s American film and the social mobility their sartorial knowledge gave them.

6

Cinderella Stories: Oral Histories of Seamstresses

'Please take the private lift … or the stairs if you prefer', were the words with which I was greeted upon arriving at the atelier Oriana Neri. They were enough to make me wonder whether I should have worn a handbag, rather than a rucksack, and I was suddenly very aware of the dusty sandals that had brought me across Bologna. There was, however, no snobbery or judgement among the seamstresses I interviewed for this book; only generosity, humour, and intelligence. These interviewees had opinions and stories, and spoke with authority and sensitivity.

Where women's work was commonly viewed as having 'little or no "value"' (Maher 1987: 133), we have seen how seamstresses gained space and fame in cultural materials in the post-Second World War period. Seamstresses's renown peaked with the rise of Made-in-Italy fashion brands in the 1960s (Paulicelli 2015: 5). It is easy, then, to pick these women out as occupying a 'peculiar position' (Maher 1987: 137) as workers and women. Why this exception for *sarte*? This chapter argues that the work of the *sarte* 'was seen as a kind of extension of their exquisitely feminine nature' (Maher 1987: 138) and that the feminization of the *sarte*'s work allowed women to occupy unprecedented spaces, while to a great extent avoiding the transgressive reputation of other female workforces such as the *mondine*.

This chapter continues the investigation begun in Chapter 5, asking how the work of post-Second World War *sarte* is remembered, this time by the women themselves. I present seven original oral history interviews with seamstresses who worked between 1945 and 1965. This chapter is the first where I study oral history interviews which I conducted myself. I therefore begin with a discussion of interview techniques and identity construction, engaging with oral history theory and existing studies of women's career narratives. I then move on to discuss the sources, first presenting and analyzing discussions of *sarte*'s physical working spaces, and the power dynamics expressed through them. Similarly to Chapter 5, this chapter then proceeds to examine the ideological spaces *sarte* came to occupy as a result of their professions, focusing on expressions of ambition, job satisfaction, and independence, and how these reflected and transgressed post-war social and historical norms. This section also notes the interaction between participants' identities and onscreen media portrayals of *sarte*. Finally, informed by Pierre Bourdieu's (1985) theories of symbolic cultural capital, the chapter explores interviewees' reflections on social mobility.

Interviews

The oral histories in this chapter come from individual interviews with seven women born between 1924 and 1945 who lived in Emilia Romagna. Six of the seven interviewees had worked in Bologna, and the other in Rimini. Time and financial factors limited my study to the area around Bologna, but there is something to be said for the fact that, although an urban hub, Bologna is not a remarkable location for fashion and textiles. This lends a certain 'normality' to the subjects interviewed, rather than marking out their experiences and successes as professional seamstresses as exceptional in the field. It is also interesting to note that Bologna belongs to what historians have called the 'Third Italy', notable in the post-Second World War period for its small-scale mirroring of the wider economic and social change of the so-called northern Industrial Triangle (Ginsborg 1990: 254). Interviews took place in interviewees' businesses or homes (and once in a café). As mentioned in the introduction to this section, the term *sarta* incorporates a wide range of work and professional status, and this is true of the subjects I interviewed. In setting out to find interviewees I imposed only two restrictions: that they were women who had worked outside of the home, and that they self-identified as *sarte*.[1] Despite limiting my inquiry to seamstresses who worked in ateliers, there are nevertheless other variables among the women selected. For instance, five of the women had worked in women's fashion houses, three of whom had gone on to found and run their own *sartorie*, and the other two had their own tailoring schools. The remaining two women had worked in men's tailors. This may have produced significant differences in the way in which interviewees narrated themselves as professionals, as research has shown that the predominance of male or female employees in a work environment significantly affects employees' notions of success, performance, and identity (Ely 1995). We should also note that the women I interviewed had achieved varying degrees of professional success and this is likely to colour how they remember their work.

Even in the larger group of women's seamstresses participants were heterogenous; Norma Tassoni, aged 90, had trained at the prestigious Scuola di Taglio e Confezioni Maramotti, and became a partisan *staffetta* [dispatch rider] during the Second

World War. Tassoni spent most of her life teaching rather than selling her own creations. Anna Tinti, 68, another of the interviewees who worked in a *sartoria da donna* specializing in lingerie, was the wife of the owner, and designed garments without sewing or constructing them herself. Oriana Neri, 84, owns a successful *sartoria di alta moda* in central Bologna; she directs the *sartoria*, designs, creates, and markets the garments. The same can be said of Luciana Torri, 78, a successful *sarta* with her own high-fashion bridal *sartoria* in Rimini. Which term to use to describe these women? Among them, there is an evident blurring of identities between designer, owner, and creator. This begs the question: what do we mean by the term seamstress or *sarta*? This is a common issue in fashion studies, and as fashion sociologist Yuniya Kawamura says, 'when one studies to what extent the designer is involved in the actual manufacturing and designing process of a garment [...] then the job of designer becomes questionable, and then the meaning of creativity also' (2004: 63). The element which all the participants in my study share is their self-perception as *sarte*; it is their perceived identity which unites them as a group. If it is true that subjects who self-categorize go on to 'adopt the norms, beliefs, and behaviours of the in-group through depersonalisation and self-stereotyping processes' (Bothma et al. 2015: 30), it is interesting to see how they construct identity in oral histories, and how this sits within a wider discourse about working women. This chapter assesses how working identity is elaborated, and how career and work narratives involve performances which move 'between the changing biographical history of the person and the social history of his or her lifespan' (Plummer 2001: 39–40).

Interview, memory, and identity construction

I chose to conduct oral histories of *sarte* because oral histories provide memories which fall within individual, collective, and cultural memory, as discussed in the introduction to this book. Recalling that 'work ordinarily performed by women [...] (paid or unpaid) is not usually discussed in labour histories' (Ruberto 2008: 4), it was my intention not only to engage with the 'reusable texts' (Assman and Czaplicka 1995: 132) provided by filmic representations of seamstresses but also to create a body of recorded and transcribed interviews which might be put into the public sphere and become a source of cultural memory in itself. As in the case of the *mondine*, the desire to retell history 'from the bottom up' is also key to my choice to conduct oral history research. Like the *mondine*, *sarte* were female and mostly from the working classes, and, as such, they represent a social group that has rarely been given a voice in historical narratives.

When preparing to conduct the interviews, I was influenced by Alistair Thomson and Robert Perks's theoretical reflections on the interview process and their argument that 'the content of oral sources [...] depends largely on what the interviewer puts into it in terms of questions, dialogue and personal relationship' (1998: 70). Similarly, Laurie Cohen's instructive study of women's career narratives informed the approach I took to interviews. She recounts of her study that 'explanations for career moves and decisions often draw on experiences that sit outside the actual work setting, thus the methods we use must enable respondents to move around their lifeworlds in this fluid way' (2014: 19–20). Given these considerations, I adopted a holistic approach which listens to interviewees' life stories. Although my interest lies in narratives of work, this book is inspired by and informs the notion that life narratives are closely tied to career narratives and vice versa. I was the person to introduce the term 'career' into these interviews, and this itself may have had a transformative effect as 'it could be argued that career is a retrospective concept' (Cohen 2014: 18). The ambiguity of the *sarte*'s class position between working-class and professional may also explain why they engaged with but did not propose the traditionally 'white-collar' notion of career.

My interview technique focused on giving space and agency to interviewees to direct the flow of conversation. As Luisa Passerini asserts, 'to respect memory also means letting it organise the story according to the subject's order of priorities' (1987: 8). My own questions intended to develop subjects, themes or comments brought up by participants themselves. Personal relationships with interviewees were also considered. The relationships I formed with interviewees were for the purpose of interviewing them, although in the case of four of the seven women we had a mutual acquaintance. I would assert that our brief acquaintance, as well as my status as foreign, young, and – perhaps most significantly – female, influenced interviewees' production. Initially, I was concerned that these factors would lead to formality or reticence in interviewees, but I would now argue that participants were not hindered by our lack of intimacy. On the contrary, I observed what Celia Kitzinger calls the 'immediate short-term benefits' (1987: 75) and participants' explicit enjoyment of being interviewed. I found participants to be pleased to talk about their lives, for reasons of nostalgia and recognition. This is evidenced by Giordano's enquiry as to why I was undertaking this project, and her approval when she says, 'You should go among these people because people from my generation are no longer here' (2016).

At the heart of western society is the notion that, unlike labour, which 'is the actions necessary to fulfil our needs' (Arendt 1998: 4), work serves more profound goals. Across disciplines, we find similar reflections that work 'determines our worth and purpose as citizens' (Arendt 1998: 4) and offers us a means to define our identities (Bothma et al. 2015: 25). But narrating one's career is not only about remembering the individual but also society. This chapter analyzes how *sarte*'s personal and social identities intersect. I wish to consider how the retrospective nature of oral histories affects identity construction. When a subject remembers a past identity they both perform and reinforce that identity. Oral histories activate identities, externalizing, strengthening, and creating identities that are at once historical and contemporary. Much of the scholarly enquiry regarding professional identity construction has been published in journals of management and business studies, or psychology; this chapter demonstrates the interest of this approach in cultural studies.

Physical space in interviews

In interviews, as in films, class dynamics and power are expressed through spatial demarcations. Interviewees commonly describe the *sartoria* as a substitute or alternative space to the schoolroom. Frequently, they highlight exploitation, menial labour, and sacrifice, although never in such terms. Neri comments, 'anything I earned I did so in the evening, […] that's how you start out, […] they didn't pay you – not even your insurance, nothing. You were learning from them' (Neri 2016). Coppola also remembers her initial work as sometimes seemingly unrelated to the development of professional skills, saying 'they didn't put me on sewing, I was the one who had to do whatever they needed. I had to go down to the haberdashery, get the thread, the buttons, this and that, welcome clients when they arrived' (Coppola 2016). Both Neri and Coppola's descriptions of their work highlight the determination and perseverance necessary for seamstresses, yet they also recall Maher's idea of seamstresses's mobility, as both women are enterprising in their work, moving nimbly through the professional and public space. These comments are contrasted with a general lack of, or distaste for, formal schooling among interviewees. Neri notes, 'I didn't like going to school, I didn't want to go, I didn't like studying' (2016), and Giordano underlines, 'I repeat, I have no schooling, I only got to fifth grade' (2016).

Nuns often describe the convent as a privileged space for women's education during the Second World War. Quite the contrary is recounted of seamstresses' workplaces. Not only do many participants remember their education as of a more vocational nature, but they describe the *sartoria* as strictly hierarchical and devilishly difficult to navigate. Although they may have been called apprentices, and describe the workplace as a school, in interviews there is an evident lack of discernible instruction in the *sartoria*. Apart from Tassoni, who went to a dedicated tailoring school, young employees were expected to learn the trade through watching; any verbal instruction was either forbidden or seen as a waste of time, and perhaps an attempt to usurp more senior *sarte*.

We find multiple references to the power dynamics of looking and gazing in the workspace. Interviewees state, 'even if they made me pick up pins from the ground,

I was just happy to set my eyes on what they were doing' (Coppola 2016), and, '[the owner] would take me to fittings because I was a good girl and would keep quiet. I just stayed there with my eyes wide open seeing how she did it and I was very happy' (Neri 2016). Similarly, Tinti describes her training by saying 'I just watched – I did – I liked doing little drawings by hand, and so I started designing' (Tinti 2016). Neri's identification of her silent watchful obedience as being 'a good girl' evokes the gendered trope of female silence as desirable. Far from bitter invocations of an exploitative system, interviewees' statements are intended to highlight the opportunity accorded to *sarte* who knew how to utilize gazing to their advantage. Coppola's account of her apprenticeship highlights this:

> They showed me an embroidery stitch, and I did this embroidery stitch, as well as a chain stitch, but I didn't understand the importance of it [...]. And I understood, a while later, that I had acquired a certain dexterity and I could use that dexterity when I needed to do certain things; [...] and when I started to love this profession I then changed workplace straight away and went to a large *sartoria* where I was welcomed. [...] And that's when I began to understand that if I learned well, in the future I too would be able to have my own *sartoria*.
>
> (Coppola 2016)

As Maher argues of seamstresses's emphasis on watching, 'this gaze [is] a practise linked to a certain *style of social philosophy* [...]. As such, attention to dress is part of a system of knowledge, judgement, and values, that creates and structures social relations' (2007: 28). As in Maher's reading, my interviewees' ability to gaze bestows them with new possibility and potential.

It is important to problematize the link that the *sarte* make between their effacement and exploitation in the workspace and the notion of opportunity. Given the increasingly liberalized employment market in which these *sarte* were working, we might reflect on what interviewees' positive attitudes towards professional struggle say about the social context. In the years between the late 1940s and the economic boom in the late 1950s, the Christian Democrat government embraced the 'free play of market forces' (Ginsborg 1990: 153–54). We can note from collective contracts held in the Confederazione Generale Italiano del Lavoro (CGIL) archive in Bologna that in *sartorie*, the pay gap between male and female tailors in the highest (*lavoranti di 1' categoria*) and lowest (*apprendisti/e*) categories was over 50 per cent in the period between 1945 and 1954, and the pay gap between male and female workers existed and widened in the period between 1945 and 1960, only beginning to close from 1960 onwards. The gender pay gap was more keenly felt in higher-ranking positions, as can be understood from Figures 6.1 and 6.2. Curiously, in 1963 the salary tables show that men and women working as

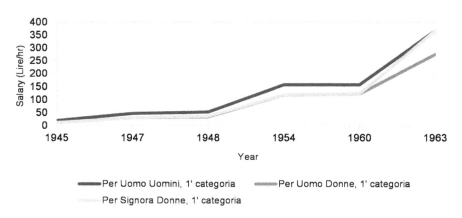

FIGURE 6.1: Salaries for First Grade Workers in *sartorie per uomo/per signora* between 1945 and 1963. Personal drawing, Flora Derounian, 2017.

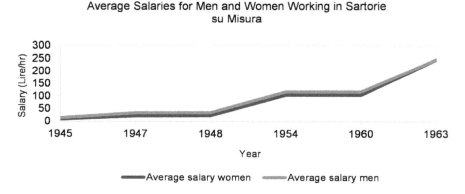

FIGURE 6.2: Average salaries for men and women working in *sartorie su misura* between 1945 and 1963. Personal drawing, Flora Derounian, 2017.

first-category workers in women's tailors received the same wages, whereas the opposite was true in men's tailors.

Interviewees' acceptance, and even enthusiasm, for a free market system where they experienced these obstacles and inequalities mirrors Italy's embrace of liberalism. This confirms Cohen's argument that historical context is an inextricable part of career narratives and that we can read social and political history through the ideologies narrators expound concerning their work (Cohen 2014: 14).

Interviewees suggest that the payoff for long hours and menial tasks was entry into the precious space of the *sartoria*. As in films, interviewees mark an ideological and hierarchical division between the spaces of the private workroom [*laboratorio*], the semi-public showroom and the urban public space outside, and underline the mobility their work gave them to move between various spaces. The *sarte*'s ability to occupy alternative spaces marks them out as independent and exceptional. Several of the *sarte* make references to their physical mobility. Coppola remembers travelling between her school and the *sartoria* every day, saying, 'I had to continue going to school because you can't stay ignorant […]. I would come back from school, do some homework, and then go to the *sartoria* in the afternoon' (2016). Here, Coppola links the ideas of increased physical freedom with greater intellectual, and thus social, mobility. Tinti confirms the increased mobility her work gave her, saying 'I wasn't interested in domestic life, the life of a housewife […]. I've always loved going out to work' (2016). Tinti makes the case for a professional life leading women to break through spatial and gender norms, calling to mind Massey's thesis that 'the limitation of women's mobility, in terms of both identity and space, has been in some cultural contexts a crucial means of subordination' (1994: 179). Finally, Neri recalls how 'they gave us these big wooden boxes and we would go by tram to deliver garments. […] Ah well, it was safer back then too. Back then you could go out in the streets and get back home' (2016). Neri's statement evokes an ease travelling through the urban space which is underlined as exceptional in its contrast with the contemporary urban space. In her research on oral histories with women strikers in 1930s Canada, Joan Sangster remarks upon women's tendency to downplay the dangers of the past in testimony, 'yet, from other sources and research, I knew that violence in the streets, and in women's homes, was very much a part of daily life' (1994: 9). Interviewees' erasure of potentially difficult professional realities as positive perhaps highlights its importance to their lives and careers.

Ideological space: Struggle, ambition, passion

Historian of the Italian textile industry Fiorella Imprenti notes that 'prioritising and being attached to one's work […] when applied to women took on ambiguous connotations' (2007: 168); this section examines the importance of work to my interviewees and how they articulate this. Coppola told me that 'you get into fashion by being among fabric offcuts from a young age' (2016), and this journey from humble social origins to professional success is reiterated by many. Without fail, interviewees specify their age at the time they began to work. The ages referenced are, historically speaking, remarkable because they indicate a contravention of laws in force at the time; of the women who began working independently (as opposed to in their husband's business, in the case of Tinti and Giordano), the average age at which they started work was 13.6, with a range between 10 and 20.[2] The legal minimum age at which a *sarta* could be employed was fourteen.[3] Lucia Garagnani, who worked in a men's tailors for her entire professional life, narrates how she lied to the owners in order to be hired, saying, 'when she saw me, she said: "look you can't come here you're too little". I said, "I'm twelve. I'll be thirteen in February, so I'm practically thirteen"' (Garagnani 2016). I would suggest that the frequent mention of their young starting ages feeds into the creation of a more general narrative of struggle and ingenuity. It intertwines with narratives which illustrate participants' passage from working-class, unskilled, and poor to personally, artistically, and economically independent.

Another way in which *sarte* express their professional journeys from humility to success is through identification with media portrayals of seamstresses. Although none of the interviewees spontaneously volunteered comments on screen representations of *sarte*, my suggestions of media portrayals were mostly met with enthusiasm and opinion. The most recognized representations were those of the *Sorelle Fontana* (Milani 2011), *Coco Before Chanel* (Fontaine 2009), and *Luisa Spagnoli* (Gasparini 2016), all well-known designers in Italy. Other television series mentioned include *Velvet* (Campos and Neira 2014) and *Le ragazze di piazza di Spagna* (Sánchez 1998). One *sarta* observed critically of the portrayal of Luisa Spagnoli, 'you don't get into fashion if you've grown up in a chocolate factory' (Coppola 2016). Poverty and hard work were the characteristics which interviewees most identified as being representative of a 'true' *sarta*. Neri comments:

> The story of the Fontana Sisters? Marvellous! It's a bit like that eh? It's not too far from reality. [...] Yes, they too came from a village, they too go to Rome, they start- I didn't have their huge success, of course not! But in my small way I'm happy with what I managed to do, where I come from, without anyone backing me who gave me- everything you see around me I earned with my own needle. No one gave me anything. I got nothing, no one gave me anything, so it's really like this eh.
>
> (Neri 2016)

Similarly, Coppola says:

> What I liked, and is admirable, no question about it, was the story of Coco Chanel [...]. She's a girl like me, eight or nine years old. They put her to work at the *sartoria* among the offcuts. And she created, put outfits together, made. And then she earned, she earned a pretty packet.
>
> (Coppola 2016)

Coppola's is actually a false memory; the film portrays Chanel as a cabaret singer in her youth before becoming a seamstress. Coppola's alternative memory highlights the importance of the transformation-through-fashion-work trope in *sarte*'s career narratives. Lucia Garagnani says of the protagonist of *Velvet*, 'Anna is like me. So much so that in the last episode she becomes a designer, she became [great]' (2016). These testimonies underline the importance of humble beginnings, independence, and persistence in *sarte*'s career narratives.

The transition from humility to success that interviewees construct in their career narratives is mirrored in descriptions of their move from rural to urban contexts. Torri describes the rural origins of her profession: 'my parents lived in the countryside, we had a rural house […] and I didn't have any materials, I dreamed of making clothes, and you know what I used? Leaves and flowers that I found in the fields' (2016). Neri notes that her rural background was seen as inappropriate for an aspiring seamstress, and that at the beginning of her job hunt she was turned away by owners who said 'no, you're from the countryside. You don't come from a *sartoria* background' (2016). Neri's story confirms the link between seamstresses and urban spaces which I underlined in Chapter 5, and reinforces the idea that the urban space gave women a degree of opportunity and the chance to break out of conventional gendered destinies.

Several of the *sarte* portray their entry into work as an economic and familial necessity. Giordano, who was a stylist in her husband's tailoring business, describes the beginning of her career, saying 'we started working immediately and we neither of us had a thing' (2016). Neri recounts the dramatic circumstances of her own financial need. The sixth of seven children, Neri saw her house destroyed and her father killed in a bombing during the Second World War. She recalls, 'I was thirteen in 1945. At that point, my mother sent me to a seamstress in the village, she was called Venusta' (2016). Both Giordano's and Neri's testimonies portray their entry into work as a result of necessity and relative hardship.

Yet, narratives of working for survival among my interviewees are insignificant in comparison to those of working for artistic fulfilment. In this way, my oral histories break with Fascist discourse of women labouring to serve the family and the nation state (Willson 2010: 85–86), and Christian Democrat rhetoric stated clearly 'that woman's role as mother and wife was both "essential" and "natural"' (Bonifazio 2011: 44). In contrast, my interviews evidence the occupation of a new ideological space and identity – that of the fulfilled female professional. Neri's approach to her work was far from what we might expect from her initial economic motivation. She describes how at the beginning of her career she changed workplace frequently, seeking out a more urban, industrialized model of *sartoria*, because she did not wish to work with domestic *sarte*. She recalls how her mother sent her to a seamstress, who also worked from her home with the smells of cooking all around, I didn't [like it]. So I took the phone book, I looked through all the *sartorie*. And I went and rang their doorbells, I did, I went for free.

(Neri 2016)

Neri's approach, prioritizing an artistic preference for high-class environments rather than the necessity of earning a living, moves away from the image of the *sarta* as manual labourer and towards the *sarta* as artist or artisan. Coppola, owner of a number of *scuole di taglio e cucito*, paints her entry into the workforce as motivated by ambition, saying 'I remember that it was during adolescence when you are trying to make a future for yourself. I mean more than anything it was families who wanted to send their daughters to learn the profession for their futures' (2016). Anna Tinti, who began working as a designer in her mother-in-law's lingerie business recounts how, 'at some point I got bored at home and I said [to my husband and sister in law]: "can I come to work with you?"' (2016). Even Tassoni and Garagnani, who began work during the difficult periods of Fascism and the Second World War, reference artistic ambitions. Tassoni frequented a renowned high-fashion school, while Lucia refused very early on in her career to complete only basic tasks, saying:

> I was one of the youngest. But I wasn't keen on those simple stitches. One day at thirteen years old I went to work, and I said to a colleague 'from tomorrow I'm not coming any more I'm fed up of these simple stitches, [...] I want to make a pocket', but he said to me 'Did you dream that up in your sleep last night?' [I replied] 'No, no! I want to do it'.

(Garagnani 2016)

Although the testimonies suggest a degree of necessity behind the women's choice to work, particularly for those who worked before and during the Second World War, a strong sense of artistic drive and ambition also emerges. These oral histories begin to show women as dynamic and driven, occupying ideological spaces which reflect the newfound liberalism and social flexibility of the post-war period.

Passion and independence

Not only do themes of pleasure, satisfaction, and fulfilment emerge strongly from the testimonies, but they are framed in language which elevates the *sarte*'s work. Competence is described as 'innate', ambition is 'love', and fulfilment is a 'dream'. Seamstresses frame their memories of work in terms of realization, affect, and fairytale. To first look at ideas of ability or competence, we can observe many instances of this being described as 'an innate ability probably [...] you don't learn it' (Tinti 2016). Coppola continues this discourse, saying of her aptitude, 'you feel it in your soul' (2016). There are also observations that 'you need to be gifted. If you're not you can't make it up' (Giordano 2016). These testimonies have the effect of painting the *sarte*'s work as the fruit of innate ability. The overlap with vocation narratives of nuns in Chapter 9 is striking. Vocation is a sense of divine calling corresponding to an innate ability and is significant because it removes a sense of personal drive or accountability in professional success. In this way, *sarte* avoid the traditionally masculine domain of ambition, keeping their career narratives feminine in lexis.

There is also a strong emphasis on the idea of passion in the interviews, with the word *passione* occuring nineteen times, and being employed by five out of the seven interviewees, in statements like, 'it's a passion for me, it has always been a passion' (Torri 2016). Interviewees urged me to follow their suit, saying, 'think about what your passion is, what gives you pleasure, what work you like' (Coppola 2016). Descriptions of the *sarte*'s work in emotional terms often reference the pleasure, even love, which they experienced for their work, saying: 'you need to love this work' (Neri 2016). Coppola affirms, 'you need love, passion, you're like a painter, if you feel it in your soul you become great, but if you don't feel it there's nothing you can do' (Coppola 2016), intensifying a sense of drive born of emotion. In two cases, the *sarte* describe falling in love with the fashion world, once when Torri recalls how as a child watching Cinderella she 'fell in love, *not* with the prince [...] [but] with the fairy godmother', because of her costume (Torri 2016). Neri, too, stated, 'I fall in love and instead of buying a painting I'll buy a fabric' (Neri 2016). It is interesting to note that, in both instances, the women contrast their behaviour – motivated by love – to an imagined appropriate behaviour. We could argue that these descriptions both highlight the emotive character of the *sarte*'s work and simultaneously underline it as a digression from usual or suitable behaviour.

There are also frequent references to interviewees' professional experiences as unreal, describing them as *sogno* [dream] and *favola* [fairytale]. Neri describes her ambition to have her own *sartoria* as 'the dreams you dream up' (Neri 2016). In two instances, interviewees comment, 'our life was a fairytale' (Tinti 2016; Neri 2016). In Maher's investigation of *sarte* working between 1980 and 1960, she highlights precisely the same linguistic trends and usages as those which occurred spontaneously among my interviewees. Maher comes to the conclusion that, 'seamstresses attribute their abilities to the "force of will" and "passion" with which they were gifted: the ability to experience *emotions* that others didn't, to have a creative outlet. "Passion" transformed their work into a gift, a vocation' (Maher 2007:

202). In other contexts and timeframes, the same trend in female interviewees has been observed (Cohen 2014: 8). We might argue that the *sarte*'s descriptions of their work in terms of dream or fairy tale are symptomatic of shaping an identity – that of the successful working woman – into a socially-acceptable form. Echoing Meisenbach's findings, the interviewee takes pains to '[make] sure the interviewer knows that she did not engage in any (masculine) pursuit of power' (2010: 8). Framing success in the unreal and fictitious terms of a dream or fairy tale in some way diminishes that success in narratives, turning it into something less tangible and more a result of chance. It is interesting to note that the more successful the *sarta* being interviewed, the more she frames her life in terms of dream or fairy tale; Tinti, who worked with national department store COIN, and Neri, who successfully opened her own high-fashion *sartoria*, are probably the most economically successful of the *sarte* with whom I spoke, and also those who most frequently employ the dream or fairy tale image.

Maher suggests, as I have, that we might read the *sarte*'s language choices in this case as attributing their work to a certain 'weakness and irrationality where "emotion" indicates lack of logic and chaos' (2007: 203). Similarly, in interviews the *sarte* do not describe their work in terms of logical or ordered process. Luciana Torri inaccurately described her workroom to me as 'chaos!' (Torri 2016). In fact, only Garagnani who worked as a seamstress for men, and Coppola, who produced both men and women's garments, underlined order and protocol as part of their work. Coppola even went so far as to say 'the most important thing this work can give you is a sense of precision. Order. Above all, order' (2016). Even wage tables and collective contracts produced between 1945 and 1965 and held in the CGIL archive in Bologna reflect the idea of men's tailors following an ordered structure. These legal documents set out the amount of time each garment would take to make, and how much it would cost. No such provision is made for women's dressmakers, presumably because of the infinite range of garments which they might produce, and the fact that the 'chaos' and 'imagination' which thus ensued made it impossible to fit their work into an order. The fact that seamstresses who worked in more male environments favour traditionally masculine attributes in their career narratives is typical, as Robin Ely has elucidated in her study of male-dominated vs. sex-integrated law firms. In her study, Ely found that women in male-dominated firms are more likely to associate traditionally masculine characteristics with success. If it is true that through the narration of one's career one 'articulates and performs' identity (Lapointe 2010: 2), seamstresses are mostly commonly performing a specifically female identity which reflects social preferences for female emotion and 'soft' skills.

I now wish to discuss *sarte*'s expressions of independence, arguing that they represent seamstresses' occupation of new ideological spaces. Although independence is a theme which emerged strongly from the interviews, the term itself was only used by the *sarte* after I suggested it as an interpretation, for example:

> COPPOLA: I was able to fulfil my own desires [...]. I didn't need to go to my parents or a man [...]. I never wanted for money because I always earned. [...]
>
> INTERVIEWER: So your work gave you independence?
>
> COPPOLA: A great deal of independence! I can freely say 'I can live on my own' [...] because I can count on myself.
>
> (Coppola 2016)

Although the *sarte* never spontaneously offer the term 'independence', I have identified several key ways in which they frame the subject: through references to self-realisation, rebellion, and mobility.

Tinti asserts that her work allowed her to escape the domestic sphere, saying 'we only went home to sleep' (2016), and Giordano states that although she had no formal education, her profession meant that 'I knew how to stick up for myself' (Giordano 2016). These statements allow us to see how work provides individual independence which breaks with conventional gendered destinies. Other *sarte* explain their ambition and self-fulfilment through work. Coppola describes her passion for learning, saying '[I always had this taste] for learning [...] I would stay two or three months in a *sartoria* and then move on' (Coppola 2016). She explains that 'I was so driven, [...] in our day, women were trying to progress, so I wanted to work either in fashion or in cinema' (Coppola 2016). This statement echoes ideas that in the 1950s and 1960s the professions which offered women radical life change were few and often linked to their cultivation of body and beauty. Other interviewees had more fundamental ambitions for their work. In animated terms, Tassoni describes her choice to work because,

> I wanted to be considered a person. I didn't want to do as they told me. [striking her fist on the table] [...] I wanted to decide for myself, make my own choices [...] not always say 'yes Sir, no Sir'.
>
> (Tassoni 2016)

These statements narrate the *sarte*'s work as an opportunity for empowerment and independence. Interviewees echo Maher's observation that through their work seamstresses 'maintained a vivid sense of self and their own ability to act' (2007: 196). The very notion of women's self-fulfilment not orbiting around the family, domesticity, or sexual attractiveness diverges from filmic representations, and social, political, and religious discourse of the post-war period and points instead to the *sarte* occupying novel ideological spaces. Acknowledging Cohen's argument that 'career is a retrospective concept' (Cohen 2014: 18), we might also posit that interviewees entwine elements of contemporary discourse, where work has been a core component of feminist notions of emancipation, into their narratives.

In her investigation into female workers in Turin, Luisa Passerini notes that the women often described themselves as *ribelli* [rebels] (1987: 21–2). Maher states that this is not the case for *sarte*, saying, 'Torinese seamstresses seem to experience their profession as suitable to their female gender' (2007: 216), a statement which my testimonies refute. The term *ribelle* is spontaneously employed by two interviewees, Tassoni (who repeatedly uses the term), saying, 'I was always very rebellious [...] against those who wanted me to obey' (2016), and Neri, who laughs, 'I've always been a bit of a rebel' (2016). I agree with Passerini, who suggests that interviewees self-identify as rebels because they acknowledge how they transgress gender norms (1987: 27).

Aside from direct descriptions of being rebels, seamstresses provide anecdotes which suggest transgression of gender norms through their work. One such narrative involves romance being replaced by work. Torri's anecdote about falling in love with the fairy godmother in Cinderella rather than the prince is a humorous example of her rejection of expected gender behaviours. Laughing, she states 'I couldn't have given a flying fig about the Prince!' (Torri 2016). Neri similarly recalls replacing love with self-reliance and passion for work:

> I found a boyfriend. He was so handsome, tall. He was my first love, it was wonderful, at seventeen years old. When I was about twenty [...] he came to me one fine day and said 'I'm getting married'. Because his other girl had gotten pregnant. [He went on] 'because before you, I had another girl'. 'Ok, go then', I said. And I understood something in that moment. I saw him a long time after and I said, 'I should send you flowers because you changed my life for the better, [...] you made me understand that I should only ever count on myself'.
>
> (Neri 2016)

Neri then goes on to discuss how this experience made her fiercely independent; at 30 she decided to have a child and rejected the idea of marriage saying 'I was married to my work' (Neri 2016). These statements underline *sarte*'s transgression of expected female behaviours. Recognizing that 'the image of [...] the worker whose identity is subsumed in the product, [is] traditionally part of masculine stereotypes' (Passerini 1987: 51), my interviewees re-appropriate the conventionally male notion of being romantically attached to one's work.

To tie together the ideas in this section, there is evidence and reference to the *sarte*'s independence and the new opportunities which their work gave them. Yet, there are implicit recognitions by interviewees of the transgressive nature of this independence. Unlike the fictional representations of seamstresses in Chapter 5, these interviews are not rehearsals of new gender behaviours (Wood 2006: 60) that can be driven to reassuring traditional conclusions, and as such are exceptional in their positive exhortation of female work and independence.

Class, clients, and status; 'Tell me how you dress and I'll tell you who you are'.

One of the most striking aspects of the interviews is participants' complex attitudes to social class. Like films with *sarte*, oral histories demonstrate the *sarte*'s understanding of the class system. The relationship between fashion, social class and identity construction is acknowledged by fashion scholar Diana Crane, who states that 'clothing is an indication of how people in different eras have perceived their positions in social structures and negotiated status boundaries' (Crane 2001: 1). Or, as Garagnani simply puts it, 'tell me how you dress and I'll tell you who you are' (2016). This section looks at how *sarte* narrate class and social change, their relationships with clients and the social mobility at stake in their professions.

Explicit references to class emerge in the interviews in response to the question, 'what were your clients like?', with most replies referencing clients' economic or social superiority. Clients are referred to as 'high-class people' (Torri 2016), and 'people who were pretty … propertied' (Giordano 2016). In addition to these descriptions of clients' wealth, interviewees demonstrate a nuanced understanding of the political and social change which impacted upon the fashion industry and the relationship between the *sartoria su misura* [made-to-measure *sartoria*] and social mobility. Oriana Neri details the evolution of the class system in Bologna between 1945 and 1970, saying:

> We began with nobles, it was the nobility who came to the *sartoria*. Then the nobility fell, and the industrial class started coming, […] wives of industrialists started coming to us. Then the politicians. And then we began to see generations of all different kinds of people coming through.
>
> (Neri 2016)

This is a potted history of the social changes occurring in what Ginsborg calls the 'Third Italy' between 1945 and 1965 (1990: 254). Neri's relation of class to profession, and her demonstration of class privileges gradually extending to a wider demographic, mirrors the 'radical changes in employment patterns and class composition of Italian society' (Ginsborg 1990: 235). Other interviewees comment, 'going to the *sartoria* wasn't for workers' (Giordano 2016). The implication in these oral histories is that increasingly the *sartoria* was a space for the *nouveaux riches* to assert their status via the acquisition of what Bourdieu has called symbolic capital (1985). In the changing context of post-war Italy, new money was still seeking old expressions of status through embodied cultural capital and the *sarte* were instrumental in that process. They advised and facilitated access to appropriate products for the construction of class identities.

Interviewees describe a rigid class system, where specific items and garments become signifiers of cultural capital and class. Neri notes how clients instructed her in this system:

> You learn a lot from clients. I may have taught them how to dress, but they also taught me a lot; [...] if you listen, you understand what is right, what is wrong. Even when they put on a garment, the good ones tell you, 'no, it's done like this'.
>
> (Neri 2016)

Neri seems to corroborate fashion sociologist George Simmel's theory that fashion is dictated by the upper classes and imitated by the lower (Simmel 1957). More recently, Kawamura has observed, 'fashion both requires a certain degree of mobility and fluidity within a society and promotes a more egalitarian society and erases class boundaries' (2004: 4). If there is a set of class signifiers, these can be imitated and thus social mobility is possible. The *sarte*'s recollections exemplify this process. Neri is not the only *sarta* to observe some of the trappings indicative of cultural capital. Coppola paints a similar picture in descriptions of her working environment, saying 'we had luxury clients, luxury salons with carpets, red carpets, gold mirrors, [...] fashion magazines from France' (2016). These signifiers of class in the fashion environment also emerge in wider discourse on *sartorie di alta moda*; Micol Fontana, legendary *sarta* of the Roman *Sartoria Sorelle Fontana*, in fact named her autobiography *Specchio a tre luci* (*Three-Way Mirror*) (1992), choosing the iconic backlit mirror as a signifier for her career in high fashion.

Recollections of a class system so rigidly based on material signifiers such as dress and decoration tie in with interviewees' comments on branding. Giordano describes how she gave clients a branded label to be sewn into garments:

> INTERVIEWER: Was it important to have the label?
>
> GIORDANO: Certainly! If it was a Blumarine or Oscar Valentino. [...] The brand was really important. Now it's a bit different. [...] You can't tell real from fake. They've changed how they think here in Italy.
>
> (Giordano 2016)

The nostalgia and evocation of social change that ventures beyond fashion into politics is clear in Giordano's statement, suggesting that if the class system has changed, so too have its symbols and signifiers. I would argue that part of the reason that discussion of class is so prominent in these oral histories is because it marks and is marked by a nostalgia for a social reality that no longer exists in the same form.

Clients emerge as protagonists in the *sarte*'s oral histories. Paulicelli underlines 'the importance of the relationship between a customer and a tailor or dressmaker' (2015: 2). More than any other element of their work, clients are the pivotal point around which the *sarte* narrate their careers. What is perhaps most notable is the binary way in which clients are presented; between personal emotional relationships and impersonal financial transactions.

On the one hand, it is clear that many of the *sarte* have fond memories of personal relationships with clients. Torri remembers how clients 'brought us gifts, even for us girls, […] perfume, chocolates, stockings, small things like that' (2016). Garagnani states 'yes, they knew me [they would say] "you have a golden touch"' (2016). Neri underlines the emotional element of the *sarta* – client exchange, saying 'I have some clients, ooh they write me letters, if I read them to you you'd cry. […] I have one client who says I've changed her life' (2016). Maher makes a similar observation of the *sarte* she interviews in post-war Turin, saying 'the rapport between seamstress and client has connotations of emotion and intimacy' (2007: 232). These accounts mirror the autobiography written by Micol Fontana (1991), in which she structures her own life story around her favourite customers, dedicating a chapter to each.

Yet, despite the evident emotional exchange between seamstresses and their clients, interviewees also point to a divide between the client and the worker; one which cannot be surpassed by friendship or intimacy. Revisiting the theme of the letters she receives, Neri observes, 'they are the protagonists. You are the one who serves them. Then there are those that write me letters, send me flowers […]. No, I'm extremely fortunate' (2016). This statement puts a different slant on her original comment; although she considers herself fortunate to receive affection and appreciation from her clients, she precedes this with an acknowledgement of the difference in their relative statuses. Similarly, Torri recounts of the same singers who would send the *sarte* gifts or tips:

TORRI: Many of the singers who came here to the seaside […] like Milva [Maria Ilva Biolcati], and Mina [Anna Maria Mazzini] […] we would have loved to have got their photo and an autograph.[4]

INTERVIEWER: And did you?

TORRI: Absolutely not! It was forbidden!

(Torri 2016)

These interviewees highlight a differential in power dynamics which Neri summarizes in the following observation:

> My story, I think you [the researcher] are the only one who knows it, because I've never told it. They [the clients], don't get to know your soul. They talk about themselves. You have to become their psychologist. Because as they undress, they also undress their souls, they tell you and you have to remember for next time.
> (Neri 2016)

For all the stories of clients appreciating seamstresses, there is something deeply affecting about an 84-year-old woman telling a 26-year-old researcher that she is the first person the seamstress has met in her professional life who has been interested in hearing her story. In all the above statements, there is a sort of one-way intimacy between *sarte* and clients which, although unequal, is ultimately portrayed as benefitting both parties, whether emotionally or economically.

Neri's description of becoming a psychologist to her clients evokes the concept of emotional work. Emotional labour, first theorized by Arlie Hochschild in her seminal work, *The Managed Heart: Commercialization of Human Feeling* (1983), is defined as the performance of emotion required in a professional role, or 'the work involved in dealing with *other peoples*' feelings' (James 1989: 15, my emphasis), as Neri's interview demonstrates. Hochschild reads the performance of emotional labour as gendered, arguing that 'lacking other resources, women make a resource out of feeling' (1983: 163). This emotional–financial exchange is underlined by Neri who elaborates, 'if they don't have a psychologist you don't come far from becoming one. Because they pay you – they certainly pay you – but you have to listen to them' (2016), confirming the necessity for a *sarta* to perform emotional labour. The *sarte* recount performing dual identities, one in the new superior social space which their profession allows them, the other still occupying the position of social inferior.

Much of the gratification which the *sarte* glean from their jobs is remembered as being personal rather than financial. In my interview with Coppola, I observe that she experienced much success in her career, to which she replies, 'yes, I had success, but more importantly I had satisfaction because that's what keeps you alive' (2016), defining success as emotional. *Sarte* particularly articulate their success and satisfaction through comments about how appreciated their work was. When prompted to elaborate on whether the work of *sarte* had been appreciated, most responded positively, saying, 'they queued up to see me' (Garagnani 2016), and 'people held me in very high esteem' (Tassoni 2016). Torri underlines the social importance of becoming a *sarta*, saying, 'being a seamstress meant a lot [...] it was a respected profession, it meant a lot to families' (2016). These narratives express financial and professional success in emotional terms.

Interviewees provide numerous examples of how their work affected their social status and mobility. Torri comments, 'I never felt awkward, because I was the owner's assistant. *Basta*. I wasn't phased by who the client might be' (Torri 2016). Her professional identity protected her from the implied embarrassment of frequenting other social classes. Reflecting Bourdieu's theory that 'possession of a durable network of more or less institutionalized relationships' (1985: 248) is a passport to social mobility, Coppola told me, 'I chose my clientele carefully, because I was trying to get into circles I wouldn't normally have been able to integrate' (2016). Both Torri and Coppola recount how their own self-perception was radically transformed through their work; Torri twice comments: 'I thought I was Christian Dior! Dior, and I was just an apprentice!' (2016), and Coppola notes that 'at that time, to say "I'm going to train to be a designer" was like saying you were going to outer space' (2016). Although these statements might suggest a positive side to the *sarte*'s social mobility, it is also revealed as problematic. Torri goes on to explain that her status as a seamstress marked her out as different:

> In my generation, they made you feel different [...]. I was twenty when I opened my shop. My father was a machinist on the public railways, he earned sixty thousand Lire a month back then [...]. But me, in one dress I could make one hundred and twenty thousand. My father worked a month for what I earned in two days [...]. So that was something my father experienced as [...] how can I say it? As a humiliation.
> (Torri 2016)

Although *sarte* evoke the advantages of social capital, intimacy with clients is also problematized. Seamstresses' work rendered social hierarchies more fluid, creating spaces in which they could be a servant, a counsel and a friend. Yet, seamstresses express a certain distance from their clients, in comments like 'I never wanted to be one of them' (Neri 2016) and 'clients are like stomach pains, one goes and another arrives' (Coppola 2016). The *sarte*'s double status is narrated as leading to problems, in the sense that although *sarte* may have enjoyed a degree of social promotion, their success neither fully promoted them to a new class, nor was it looked kindly upon by their original social class. Maher notes a similar double-bind of *sarte*; *n*ot the equal of their clients, yet estranged from religious and working-class institutions (2007: 242).

Despite the evident social mobility their work gave them, none of the interviewees ever cite social climbing as a motivating factor. At most there are references to the appeal of '[being among] dynamic people' (Giordano 2016), the excitement of seeing famous singers and actors, the desire to work in luxurious *sartorie* rather than domestic ones, or the desire for economic stability. Self-representation points to *sarte* as ambitious artists rather than social climbers and their social mobility as a result, rather than a goal, of their work. Like their accounts of professions as fairy tales, interviewees shy away from narratives which explicitly state traditionally masculine pursuit of ambition or status.

Conclusion

This chapter has revealed the sometimes ambiguous nature of seamstresses's accounts of occupying new physical, ideological, and social spaces. The chapter has shown the significance of social context in subjects' career narratives, and to what extent their work was perceived as transgressing social, political, religious and gender norms. Unlike films, oral histories idealize women's spatial freedom. Despite many evocations of newfound independence, satisfaction, mobility, and agency through work, oral histories mainly avoid direct expressions of transgression or ambition. Rather, interviewees often employ strategies which gender their work as conventionally feminine. This tendency reflects Maher's thesis that the work of the *sarte* was seen as inherently feminine (1987: 138) by women themselves as well as wider society. Rather than interpreting this discourse as devaluing their work, this chapter underlines the need to interrogate women's career narratives by considering how they interact with, and are informed by, historical context and gender norms.

NOTES

1. To source interviewees, Elisa Tolsi Brandi's book (2009) was very helpful.
2. Respectively, interviewees reported ages upon starting work were 11, 20, 12, 12, 13, 12, 15.
3. According to the 1945 *Verbale di accordo per la sistemazione dei lavoratori dipendenti di aziende industriali esercenti l'attività di sartoria per signora,* consultable at the CGIL archive in Bologna.
4. Milva was an Italian pop singer and famous redhead who was active during the 1960s. Mina was also famous during the 1960s as a pop singer with a three-octave vocal range.

SECTION 3

RELIGIOUS WORK – NUNS

7

A Brief History of Nuns in Post-war Italy

There were 144,171 women religious, or nuns, in Italy in the year 1951, accounting for 20.1 per cent of the unmarried female population (Rocca 1992: 53).[1] In regions such as Umbria and Basilicata, women religious accounted for over half of the unmarried female population (Rocca 1992). Scholars of women religious widely agree that the activity of nuns can be qualified as work, labour, and often profession. Particularly given the Church's encouragement in its 1950 *Sponsa Christi* for religious to engage in remunerated activity, and the professionalization of much social work – historically undertaken by nuns – in the nineteenth and twentieth centuries. Women religious have historically dominated the sectors of care and education in Italy and elsewhere. This data begins to paint a picture of why women religious are so significant to women's labour history in Italy. As John Pollard notes, 'religion and politics in Italy have been inextricably intertwined […] in a way that is not comparable in other European countries' (2008: 4), foregrounding the influence of religious ideas around gender to wider socio-political attitudes in Italy between 1945 and 1965. The chapters in this section assess the interaction between religious and secular discourse around women, and how it permeates cultural materials like film, and women's accounts of themselves in interviews. This section on nuns asks the questions: who were the Italian women religious living and working between 1945 and 1965, and how do they remember their lives? How are women religious portrayed and remembered as workers? What features of representations and testimonies recur, and what might this say about post-Second World War and contemporary society? What challenges, if any, do portrayals and testimonies of women religious pose to gender norms?

The information presented here provides a background against which the two following chapters develop. Chapter 8 examines filmic representations of women religious between 1945 and 1965, providing a close textual analysis of the films *Anna* (Lattuada 1951), *Suor Letizia* (Camerini 1956), and *Lettere di una novizia* (Lattuada 1960). Chapter 9 presents a corpus of oral history interviews collected with women religious who worked between 1945 and 1965, presenting and analyzing the memories they exhibit.

Research on Italian nuns working between 1945 and 1965 is important because nuns represent a sizeable all-female workforce which has been largely ignored. Existing literature about the work of women religious is mostly – although not exclusively – restricted to convent records, or histories of individual convents, foundresses, or saints. Although the scholarly network History of Women Religious of Britain and Ireland has made important steps in valorizing their work, inquiry has not, according to Tom O'Donaghue and Anthony Potts, 'been accompanied by a major corpus of serious scholarship on the social history of the lives of the "religious"' (2004: 469). Particularly in Italy, the drive to record or celebrate the work of women religious comes from within institutions themselves, rather than from academia. Their study is also important because it pursues oral history's goal of giving silent people a voice (Foot 2008: 165).

Nuns present a special case in terms of memory and representation, since often their beliefs cause them to shy away from both. A core drive of nuns' lives, the abnegation of the self, means that they do not often tell their own histories, particularly during their lifetimes, and historical or popular interest and enquiry are most often posthumous. Visual representations of nuns have most commonly been found in cinema and pornography, both of which have been historically problematic for the Church. Particularly in Italy, in the period following the Second World War, the Catholic Church responded to a cinema industry it disapproved of by developing a highly influential network of *cinema parrocchiali* [parish cinemas] which accounted for a third of all cinemas in the 1950s (Bayman 2014: 66) and exclusively showed works approved by the Vatican (Treveri Gennari et al. 2016: 220). Nuns on screen were mostly created by secular directors and played by secular actors; representations of nuns in film are therefore more a mirror of society's image of women religious than their reality.

Catholicism, and its influence and ideas regarding women were in a period of change after 1945. In her work on the British case, Carmen Mangion points to a 'noticeable shift' from the 1940s and an encouragement from the Holy See to prioritize 'engagement with the modern world: adaptation, renewal, and change' (2020: 4). Both secular and religious ideals for women were mutating; previously inspired by saints, women of faith were now beginning to move towards self-determination. A survey of women by the *Gioventù Femminile* [Women's Youth] (a branch of *Azione Cattolica* [Catholic Action]) in 1958 demonstrated that 'only 26 per cent of teenagers chose saints as role models' (La Scuola 1988: 282), marking a shift in Catholicism's influence on gender ideals. However, we should not overestimate the progress made by the Church in the matter of female emancipation. Adriana Valerio notes of the Church, 'even after Vatican II the Church, the "perfect society", presented itself as monarchical, gerarchical, clerical, and masculine […] to which we can add the institutional invisibility of women' (2016: 174). Italian society was somewhat moving towards secularization, and although at the end of the Second World War 'some 95 per cent of Italians were baptised into the Catholic faith, the proportion of practising Catholics was significantly less (circa 60 per cent)' (Allum 1990: 80). Thus, we see an increasing distance between the Church and the Italian people, and with this, bifurcating notions of ideal womanhood.

What was the state of the Church following the Second World War? In the aftermath of war, popular Italian opinion of the Church was complicated and not helped by the ambiguous position which the Church had occupied in relation to the Fascist regime (Montagnolo 2016). Despite this ambiguity, in the immediate post-Second World War years – before much speculation about the Church's role in Fascism was aired – Catholic morals and institutions played an important role in post-war reconstruction. The year 1945 opened up new political and social identities for Italian women and men but the Church struggled to do likewise. In the period between 1945 and 1965, there were two major challenges to the relationship between Catholicism and women: the Second Vatican Council (Vatican II) and feminism. Catholic models of womanhood were hugely important to women, who were more likely than men to be socially and politically Catholic. According to a 1962 DOXA survey, '61 per cent of women had attended Mass [in the last week] in contrast to only 39 per cent of men' (Willson 2010: 200).

Vatican II, held between 1962 and 1965, aimed at renewed integration of the Church in the world but, in terms of its treatment of women, it was problematic. Excluded from the first two sessions of the Council, women were eventually admitted as auditors to the final two sessions, after the apt observation of Cardinal Léon-Joseph Suenens, the author of *The Nun in the World* (1963), who objected to the absence of women, saying 'it seems to me that women constitute 50 per cent of humanity' (Valerio 2016: 179). Female auditors came from a wide range of religious, secular, and professional backgrounds and – contrary to the expectations of many attendees – participated actively in Council proceedings (Valerio 2016: 195). There is still a question over how much the Council changed the Church's attitude to women. The sources examined in this section are produced in the runup to Vatican II; the films in Chapter 8 were all made and released pre-Vatican II, and the interviewees in Chapter 9 were all born and taken into orders by the end of the Council. As such, an effort will be made to detect the winds of change which were blowing towards Vatican II; principally, the modernization of religious, social, industrial and gender norms.

More explicit is the line the Church took in response to feminism, and it is useful to understand the religious ideals of femininity which appear in both chapters of this section. Obviously, the Virgin Mary is the central female figure of Catholicism and behind the Catholic idealization of motherhood. Lesley Caldwell notes that in post-war Italy, 'the Christian representation of femininity was almost completely identified with motherhood' (2006: 225). Key concerns of Italian feminism in the 1950s and 1960s, such as birth control, access to the workplace, and economic and legal independence, were regarded with disapproval by the Church, which, 'suspecting the subversion of its doctrinal and social order condemned outright all of women's claims, conflating them with secularism, free-thinking, and socialism' (Valerio 2016: 176). Although in word the Church claimed to value women, in deed it continued to overlook them. Up to and beyond Vatican II, a number of the Church's priorities remained largely unchanged, including 'the family and the subordinate position of women' (Allum 1990: 82). Catholicism – and indeed Italian society at large – reverted to traditional gender roles after the Second World War, promoting the female roles of 'wife and mother, bride of Christ, and apostle' (La Scuola 1988: 238). The root of the Church's inflexibility is to be found in its insistence on the essential difference between women and men which it used as an alibi against modernization and feminism. Tied in with maternity was the valorization of female sacrifice, citing 'feminine gifts of maternalism, family-spirit, and sense of giving and sacrifice' (La Scuola 1988: 278). The Church often foregrounded maternity and sacrifice as a way of supposedly valorizing women.

How did the Church perceive women's work? Despite apparent traditionalism in the Church, the subject of women's work was a subject which divided cardinals between 'the possible overturning of roles' and the 'riches that the female universe could offer to reinvigorate the Catholic faith' (Valerio 2016: 174). On the one hand, women's work was linked to feminism and modernity. The Church repeatedly underlined the dangers of work for women. An example of this is the magazine of the *Gioventù femminile*, which warned working women in 1952, 'our environment is peppered with dangers' (La Scuola 1988: 287). On the other hand, there were definite shifts in the perceived value of women's work. Apostolic work and missions were common for women religious and represented a concerted placing of women in professional roles. Women's integration into the workplace was progressively encouraged by the Church, although it was never discussed as profession but rather as vocation.

Cardinal Suenens argued forcefully that 'a community of nuns often enough gives the impression of being a fortress whose drawbridge is only furtively and fearfully lowered' (1963: 17). He asserted that women religious should, instead, be to the community what yeast is to dough, leavening it (1963: 1). Recruitment figures were also directly linked to the professional opportunities provided by religious life, creating concern in the Church that women were taking religious vows in order to work. Until the Second World War, convents had seen various fluctuations in recruitment but they were challenged in the immediate post-war, leading some scholars to argue that this was due to the rise in alternative career paths for women who wished to work in the community (Rocca 2013: 145–46). Whilst enclosed orders maintained high levels of demand, teaching orders, and those whose work could now largely be done without the need to become a nun, experienced a drop in recruits (Campbell-Jones 1979: 77). This decrease was still greater following Vatican II. This data suggests that women sometimes entered religious orders more for the career it offered than for spiritual reasons, a theme brought to light in oral histories in Chapter 9.

These currents in the Church and Italian society are important to acknowledge because they constitute the context within which representations and testimonies of women religious are formed. The period between 1945 and 1965 marks a time in which the Church was intensely preoccupied with being perceived as being both in-step with contemporary society and simultaneously the guardian of traditional religious doctrine. Women were a pivotal group through which this dynamic was negotiated.

NOTE

1. Women religious is the term used in the academic field dedicated to their study.

8

Fallen Women: Filmic Representations of Nuns

A 'sudden and never to be repeated domination of women in religious films' (Grignaffini 1999: 299) is how Giovanna Grignaffini describes the burgeoning presence of nuns in film in the immediate post-Second World War period (Figure 8.1). Why this sudden prominence of nuns in cinema, and what do their portrayals say about post-1945 society? This chapter draws parallels between the 'three-way tug-of-war' in post-war Italy, between the United States, the Soviet Union, and the Vatican (Pojmann 2013: 6) and how this influenced portrayals of nuns in film. The social and religious tension between modernization and retrenchment is played out in film, and more specifically

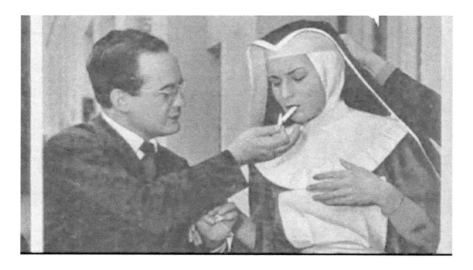

FIGURE 8.1: Silvana Mangano on the set of *Anna* (1951). Captured from the documentary Rai Edu, *Sorriso amaro*, 2009. Italy. Doc Italia. *Sorriso amaro*, Rai Edu, 2009.

in the figure of the nun. This tension mirrors the concerns of Vatican II, held between 1962 and 1965, of *ressourcement* [going to the origins] and *aggiornamento* [updating].

Cinema was a place where commercial interest met moral propaganda and was a focus for the state and Church alike in post-war Italy. The chapter assesses portrayals of nuns in the context of cinema. Pope Pius XI argued that films should be 'moral, moralising, educator' (Treveri Gennari 2009: 116); the present chapter asks what gendered morality cinema propounded, and why. How important were portrayals of nuns as alternative versions of femininity? Anna Maria Torriglia observes that in the post-Second World War period 'cinema rediscovers women' (2002: 58), and she groups *Anna* (Lattuada 1951) – a film about a nun – with a number of other films of the period that supposedly do just that. Of this attention, Torriglia says, 'film directors start to share a genuine, though at times ambivalent, admiration for the female characters they portray' (2002: 58). Millicent Marcus observes of the use of female characters that they allow 'filmmakers to apply all the dualisms implicit in traditional portrayals of women to the plight of the post-war state' (2000: 330). This chapter studies portrayals of cinematic nuns and their work, asking what these portrayals might say about the dualisms they represented, and the ambivalent admiration of the societies which produced them.

The three films studied in this chapter are *Anna* (Lattuada 1951), *Suor Letizia* (*The Awakening*) (Camerini 1956), and *Lettere da una novizia* (Lattuada 1960). I will use the French language title *La novice* [*The Novice*] for the latter film throughout, as it is the version which is still available to view. The choice of these films aims to provide a temporal spread of cultural production around women religious during the period between 1945 and 1965, focusing here on the 1950s. As noted in the introduction to this section, this period was marked by shifting social and religious ideas around womanhood, and women religious had a role to play in the negotiation of this. The tension between modern and traditional female characters has a number of sociohistorical underpinnings. Italy of the 1950s has been dubbed by historians as the Italian 'restoration', grappling with reconstruction, modernization, and Americanism. The Christian Democrat government was, to a great extent, beholden to these ideals because of its acceptance of the Marshall Plan. Ideologically, however, 'traditional Catholic social theory lay uneasily alongside liberal individualism' (Ginsborg 1990: 153), and the Christian Democrats 'preached the need to safeguard Catholic values in a changing society' (Ginsborg 1990: 153). The contradictions between American and Catholic influence can be found inscribed in portrayals of women in film. Italian cinema had to compete with popular American portrayals of women, 'for the sake of its own financial stability and well-being' (Treveri Gennari 2009: 8). Yet, the Church exerted a strong force against the 'pathological and uncontrollable eroticism' (Treveri Gennari 2009: 115) of these films.

The chapter first assesses the history of representing women religious in film. A link is drawn between filmic nuns and secular heroines in melodrama, arguing that nuns are allowed less punitive conclusions to their narratives. As mentioned in the introduction to this section, a religious discourse of ideal womanhood was restricted to praising women's maternalism and self-sacrifice. A key focus of this chapter is the extent to which the convent and the nun can be considered symbols of transgressive or emancipated femininity. Nuns are working women, yet because they represent Catholicism, I suggest that they were acceptable characters to the Christian Democrat government and Catholic Church. Because nuns represent traditionalism and care, I suggest that they were reassuring to both lay and secular audiences in the moral and social upheaval of the Italian post-war restoration.

Yet, nuns are also portrayed as unstable and desperate, and consistently victims of unbridled carnal desires. Scaraffia and Zarri argue that 'the heart of post-war cinema's representational system is the female body caught in a net of motives that far more explicitly bring out the conflicts between guilt and innocence, sexuality and maternity' (1999: 299). The final part of this chapter argues that nuns' filmic identities are in fact dominated by an interest in their bodily maternal and/or sexual urges. Female characters, 'when sexualised, provide a doubleness (new/old, virginal/experienced, pure/fallen) on which post-war filmmakers will base their critique of the national self' (Marcus 2000: 330). These portrayals suggest a national unease about perceived changes in gender politics and an underlying patriarchal interpretation of women who choose religious life as unnatural. Film allows for transgressive modern behaviours to be attempted, and then reabsorbed into conservative conclusions.

The corpus

The earliest of the films, Alberto Lattuada's 1951 *Anna*, was the second-most popular film of the period 1945–65, taking almost 500 million Lire at the box office (Treveri Gennari 2009: 114). *Anna* is set in Milan and follows Anna (Silvana Mangano), a religious sister working as a nurse in Ospedale Niguarda Ca' Granda.[1] Anna's world is shaken when her ex-fiancé, Andrea (Raf Vallone), makes a reappearance in her life after a near-fatal road accident brings him to the hospital. Through a series of flashbacks, we understand that Anna used to work as a singer and dancer in a nightclub, and had a torrid romance with one of the barmen, Vittorio (Vittorio Gasman), until she decided to accept her client Andrea's proposal of marriage. Anna prepares to become Andrea's wife by moving out to his countryside home but Vittorio, unwilling to accept Anna's new life, comes to find her at Andrea's home and attempts to rape her. Andrea discovers the two and – already aware of Vittorio's relationship with Anna – attempts to throw him out. The fight turns ugly when Vittorio pulls a gun, with which he eventually accidentally shoots himself. Distraught at having become associated with murder, Andrea orders Anna to leave, at which point she wanders into a road, collapses, and is taken to hospital. When she recovers, she takes religious orders and vows to stay in the hospital where she finds something she ambiguously describes as having 'never found before'. Anna works in the hospital as a highly competent surgeon's assistant and ward sister. The film ends with Anna refusing Andrea's supplications to leave the hospital and marry him. She returns to her work triumphant. *Anna* is described as a melodramatic *strappalacrime* [tear-jerker], and Lattuada himself says of the film's reception 'the public pulled out their tissues and cried' (Cosulich 1985: 51). We should remember the words of Gianfranco Casadio, however, when analyzing *Anna*: '*Anna* highlights the trend of superficiality and avoiding giving a personal interpretation of how to deal with certain problems' (1990: 37). It is true that the ambiguity of *Anna*'s message and character is an issue to which this chapter returns, and which should be equally considered in relation to Lattuada's film, *La novice*.

Suor Letizia is a 1956 film by Mario Camerini and tells the tale of a Roman nun, Letizia (Anna Magnani), whose return to Rome from missionary work is diverted when she is asked to close the bankrupt island convent of San Filippo. Letizia is eager to shut down the convent, dealing skilfully with its debts and debtors. However, as time passes she increasingly wishes to stay at the convent and help it thrive. Letizia develops a particular affection for one child, Salvatore (Piero Boccia). Salvatore's mother is Assunta (Eleonora Rossi Drago) who was abandoned by her first husband. When her new fiancé, Peppino (Antonio Cifariello), offers to marry her, his marriage proposal excludes keeping Salvatore. When Letizia meets Salvatore 'her maternal instinct violently explodes' (Chiti and Pioppi 1991: 351) and she offers to become Salvatore's guardian, even planning to take him back to Rome with her. Eventually, however, Letizia realizes that Salvatore's place is with his family, and she takes him to Naples to his mother. The episode is very painful for Letizia, as the motherly affection she has developed for Salvatore throws her vocation into question. *Suor Letizia* is described as a 'heart-tugging melodrama' (Moliterno 2008: 61).

La novice (1960) was directed by Italian director Alberto Lattuada and co-produced between Italian and French agencies Euro International Film, Production Les Films Agiman, and Production Les Films Modernes, and it is the French language version that is still widely available. The story is mainly told through flashbacks of the protagonist Rita (Pascale Petit). When we meet her, Rita is a novice at a northern-Italian convent, on the point of taking her perpetual vows. We learn that Rita had been schooled at the convent, with only a brief interruption at age 18 when she returned home to her country estate. This period away from the convent is the crux of the film's drama, and the content of the flashbacks to this time makes up most of the film. Through these flashbacks, we learn that Rita's father died when she was 12, leaving her young and attractive mother, Elisa (Hella Petri), to manage the estate. The estate is large and losing money, but cannot be sold until Rita reaches 20 and gains power of attorney. During her summer away from the convent, Rita meets up with her neighbour Giuliano Verdi (Jean-Paul Belmondo), a young graduate in law and her mother's secret lover. Rita learns of their relationship, as she herself begins an ambiguous seduction of Giuliano. The spectator is unsure whether Rita's attraction is genuine, or whether she is using Giuliano to marry and thus gain power of attorney over the estate. Giuliano and Elisa meet in the marshes near the estate, ostensibly for Giuliano to announce his engagement to Rita, but he fails to do so. Rita, who has been eavesdropping, is enraged by Giuliano's treachery and shoots him. Her mother learns of the murder and sends Rita back to the convent, where the film begins. In the final scene, Rita is on trial for the murder of Giuliano, but there is no credible case against her since both her mother and the priest to whom she confessed, Don Paolo (Massimo Girotti), refuse to give evidence. The final scene sees her affirming her innocence, despite our knowledge of the contrary. As in *Anna*, Lattuada chooses the theme of the fallen woman seeking refuge in the convent, and in explanation says, 'I was struck by the veil of hypocrisy [...] which is the hypocrisy of Catholicism, one of the themes against which I like to fight' (Cosulich 1985: 77). Lattuada's attitude to Catholicism should be borne in mind when assessing both *Anna* and *La novice*. The film was inspired by a book of the same name by Guido Piovene (1941), described as 'one of the most significant novels written under Fascism' (Cosulich 1985: 78).

Women religious in film

The three chosen films represent only a snapshot of global cinematic portrayals of women religious. Many other films featuring women religious were produced during this period; Laura Pettinaroli lists 49 films produced worldwide featuring women religious between 1943 and 1996 (2012: 12), and this is surely an underestimation.[2] In the period between 1945 and 1959, in Italy alone sixteen films featuring nuns were released (Pioppi 1991). We should be careful to differentiate hagiographic films, films *about* nuns and films *which feature* nuns. As Grignaffini observes, a great number of Italian films feature nuns, although in many they 'are mostly background pictures, a sort of backdrop landscape of the stereotypes of costume drama against which to project the big picture of "national life"' (1999: 194). This attests to nuns being signifiers in an imagined national landscape. A notable contemporary example of filmmakers' fascination with nuns as national symbols can be found in Paolo Sorrentino's works *La grande bellezza* (2013) and

The Young Pope (2016). These 'background portrayals' of nuns are no less interesting than films with nun protagonists and are examined in this chapter. Scaraffia and Zarri reference 'institutional reasons that go some way toward explaining this sudden and never to be repeated domination of women in religious films' (Scaraffia and Zarri 1999: 299), the obvious exception being sex films, which demonstrate a sustained interest in nun protagonists. We might recognize the technique of using women to embody national change from previous chapters and note that while the Church was in turmoil in these years leading to Vatican II, it is religious *women* whose image is used to portray Catholicism.

It is difficult to share Grignaffini's judgement that Italy's filmic portrayals of nuns are 'completely marginal' to the global body of films showing women religious (Scaraffia and Zarri 1999: 294), although they have certainly received less scholarly attention than their American counterparts. A number of excellent works have been written about women religious in anglophone film, but academic literature on nuns in Italian film is scarce and brief.[3] Nuns have represented figures of intrigue and entertainment in cultural materials since their existence, particularly the much-reproduced character of the Nun of Monza, first fictionalized by Alessandro Manzoni in 1827, and before this, Giovanni Boccaccio's naughty nuns.[4] Others have noted the 'explosion of interest in such topics during the immediate post-war period' (Nerenberg 2001: 85), so why the renewed interest?

Not all representations of nuns have historically belonged to high culture. As Pettinaroli points out of portrayals of women religious, 'the importance of "sex films" must be underlined [...] that is to say pornographic films which constitute a fifth of the global corpus: all produced between 1971 and 1986, most often in Italy' (2012: 4). Both in terms of plot and aesthetic, we could tentatively consider the films studied here as precursors to sex films, in their interest in women religious' sexual and reproductive urges. We might also recognize traits of 'nunsploitation' films, defined by Tamao Nakahara as 'any exploitation film that takes as its main content nuns and, more often than not, naughty nuns' (2004: 125). Although the majority of nunsploitation films – of which Italy is the biggest producer – are pornographic, many fiction films might also fall into this category. As Babini argues, 'due to their being "emotionally and physically inaccessible to male coercion", nuns have always been considered as particularly appealing cinematic subjects, as "an underground sexual fantasy [...] whose intolerable purity invited defilement and innocence abused"' (*Talking Points*, in Babini 2012: s33). The nunsploitation films which Nakahara studies appear during the 1970s, but I argue here that the current films which represent 'mild to pornographic transgressive sisterly behaviour' (Nakahara 2004: 125) can be seen to spring from the 1950s. It is not coincidental that Lattuada, for example, later went into sex films. The sexualization of nuns contributes to the ambiguity of their portrayals.

Nuns and melodrama

The films *Anna* and *Suor Letizia* have been defined by scholars as melodrama, but with neorealistic nuances. In their book, Chiti and Pioppi describe *Suor Letizia* as 'neofasullismo [faux neorealism]' (1991: 351), and Casadio calls *Anna* 'popular neorealism' (1990: 23), although elsewhere both films are categorized as melodrama.[5] This section asks how nun characters fit with the archetypal melodramatic heroine, and what the use of melodrama to portray nuns might say about attitudes to women's work.

Bayman argues that post-war Italian melodrama 'truly meant something to those who made up its audience, and that to do so involved both a certain artistry and engagement with the significant experiences and conceptions of its day' (2004: ix). Melodrama was very much a genre of the 1950s, and one of the reasons suggested for this is that it enabled the articulation of culpability and trauma from the Second World War, displacing male guilt onto female characters (Garofalo 1956; Hipkins 2007). Another feature of melodrama is the role it played in negotiating gender relations. The changing roles of men and women in Italy after the Second World War have led some to ask whether melodrama provided a forum to overturn gender relations or offer 'deplorable tale[s] of moral transgression' (Bayman 2004: 1) which created polarized categories of right and wrong.

Melodrama has been argued to be a 'form for secularised times' (Brooks 1995: 205), precisely because it harks back to times of religious moral certainty. Melodrama instates clear models of morality, whilst giving space to divergent ones. This may explain the popularity of the form in 1950s Italy, still recovering from post-war instability, but simultaneously exploring new social models. Catholicism in melodrama 'showed itself to be victorious' (Morreale 2011: 258), and 'the Church is as present as parsley' (Baldelli 1999 in Bayman 2004: 64). Melodrama's connection to Catholicism makes it the perfect genre to articulate ideas about women in 'a rigid value system in which Good and Evil come face to face' (Cardone 2012: 11). This system was symbolic of both national and female choices in post-Second World War Italy, between traditional and alternative modern roles.

Melodramas simultaneously foreground and repress female desire, presenting both modernizing (female sexuality) and traditional (Catholic) resolutions. Convents act as a symbol of this contradiction; they represent threatening spaces of female solidarity and asexuality and simultaneously the reassuring containment of women and their desires. Maggie Günsberg suggests that melodramatic heroines see their desires 'forcibly subsumed into procreation, [...] within marriage, and female economic desire diverted away from the possibility of autonomy through work outside the home' and that 'domestic bliss is presented by the melodramas as the only legitimate goal for femininity' (2005: 19). This is clearly not the case for nuns in film. The question then is how the convent space, which replaces the domestic as the final destination for protagonists, is different. Günsberg elides the convent space with the family unit, saying that these are the 'only viable context[s] in which to show female desire and oppression' (2005: 19–20). Convent and domestic spaces are, for Günsberg, 'repressive macro-institutions like the prison' (2005: 32). This is a broad-brush interpretation of the convent space. Despite some historical evidence for Günsberg's argument that the convent represents a 'relentless patriarchal containment of femininity' (2005: 24), she overlooks the aspect of choice in vocation. What is more, even if we agree that the convent might contain women's sexual desires, we cannot ignore the more varied options and destinies it often gave women. Spinazzola argues that melodrama refused its female protagonists any agency, and rather featured the male character as the 'dynamic agent' (1985: 82). This is not true of melodramatic nuns. In *Anna*, *Suor Letizia*, and *La novice*, women take action and make choices, often going against the wishes of male characters. In this way, nun characters represent a departure from traditional heroines and gender norms, contradicting ideals of domesticity, while staying within a lexis of Catholicism.

That melodrama was a female genre has been repeated by many scholars (Cardone 2012: 9). Melodrama was linked to other popular 'female' genres, particularly the *fumetto* [comics] and *fotoromanzo* [photo comics], which were associated with young women in the post-Second World War Italy and often denounced as overly American and modern by both the Church and the Left Wing. As such, melodrama fits well with the plots' negotiations of women's sexual behaviour.

Like traditional melodramatic heroines, Anna, Letizia, and Rita are women who cannot or will not fulfil their 'proper' roles as 'wives, mothers, [or] brides of Christ' (La Scuola 1988: 238). However, unlike other melodramatic heroines, nuns are redeemed within the space of the convent. Melodramatic nuns are still the emotional women represented in wider melodrama, but their character resolutions are a far cry from the marriage/death paradigm of traditional melodramatic heroines. This may be for reasons of historical context. Marcus offers the idea that films made in the 1950s showcase Italy's 'new-found ideological complacency, together with encroaching affluence, mean[ing] that representations of the body politic, even sexualised ones, will be far less fraught with tragic potential' (2000: 339). These melodramas do not just stimulate emotion in the – supposedly female – spectator, but propose alternative behaviours, choices, and conclusions for her, in line with the experimental conservatism of 1950s Italy.

At first glance, we might suppose that the three melodramas I study here were intended for a principally female audience. Yet, recent studies of Italian audiences of the 1950s suggest that 'male audiences did dominate in this period' and that 'melodramatic conventions were needed to negotiate the reconstruction of gender identities' (Hipkins 2007: 84). This would suggest that although tears are supposedly female, and, as Marina Warner argues, 'a woman who weeps always becomes, in the very act, a mother' (1990: 223), what is actually happening within the melodramatic spectator is a maternal concern not for a child, but for a nation. Melodramatic nun characters, who are both sexualized and resolved into traditional Catholic models, are doubly reassuring to the male spectator as mirrors of the Madonna/whore paradigm.

Unsanctimonious women

This section studies the pervasive representations of nuns which occur in the background of the films; in the supporting characters and contexts of the films. Remembering that filmic nuns often function as a backdrop 'against which to project the big picture of "national life"' (Scaraffia and Zarri 1999: 194), portrayals of supporting characters and contexts may tell us more about social perceptions of nuns in post-Second World War Italy than nun protagonists. The first aspect of nuns' portrayals that merits comment is the overall positivity with which the women and their communities are depicted. Anna is shown as having been welcomed into the protective bosom of the hospital convent at her most vulnerable; having caused the assassination of Vittorio and losing Andrea's love. Those other nun characters with any development are shown to be benevolent, particularly the mother superior, who is inflexible but has Anna's and the hospital's best interests at heart. This is evident when she refuses Anna's precipitous request to take her perpetual vows, and later when she emphasizes to Anna:

> There is only one thing we fear more than sin, and it is scandal. The life of hospital sisters isn't only a question of faith. Here, you are not only accountable to your conscience like in the convent: a thousand eyes watch you, every patient judges you. You must be an example to everyone.

This moment speaks of not only a moral strength, but of a pragmatic understanding of the place of the hospital, and of women religious, within society. The attitude of the mother superior echoes discourse coming from the Church about its role in society. Particularly as a result of Vatican II, the Church began to argue for itself as 'more humble and pastoral' (Madges 2003: 88), reinforcing the need for its disciples to be moral examples. I refute Morreale's assertion that the nuns in *Anna* are 'highly unpleasant' (2011: 261), and 'the doctor, [...] is the central figure of the set-hospital, not the nuns, who are furthermore seen with a certain dislike' (Morreale 2011: 259). This analysis does not tally with my view of the text and perhaps points towards a phallocentric reading of the film. On the contrary, supporting nuns in *Anna* resound with goodness and morality. Bayman supports such an argument, commenting on the nuns in *Anna:* 'anonymous groups of women [...] uphold the most rigid sexual morality' (2004: 49). The convent portrayed in *La novice* is, as in *Anna*, a refuge for the protagonist Rita. The mother superior is, again, a benevolent character, shown socializing easily with the families of postulants and distributing gifts to novices. She also shows sensitivity to the feelings of those unused to the religious life, saying 'when you take the veil, it is lovely to know that there is someone outside the walls who loves you. I know from experience'. It is interesting that Lattuada, who despised the 'hypocrisy' (Cosulich 1985: 77) of Catholicism, nonetheless portrays women religious as moral, kind, and worldly.

Similarly, the religious communities represented in *Suor Letizia* demonstrate benevolence, cohesion and pragmatism. The island convent immediately accepts Letizia and treats her with deference. We see many scenes in which the convent community is presented as collaborating, at meal times, when looking after children, and particularly in the scene in which they labour together to build and sail their boat. Not only do the sisters form a cohesive team but they collaborate with the local community in order to revive the island's floundering fishing industry. The nuns initially give their catch to the fishermen, saying 'take it to market, sell it, and let's share the profits, ok?' They then go on to sell their fishing net to the local fishermen and set up a scheme to share the profits of the fishing as a regular source of income. Such portrayals represent a community of women religious who are pious, yet in tune with the local community and capable of getting their hands dirty in order to better it.

Humour also makes a subtle appearance in supporting nun characters. In *Anna*, Dina Romano plays Suor Paolina and brings her usual peasant-with-a-heart-of-gold character to the role, grumbling about Anna's infraction of rules, but humouring her nonetheless. There are other glimpses of humour, such as the ward sister who hurriedly asks a passing hospital visitor, 'excuse me, have they sold the Swedish center-forward to the Milan team? [...] For how much? [...] Hmm, too little!' The football player to whom she is referring is likely the famous Swedish player Nils Liedholm, who was known and loved in Italy at the time of the film's production. Such an inclusion would doubtless have signalled to the audience an unlikely secular interest in the character of a middle-aged nun.[6] In a striking coincidence, the nuns in *Suor Letizia* are shown actually playing football with the school children, hiking up their habits and getting into the action.

This scene is set up for comedy and includes slapstick moments, such as the ball striking another nun on the head when Suor Letizia takes a corner. Footballing nuns seem to be a lasting aesthetic interest in Italian film, with Sorrentino including a scene of young nuns playing football in the gardens of the Vatican in his cult series *The Young Pope* (2016) to the tune of *Ave Maria*, highlighting the juxtaposition of sacred and secular worlds. Such scenes continue to provide a sort of aesthetic background to the films, rather than directly influencing plot, recalling Grignaffini's statement that nuns mostly play a symbolic role in cultural materials (1999: 194). The portrayal of pious women as engaging in vigorous, popular, masculine leisure pursuits was probably both incongruous and gratifying to secular audiences. Cardinal Suenens (1963: 18) maligned the comedic effect that nuns had in popular culture, yet in the films, it serves a positive purpose. Rather than ridiculing the nuns, humour is used to point to humility and connection with contemporary Italian people. These portrayals served the double purpose of evoking new gender behaviours within the safe space of conservative Catholic roles.

The convent space

Although nuns are often portrayed positively, their choice of profession is attributed to a lack of choice or punishment. The convent space in the films is invariably discussed as one of isolation or refuge, unreality and punishment. In the increasingly secular and neoliberal Italy of the 1950s, 'the Church and its institutions cannot but represent a self-abnegation that is felt as the greatest possible loss, because it is the loss of the possibility of individual fulfilment' (Bayman 2004: 70); the filmic convent is a spatial demonstration of this. We should nevertheless recognize that the choice of the convent space may be a source of freedom and joy for some women.

It is important first to point out the protagonists' isolation which is communicated through their backstories, either explicitly or through omission. Anna, before she becomes a nun, is pictured as sharing a small room with her sister. Her sister detests Anna's lascivious lifestyle which involves late nights and an ever-ringing telephone. No mention is made of the sisters' parents or any wider family. Letizia of *Suor Letizia* is also portrayed as without family or connections. Rita of *La novice* is an only child, having lost her father when she was twelve and has an almost electral relationship with her mother, who is shown as neglectful and inappropriate by turns, and competes with Rita for younger man Giuliano. Elisa calls Rita 'my sister', highlighting hows she refuses her maternal role. All of the protagonists are women cut loose from the traditional family unit, unplaceable in the conventional melodramatic schema of the family.

The convent is a place where women go unwillingly, or as a last resort. First, taking the case of *Anna*, it is made explicit that her taking refuge in the convent space (which here is in fact a public hospital) is a direct result of the collapse of her engagement. Her sister attributes Anna's insistence on staying within the hospital to fear, saying to her fiancé, 'I told you, she's afraid to step out of here'. These details set up a clear link between desperation and inhabitation of the convent space, an idea which is also present in *La novice*. Rita is initially sent to the convent school after the death of her father, and latterly she is returned to the convent as punishment and protection for having seduced and murdered her mother's lover. As her confessor, Don Paolo observes to her, 'you took refuge in the convent in order to escape imprisonment'. Both Anna and Rita's cases echo the notion so oft repeated in cultural materials that women became religious 'as an almost passive response to the scarcity of eligible bachelors' (McKenna 2006a: 195–96), or indeed a flight from them. Suor Letizia, too, sets up her move to the island convent of San Filippo as punishment, and the result of coercion: having recently returned from a mission in Africa, Letizia is evidently excited about the arrival in her native Rome.[7] Letizia exclaims enthusiastically over her view, 'even when I'm lying down I can see Saint Peter's, and if I get up I can see all of Rome!' However, when she is asked to immediately depart for San Filippo, she is pictured outside the superior's office saying – eyes cast to heaven – 'Jesus, forgive me, but I'm saying no'. The undesirability of the San Filippo convent space is made clear.

What is more, the convent space is presented as cut-off, unreal and isolating to the point of being tomb-like in the films. In *Anna*, Anna's brother-in-law-to-be, asks her, 'don't you sometimes want to see the world, see people?', deeming the hospital to be isolated and lonely, despite the evident daily passage of many lay people through its doors. Anna's rejection of the outside world is also suggested by the scene in which she takes her first vows, where she is told 'the moment has come to choose between the world, or God'. The spatial organization of the film also evokes strong and irrevocable borders between the hospital and the world. In the final scene in which Anna gazes out at the possibility of a secular future with the waiting Andrea, she is pictured through the barred gates of the hospital. When the camera cuts to look at Anna from within the hospital precinct, the city walls of Milan are immediately recognizable on the other side, juxtaposing the isolated hospital and the urban metropolis. More dramatically, her confinement within the hospital is described by Anna as a death. She says, 'you told me to go and die one day, Andrea, and that's what I did'. One of Anna's patients exclaims, 'I can't wait to get out of this hospital. Yes, to go back to the world, to living', suggesting that the hospital space is both disconnected from the rest of the world, and from life itself. The mise-en-scène of *Anna* similarly suggests the alienating and chromatic existence of women religious; Morreale describes the 'blinding whites and towering blacks' which throw into relief the 'strangeness of a "body", the body of Silvana Mangano, suffering and restricted' (2011: 260). Morreale here refers to the critical trope of the fertile body of Mangano, so recurrent in criticism of *Riso amaro* (1949), represented within the hospital space as alienated and stunted. In *La novice*, Rita is similarly shown to be outside of the real world when within the convent. She goes there supposedly because this grants her immunity from the law, although in reality laws passed in the mid 1800s gave police the right to make arrests in any place on Italian territory. Before this, the *diritto di asilo* [right to refuge] was respected in many areas of Italy, particularly Naples (Treccani 1929: n.pag.). Rita herself says 'religious life would be like dying for me', once again comparing religious enclosure to death.

There is a vested interest in portraying women religious as alone and desperate in the world, and when then inside the convent space as having died, or having transformed into sub-human, sub-women, ghosts of the 'real' version. The films suggest that women like Anna and Rita, when free to roam the real world, create moral decay and mayhem. As Bayman suggests, in this way melodrama serves the purpose of first showing and then resolving transgressive female behaviour (2004: 1). These portrayals suggest anxiety and incomprehension around women religious and their choices. Enclosure – which is amongst other things a rejection of men – is only allowed to be chosen in cases of desperation in films. If it is true that melodrama engaged with meaningful aspects of post-war life (Bayman 2004: ix), the convent expressed social unease about female agency. In a way which would have made sense to 1950s audiences – particularly ones dominated by men – enclosure is shown to be a flight from reality and life, refuge in a sort of death. We should acknowledge that such comparisons do not come from lay society alone; in religious institutions 'religious profession is a new "burial in the death of Christ"' (Council of Major Superiors of Women Religious 2009: 22). Nonetheless, these filmic readings of the convent space reflect a testing of secular ideas, but an ultimate reinstatement of traditional gender roles. This may be considered unsurprising in the 'renewed conservatism' (Bayman 2004: 1) of gender roles pushed by the Church and the DC in 1950s Italy.

Although the films may claim religious enclosure to be a death-like state, this is somewhat discredited by characters' agency within them. Once wearing the habit, the women are shown to be dynamic and driven, differentiating themselves from domestic melodramatic heroines. We should consider the possibility of the convent space used as a resolution to problematic women characters because it was every inch as reassuring as the domestic idyll, but we should also reflect critically on what audiences might have understood beyond this. As Bayman argues, melodrama may make traditional conclusions for women, but it also gives space to the 'language of resistance in the renewed conservatism prior to Feminism' (2004: 1). As we will see in Chapter 9, many women were made aware of the freedoms of the religious life by those they saw around them. Films showcase some of these aspects of freedom, almost despite themselves.

Sin, sexuality, and maternity

Instead of the Catholic rhetoric of the nun being elevated by her piety, the films turn nuns into fallen women. Their falls are caused by their maternal and sexual urges, reducing them to the two extremes of the Madonna/whore paradigm. Maternalizing and sexualizing female characters reflect the rhetoric of the Church and the government at this time, where 'femininity was almost completely identified with motherhood' (Caldwell 2006: 225). Although overall it would be reductive to include these films in the category of 'nunsploitation films', they do revolve around 'improper nun behaviour' (Nakahara 2005: 169). In this section, I examine the extent to which post-war cinema uses nun characters to connote 'the conflicts between guilt and innocence, sexuality and maternity' (Scaraffia and Zarri 1999: 300), and the consequences of this.

In terms of narrative, all three protagonists are subject to an overwhelming carnal urge which leads to their moral decay. In *Anna* and *La novice* these desires are sexual, and in *Suor Letizia* they are maternal. In *Anna*, we are left with no doubt as to the protagonist's previously condemnable character. Anna states, 'I am contractually obliged to do dance numbers, not to sit with your clients', refusing to be bought by patrons of the nightclub. Yet, the film implies that she in some ways sold her sexuality. We must recall that in post-Second World War Italy 'female work is considered exploitation [...] it exists close to sexual exploitation' (Bayman 2004: 51), and suitor Andrea comments of the bar's clientele, 'I don't like being among these people who only have the right to look at you because they pay'. The implication here is that even looking is a form of possession. Laura Mulvey's theory of the Male Gaze (1975) corroborates the notion that in gazing at the female body, the spectator objectifies, and to some extent gains possession of the woman. Anna is perceived as earning money from 'giving' herself to clients. Wood reminds us that prostitutes in post-war Italian film were 'the ultimate metaphor of capitalist consumption' (2006: 56). Anna's nun character is framed as one which can test modern secular behaviours, but who ultimately returns to chaste traditional ones.

Anna's sexuality is not only something which she is suggested to market but also a force which she cannot manage. Her relationship with Vittorio, characterized by self-loathing and passion, is the cause of her downfall. Of Vittorio, she says, 'if I see him, hear his voice, something awakens in me, something I can't name. If you knew how many times I tried to escape, but it was useless'. This sounds very much like an avowal of what Morreale describes as Anna's 'irresistible erotic (purely erotic, the film underlines) passion' (2011: 258). It is even suggested by Vittorio that Anna threw away the keys to his flat, saying, 'you didn't want to be able to come back, did you?' It is Vittorio's conviction that Anna wants to be with him that leads him to stay and fight Andrea, who ultimately – and accidentally – kills him. Anna's uncontrollable sexual urges are set up as the catalyst for her downfall. Like the action of throwing Vittorio's keys down the drain, Anna's entry into the convent is represented as motivated by the same desperation; to protect her from herself. When their paths cross again in the hospital, even Andrea observes, with implicit reference to Anna's libido, 'you put this habit on to defend yourself'. Anna's story allows the audience to indulge in the libidinous possibility of a nun taking vows only to harness her unbridled lust. Such a fantasy correlates directly with Nakahara's definition of nunsploitation films as 'film[s] that exploit fantasies about and representations of nuns' (2005: 169). This betrays a patriarchal assumption that female celibacy is motivated by unmanageable attraction to men. It is worth noting that *Anna*'s trajectory is recurrent in Italian cinema of this time; in *I figli di nessuno* (Matarazzo 1951), the protagonist also takes religious vows after a botched love affair. Anna's promiscuity and subsequent enclosure echo Wood's argument that melodrama allowed new gender roles to be rehearsed, but then ultimately contained, to restrain the 'pathological and uncontrollable eroticism' (Treveri Gennari 2009: 115) which was so objectionable to the Church.

Rita of *La novice* is also a slave to sinful desires, although they are less explicitly stated. Rita's motives for her seduction, love, and ultimate assassination of Giuliano are ambiguous. Initially, her romance with Giuliano is purely strategic: to become legally emancipated and be able to take up her inheritance and the family estate. However, she later claims, 'I love you. [...] I want to make you happy'. Rita also mentions the uncontrollable and electral desire to hurt her mother, saying 'I needed to make her suffer, it was like a fever'. Rita's behaviour is shown as motivated by sexual, or psychosexual drive. Rita's relationship with the priest, Don Paolo (Massimo Girotti), similarly suggests her corrupting sexuality. Girotti's star signification, formed by performances like Gino in *Ossessione* (Visconti 1943), connotes corrupting sexuality and sexualized physique (O'Rawe 2010: 130). In his performance in *La novice*, this signification figuratively bursts from beneath his priest's cassock and infects Rita. Their interactions are ambiguous, and at times verge on erotic. She exclaims, 'you have awoken me', and insists 'love my soul Don Paolo, love me', as she grasps his hand and gazes at him. At the conclusion of the film, the judge explains that Don Paolo has refused to give testimony confirming Rita's guilt, and has instead entered a new religious order 'which has particularly punitive rules'. There is an implication that Rita awakened a sexual temptation and moral transgression in Don Paolo which he seeks to quash with mortification. Rita's sexuality is shown as absolutely corrupting, even within the sanctified walls of the convent. These behaviours again fall into the nunsploitation *filone* which allows audiences to project forbidden behaviours on women religious.

Suor Letizia presents a different case. Magnani was not a *maggiorata fisica* [physically well-developed] like Mangano, nor was she like the chic Pascale Petit.

She was also almost 50 years old when *Suor Letizia* was made and therefore less of a fit for the 'convent-sexy' genre, as it became known in Italy in the 1970s. Yet, the focus on Letizia's sexuality is presented both through some focus on her body and more forcefully through an emphasis on her (foregone) maternity. Although maternity is different from sexuality, I argue here that both serve the same purpose of directing audiences into reflections about the female body and the inescapability of its carnal drives. Focus on maternity also maps onto the Madonna/whore dichotomy within whose boundaries these women are portrayed. Like the other protagonists, Letizia falls because of a male, but unlike the others, the culprit is a male child, Salvatore. In an early scene when Salvatore first comes to Letizia in the convent, he appears in a tree while she is praying in the garden. Letizia plucks him from the tree and brings him into the convent in a scene which mimics Eve's plucking of the apple. We are left in little doubt over Letizia's maternal urges towards Salvatore; she immediately dotes on and protects him, giving him shelter, food, and plentiful affection.

Initially, Letizia passes off her attention as part of a nun's duties, saying 'our duty is precisely to look after abandoned children'. However, Salvatore is shown to have a compromising effect on Letizia's vocation and morality. First, she uses money collected for repayment of the convent's debts to buy new shoes for Salvatore, and she defends him when he fakes a foul in a game of football. Later, and more gravely, Letizia uses her powers of rhetoric to convince Assunta (Salvatore's mother) that he would be better off staying with her, thus disrupting the nuclear family and the sacred role of the mother. In the scene just before Letizia is due to take Salvatore away with her to Rome, we see her having to be reminded by Salvatore to pray before bed, and replying, 'oh, of course, prayers', suggesting that she has become estranged from her vocation and religious practice. It becomes clear that Letizia ardently wishes that Salvatore was her own child, and calls him 'my love', 'my child', and 'my little one', suggesting some sense of possession. The narrative infers, though, that Letizia would not be saving Salvatore, but taking him away from his mother and herself away from her faith, unacceptably disrupting traditional social structures. Other characters remind Letizia of her incompetence in maternal matters, asking, 'what would you know about being a mother'.

Letizia's character arc is still a tale of unbridled desire, but for motherhood rather than sex. Magnani's star persona accentuated her maternity, since she 'remains, in all her films, an actress who can carry the complex symbolism of the Italian mother in the post-war period' (Scaraffia and Zarri 1999: 302). Magnani's role as Pina in *Roma, città aperta* (Rossellini 1945), and her future role as *Mamma Roma* (Pasolini 1962), demonstrate the blurred borders of her cinematic performances, in this case reinforcing the emphasis on Letizia as a mother. *Suor Letizia*'s plot evokes women's carnal urges as irrepressible and disastrous, uncontainable by religious life. Focus on maternity – and portrayals of corrupting female sexuality reinstate conservative and essentialist models of femininity.

To make a final point about the portrayals of women religious' transgression, it is interesting to compare it to that of the *mondine*. Whereas Mangano's character in *Riso amaro* sinned, was promiscuous, and finally committed suicide, in *Anna* she is allowed to live in the redemptive space of the convent. Rita, too, is saved from prison. In *Suor Letizia*, Letizia is ultimately allowed back to her life as a nun in Rome. In all three cases, the destiny of the fallen woman has changed and improved. Whereas before fallen women had to suffer death to atone for their sins, 'displacing a sense of guilt onto female sexual behaviour' (Hipkins 2014: 102), here, women are allowed to live on, to become new women through vocation, if in a highly restricted and removed context. We might read this as a reflection of modernizing Italian society, more open to female sexual agency. All three films were produced in an Italy still using the Fascist penal code, in which Article 559 stipulated that adultery was a purely female phenomenon and punishable by imprisonment. This law was only amended in 1968. Although attitudes were changing slowly to female transgression, reabsorption into the hyper-Catholic morality of the convent was perhaps the only way in which cinematic heroines could achieve alternative endings at this time.

Veiled bodies

What's in a veil? Historian Maureen Sabine counsels that a nun's 'religious veil and full habit that show her only in part are barriers to imagining her as a whole person' (2013: 1). Similarly, Sarah Ahmed suggests that when we perceive an individual as unknowable, they 'must be penetrated or uncovered' (2004: 97). These observations go some way to explaining film's fascination for unveiling nuns. Film reinforces the notion that only when we are allowed beneath the habit do these women become whole (again). Viewers are led to dwell on what the habit is supposedly hiding – both practically and figuratively. The bodies of the three protagonists and their actresses are instrumental to the films. The use of star figures to play nuns intensifies audiences' attention to their bodies. Bayman observes that 'diva means divinity, divine being' (2004: 71); in these films, stars are the site at which religious and secular ideas of divinity converge in the bodies of women.

Each film includes one critical moment in which the 'real' female body of the nun is revealed to signal a dramatic turn. The supposed revelation of the 'normality' of nuns' bodies is in fact a guise for their sexualization. In *Anna* and *Suor Letizia*, their normality is exposed when the veil is removed. In *Anna*, the nun reveals her hair – still fashionably coiffed – to Andrea, because he does not recognize her in the habit. She even invites him – and the audience – to truly see her, saying, 'look at me, look at me'. The suggestion is that the true Anna is the one beneath the habit, still fashionable, still sexually desirable and available for intra- and extra-diegetic consumption. We must acknowledge both Mangano's star persona, and the intertextual relevance of other of her performances such as that in *Riso amaro* (1949), discussed in Chapter 1. As argued by Richard Dyer, stars had a signification which went beyond the character they were portraying (1998: 1). I would argue that director, audience and critics were thinking about Mangano's – rather than Anna's – body. However, other scholars disagree on the use of Mangano's body as Anna; Cosulich notes that Lattuada refused to use the *maggiorata fisica* type in his films and that 'the Mangano in *Anna* was no longer the Mangano in *Riso amaro*, the process of shrivelling up that later transformed her was already under way' (1985: 90). Indeed, we might consider the penurious diet that Mangano adopted as her career progressed, her hatred of her body's fame in *Riso amaro* (*Sorriso amaro* 2009) and the signification of her later physical mortification may have played a part in her portrayal of a nun. From criticism made at the time of *Anna*'s release, we can see how Mangano's body was a central focus of her performance. One French critic first discusses Silvana's 'thighs and nipples in *Riso amaro*', then decries the fact that 'the writers, without any sense of the absurd, dress her up as a nun'. Another complains 'don't be fooled into thinking that you will see Silvana unveiled. You will only see the veil and no Silvana!' (Helauwick 1952: n.pag.). He continues, comparing the experience of watching *Anna* to going 'to a nougat seller in Montelimar with the intent of eating some nougat, and being sold the nougat locked in an iron safe as if it were uranium' (Helauwick 1952: n.pag.). Mangano's persona and past performances, but most of all her body, were on the minds of audiences and critics alike. As we can see from critiques, her body was the product audiences expected to consume. The use of stars tends the films towards nunsploitation and heterosexual fantasy as driving cinematic portrayals of women religious. By using stars with a strong signification for their sexualized bodies, the films suggest that nuns' 'true' and sexual bodies are never far beneath the surface of the habit.

In *Suor Letizia*, Letizia's body is similarly unveiled. A climax is reached in the intimacy between Letizia and the child Salvatore when they walk to a clifftop together and she embraces him. In doing so, her veil becomes unpinned, and Salvatore exclaims, 'even nuns have hair? [...] So you're like other women', to which Letizia replies, 'yes, I'm like other women'. Her face betrays fear and shock at her own sentiments, which we can read as an avowal of maternal desire. Again, Magnani's star signification is important to our understanding of her body in the film. As Wood (2000) points out, Magnani's body was synonymous with motherhood and everyday Italian femininity in a way which prefigures and supports

FIGURE 8.2: Letizia's (Anna Magnani) veil becomes unpinned in *Suor Letizia*. *Suor Letizia*, Camerini, 1956. Italy. © Cineriz.

the idea that she is 'like other women' in her maternal desires. Günsberg reminds us that the showing of hair in Italian melodramas is also a strategy to remind audiences of the femininity of protagonists, and the unbridled sexuality which they represent. She observes that 'hair has historically symbolized female sexuality and desire' but also that 'hair is usually only around shoulder length in this post-war genre' (2005: 32). Both these statements ring true in the scenes in *Anna* and *Suor Letizia*, where both characters are suddenly sexualized and gendered by unveiling their hair but their shoulder-length locks mix meanings of modernity with curtailed sexuality.

In *Anna*, there is another moment in which the libidinous gaze of the spectator is indulged by gazing upon Mangano's body. Using flashbacks, Lattuada is able to unveil Anna's body as an object of desire. The flashback fades directly from a shot of Anna praying to reveal the murky setting of the nightclub and Anna dancing. Morreale references the sexual suspense that the audience had been held in until this moment as follows: 'having been strung along for almost half an hour, here she is [Mangano]' (2011: 258). Morreale's comment only makes sense if we accept that audiences were motivated to watch *Anna* in order to see her unveiling. Whether in *Anna* gazing up through the eyes of Andrea or in *Suor Letizia* peering down through the eyes of Salvatore, Mulvey's notion of the male gaze (1975) is clearly identifiable; spectators discover the characters' bodies as if through the eyes of men.

Similarly, in *La novice*, Rita has emphasis put on her body. She participates in a cabaret-style show during her holiday from the convent, which Giuliano watches. Her body is exposed in a leotard and lingered upon by the camera. This scene marks the moment in which Rita succeeds in seducing Giuliano and begins her sin in earnest. Moreover, like Magnani and Mangano (although to a lesser degree), Pascale Petit brings her own star signification linked to her body. In reviews written around the time of *La novice*, Petit's physicality is particularly prominent. She is referred to as 'a pocket-size diva' (Istituto Luce 1960) and 'diminutive' (Hughes 2011: 213). In a report for *Settimana Incom*, Petit is reported to be 'tired of being considered too sexy' (Istituto Luce 1960). These are among the very few descriptions of Petit, in English, French, and Italian. It is important to note that in the scarce descriptions of the actress, her body is the most common element to be commented on.

The sexualizing power of these moments of unveiling is evident. In all three cases, the body of the nun is revealed to both extra and intra-diegetic audiences. It would appear that there is a drive in cinema to uncover women religious, as a device to bring them down to earth, among sinners. These scenes which focus on and reveal the bodies of nuns represent their becoming 'like other women', implying that religious life is an unnatural state for women. These films fall into the *filone* of the nunsploitation film which implies and reveals forbidden behaviours in nuns and feeds a libidinous audience urge to participate in this unveiling. However, nuns' bodies are ultimately reabsorbed into traditional conclusions (with the exception of Rita), supporting Marcus's observation that 'in the domestic cocoon of Restoration Italy, the peril is never too great and the eroticized body politic poses no threat that marriage and family cannot eventually absorb' (2000: 342). The convent is simply another option with which the threat of erotic female bodies is neutralized.

Work

Contrary to other films studied in this book, nuns' work is not a secondary aspect of characters' identities but a key facet of plot and setting. Particularly in the cases of *Anna* and *Suor Letizia*, ambiguous conclusions are reached concerning the emancipatory potential of women's work. This final section examines how portrayals of nuns' work give space to alternative representations of femininity, whilst ultimately returning women to delimited spaces.

Protagonists' professional competence is underlined in these films. In *Anna*, her skill is dwelt upon at length. The mother superior recognizes Anna's abilities, saying 'you are an excellent nurse: your zeal, your ability, they have made you indispensible here', and the doctor Professor Ferri even teases Anna in front of the medical students over her infallible judgement, saying 'I'd like it if you tripped up sometimes, Sister Anna'. These comments highlight Anna's abilities as a professional, rather than as a woman religious. However, as Paola Bonifazio has noted, 'when they do enter the space of productivity, women are confined into a feminized sector [...] which exclusively employs female workers for the type of work required "female skills"' (2011: 173). The choice of Anna pursuing a nursing career sets her character within the acceptably feminine profession of care work, atoning for her past transgressions. Women often become nuns or nurses in films of this period, for example Lucia in Guido Brignone's *Noi peccatori* (Brignone 1953), suggesting the acceptability of this female profession. Babini argues that audiences only pardon Anna's sinful past because she becomes both a nun *and* a nurse (covering both religious and lay bases for redemption); 'a sole career in nursing was likely to be judged as not rewarding enough by the Italian public' (2012: s35).

Suor Letizia also portrays its protagonist as an exceptional professional. Letizia is chosen to go to the floundering convent in San Filippo, because 'with her experience' she is 'much better suited', recalling the practical skills which she has picked up on previous missions in 'Africa'. Letizia is treated with deference by the other sisters, who declare themselves unable to manage the convent's finances. Letizia receives much praise from her colleagues, who say 'who knows what would happen if you weren't here!' She shows herself as eminently more practical than the other nuns, telling them, 'Sisters, the Lord can't pay your debts'. The truth of this observation may have been particularly striking to audiences involved in the economic reconstruction efforts of the 1950s. Letizia is also portrayed as able to integrate and collaborate with the local community; she is admired even by lay people, like the workman who observes, 'that sister is skilful!' Such portrayals, although fictitious, reflect the modernizing aspirations of Vatican II and Cardinal Suenens that nuns might integrate with local communities (Suenens 1963: 18). More than protagonists' faith, work is underlined as the nuns' passion and raison d'être. As such, films test out new secular gender roles within the safe space of the convent.

Portrayals of the protagonists with money are also interestingly present in the films and unusual for cinema of this time. Anna's attitude to money is the strongest indicator of her upright morality. It is made clear to the audience that when Anna worked as a nightclub dancer she would have been more than able to increase her wealth and popularity by consorting with clients. However, she rejects that lifestyle, pointing out that she is not contractually obliged to fraternize with clients. The audience is told explicitly how much Anna earns when the manager retorts, 'what are you complaining about? Isn't 15,000 Lire a night enough for you?' The knowledge of Anna's generous salary (approximately 200 pounds a night in today's terms) increases our admiration for the moral financial choices she makes; refusing to become a glorified sex worker, choosing the down-to-earth Andrea as a fiancé, and eventually giving up her opulent lifestyle for that of a nun.

Letizia is also portrayed as having a moral and matter-of-fact relationship with money. As well as pragmatism, Letizia is shown to have a keen grasp of financial management. In a scene set up for comedic value, she ties the two men who are buying the convent at San Filippo in knots, demanding that they pay the taxes, debts, and expenses of the convent's closure. She combines shrewd knowledge of housing law – 'that land is exempt from tax until 1986, according to the law of 3 November 1933' – with swift mathematical skills – 'fifteen Lire per year for thirty years. That makes … 450,000 Lire'. The men are aghast, and ask her, 'do you have a law degree sister?', when she holds up three fingers, they exclaim 'three degrees?!', to which she responds simply, 'three years of schooling'. Rather than Letizia's capability being portrayed as threatening, it is always a source of comedy; the unexpected and unusual nature of a religious woman dominating and turning to her advantage using financial negotiation is portrayed as amusing.

Even Rita in *La novice* is set up as a character with shrewd financial sense. In the film, she is shown as immediately interesting herself in the affairs of her father's domain, watching her mother interact with an agricultural subcontractor and asking her about the management of the estate. Later, Rita takes it upon herself to question her father's lawyer on the finances and legal status of the domain. Finally, Rita proposes marriage to Giuliano, foregrounding the financial conditions of the arrangement: 'For the estate: two hundred and twenty million, or ten million in annuities. I am obliged to leave half to mother, so there will be 500,000 Lire left […]. [T]his isn't a fairytale, it's a transaction'.

These portrayals of the protagonists managing their money suggest an agency and emancipation which allows them superiority and control over the men they encounter. Anna does not have to bend to the will of her male customers, Letizia is not exploited by dodgy dealers and Rita is not dispossessed of her inheritance. These portrayals somewhat refute Hipkins's affirmation that financially shrewd women in post-war film must always pay the price with a disastrous narrative arc (2007: 101). Instead, religious women successfully manage money – and men – to their own ends. However, Hipkins's study (2007) looks at prostitute figures in post-Second World War Italian cinema and thus examines a wholly more socially and morally threatening type of female figure than those of this chapter. Again, we must ask ourselves whether women religious are allowed this behaviour because their work is reassuringly conservative.

The role of work in the destinies of the characters, particularly Anna and Letizia, is shown to be invaluable. Bonifazio argues that 'work empowered and regenerated the male citizen' in the post-Second World War Italy (2011: 163). Can the same be said of the female citizen? In *Anna*, the protagonist expresses the belief that the convent has given her fulfilment that she could never find elsewhere, calling it 'something I didn't know existed, something I've always searched for, without realising'. Nonetheless, this 'something' may be deliberately ambiguous in the film. Anna describes her commitment in the following terms: 'the medics, the patients, the other sisters, they need me. You don't know what it means to realise you're needed'. Anna articulates her vocation through a sense of self-sacrifice and service. Both these characteristics were bastions of ideal (Catholic) femininity at this time, and Anna's statement could be read as recasting nuns' work into conservative female roles. Certainly, Morreale reads Anna's statement as such, saying: 'Anna's vocation is not to find God [...] but to care for others', and that 'above being a nun, she is a nurse' (2011: 259). I would take this observation one step further, and say that, above being a nun, Anna is a woman, because caring and emotional labour are so attached to feminine ideals, as will be discussed in Chapter 9.

Duty and service feature strongly in Anna's work. At the climax of the film, Anna is trapped between the hospital and a waiting Andrea when multiple ambulances carrying casualties arrive at the hospital gates – an occurrence that she interprets as a sign from God. Her choice to stay is one of duty. This duty is also expounded by Professor Ferri who counsels her, 'strangers arrive here and ask for our help, then they leave without ever knowing or thanking us [...] in life, you need to know how to lose'. Anna refigures this loss in the lexis of the emotional labourer who gains through sacrifice. Her reply, and the final pronouncement of the film, 'I haven't lost, Professor, I haven't lost', perfectly summarizes the ambiguity of the working woman in Lattuada's film. In one way, Anna has won – indeed the original line in the 1951 script was in fact 'I haven't lost, Professor, I've won'.[8] The accompanying image of Anna standing in front of the doctor, waiting for her surgical mask to be tied for her, suggests a personal victory and empowerment. We leave her, a confident nurse, valued by her colleagues and patients, with a strong sense of religious and moral vocation. Work, then, is shown to emancipate and regenerate the female citizen.

The adaptation of Anna's final line to 'I haven't lost', however, reflects the ambiguity of Anna's victory. Anna is not able to be proclaimed a winner, but neither is she a loser. Does Anna's triumph refer to her resistance of her own sexuality? This conclusion would corroborate Bayman's observation that melodrama offered 'deplorable tale[s] of moral transgression' (2004: 1), only to reinstate a correct (and conservative) moral order. Or, is Anna arguing that to care for others and sacrifice oneself is not a loss? This too would point towards validation of femininity as service; the woman who chooses God and duty over self and sex is victorious.

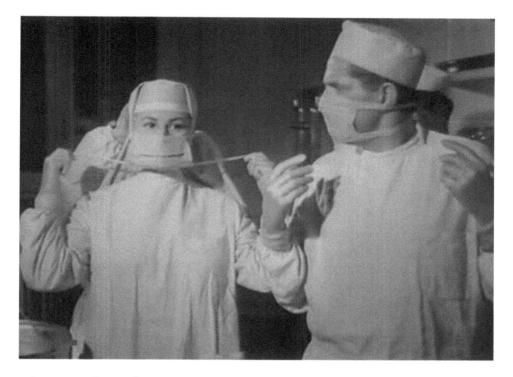

FIGURE 8.3: 'I haven't lost' says Anna (Silvana Mangano) as she prepares for surgery in *Anna*. *Anna*, Lattuada, 1951. Italy. © Cristaldi.

Conclusion

Either of the above readings of Anna's narrative valorizes reassuringly traditional models of femininity. Yet, as in *Suor Letizia* and *La novice*, these portrayals are underscored by representations of nuns as skilled, valuable and capable. It is this combination of female agency with a lexis of female service and duty which creates ambiguity around women's work in these films. Nuns present a unique example of working women; like seamstresses, they are associated with traditionalism and containment, although in reality and cinema their working lives give them access to spaces and roles of agency and variety. It is this range between transgression and reassurance which reflects the historical context in which these films were made. Films echo the ideological 'tug-of-war' (Pojmann 2013: 6) occurring between modernizing, conservative, and Catholic currents. The alternative destinies which nun characters are allowed in comparison to other melodramatic heroines may signal that society was becoming more reconciled with female agency, or that the convent was a sufficiently containing conclusion for women. Marcus argues that 1950s Italy was a cocoon, in which transgressive portrayals of women served to both exercise notions of alternative femininity and to reabsorb them into conservative society (2000: 342). This chapter may provide an answer to the 'institutional reasons that go some way toward explaining this sudden and never to be repeated domination of women in religious' (Scaraffia and Zarri 1999: 299); women religious are suitably traditional, potentially erotic, and promisingly emancipatory characters in post-Second World War Italian film.

NOTES

1. Also known as the Ospedale Maggiore di Milano and thus named in Morreale (2011).
2. Other films which feature nuns that I have discovered and which are not on Pettinaroli's list include: two different versions of *La monaca di Monza* (Pacini 1947; Gallone 1962); *Malacarne* (Mercanti 1946); *Vita e miracoli della Beata Madre Cabrini* (Battistoni 1946); *Un giorno nella vita* (Blasetti 1946); *Caterina da Siena* (Palella 1947); *Cielo sulla palude* (Genina 1949); *Margherita da Cortona* (Bonnard 1950); *Giovanna d'Arco al rogo* (Rossellini 1954); *L'angelo bianco* (Matarazzo 1955); *Il suo più grande amore* (Leonviola 1956); and *Io, Caterina* (Palella 1957).
3. For enquiry into nuns in anglophone film, see the works of Maureen Sabine (2013), Judith Wynn (1980), Rebecca Sullivan (2005), and Mary Ann Janosik (1997), among others.
4. Alessandro Manzoni's *I promessi sposi* (1827) is one of the most notable literary texts to feature the well-known tale of the nun of Monza who was imprisoned in a convent, whence she conducted a love affair and a murder. Scaraffia and Zarri attribute the 1942 Camerini film of Manzoni's literary work *I promessi sposi* as partly responsible for the renewed interest in women religious in the post-Second World War period (Scaraffia and Zarri 1999: 300). Giovanni Boccaccio included a story about carnal and canny nuns in his *Decameron, terza giornata, novella prima* (Bonghi 1997).
5. See Uffreduzzi (2017), Pettinaroli (2012: 4), Bayman (2014), Babini (2012), Pettinaroli (2012), and Moliterno (2008: 61).
6. My thanks to Alberto Del Favero for his seemingly limitless knowledge on the subject of *calcio*.
7. As well as Magnani's longstanding association with Rome, her character speaks with a Roman accent. Mary Wood (2000) argues for Magnani's Roman persona in her chapter 'Woman of Rome: Anna Magnani'.
8. The original 1951 script for *Anna* is available at the *Cinématheque Nationale* in Paris, France.

9

Professed Professionals: Oral Histories of Nuns

Silence is built into the existence of women religious, at least to a degree. They are therefore all the more important as subjects of oral history. Nuns were often taken into religious institutions at a young age, encouraged to forget a sense of self, instructed – some say indoctrinated – in an intensive didactic programme. Their memories are thus shot through with institutional discourse, not least of which is discourse around women's work (Campbell-Jones 1979: 30). I present here a body of sixteen original oral history interviews with Italian women religious. Engaging with oral history and memory studies, personal and conversion narratives, emotional and affective labour, and existing studies of women religious, this chapter asks how the work of women religious is remembered differently to that of other working women of the post-Second World War period. Historian Adriana Valerio suggests that religious work allowed women to 'reconceptualise themselves, through the unprecedented opportunities that they accessed through education, work, and missions' (2017: 186). If we have learned in the other chapters that work may have 'empowered and regenerated' the female citizen as it did the male, we have also observed that women's work is not discussed in direct terms of empowerment. Let us remember that this book seeks to prove and redress Anna Rossi-Doria's view of Italian women of the post-war period that 'the political nature of their action is not recognised either by contemporary or historical commentators, and often not even by the protagonists themselves' (2000: 361). Mirroring this, we have already seen that often women do not recognize their labour as work. This issue is assessed in relation to women religious, about whom cultural historian Carmen Mangion states 'while outsiders may have seen women religious as qualified professionals, it seems unlikely that they would have acknowledged themselves in this light' (2005: 234).

The data presented here has two goals: to reveal the work of women religious in all its uniqueness and value and to assess how it is perceived by the women themselves.

This chapter begins by interrogating the Catholic Church's attitude to women's – and women religious' – work, and how it is problematized and obfuscated. Then, examining the oral histories, I argue that women religious use a number of narrative strategies which reflect institutional attitudes, reframing their labour in religious, emotional, and traditional gender discourse. I argue that the result of these narrative strategies is to situate the work of women religious as a vocation rather than a profession, a fact which echoes wider social and institutional tensions around women's work.

Specifically, this chapter identifies four discursive strategies which situate women religious' work within wider social and institutional discourse. First, the career choices of nuns are described as vocation. Vocation is a term whose border with profession is debated and blurred and will be fully discussed below. Second, nuns' narratives of work share commonalities with conversion stories. Conversion narratives are a part of established literature on the lives and work of nuns and are doubtless familiar to women religious through sermons, saints' stories, training, and other religious materials. The section on vocation traces how interviewees narrate and make meaning from their professional lives by using the schemes provided in conversion narratives. Finally, work is described in terms of emotion. I argue here that nuns' descriptions of their work fit into the contemporary theoretical category of emotional and affective labour, but that we can historicize emotional labour for women as an extension of the discourse around female self-sacrifice and giving which has existed throughout history.

Interviews

The oral histories studied here respond to historian and Dominican sister Margaret MacCurtain's call to 'hear the voices of women religious' (1997: 58). They were collected in one-off interviews with sixteen women religious aged between 71 and 94 from three different Roman convents. The defining characteristic of interviewees is that they lived and worked in the period between 1945 and 1965. Most of the women were already in religious institutions during these years, although one entered shortly after 1965. I chose Rome for the location of the interviewees for two reasons: first, described as the 'panting heart of Catholicism',[1] and the closest city to the Vatican, Rome has a high concentration of religious. The difference that proximity to the Vatican City makes to the experiences of women religious is underlined by a scholar of English women religious, Anselm Nye, who told me, 'I remember an interview with an Italian Sister in Rome back in the 1980s which emphasised the fact that "we have to be so quiet here, all around the Pope!"' (2017). Second, and most importantly, in Rome one can find many mother houses of religious orders, meaning that at any given moment these institutions host women of different origins and experiences who are either passing through or are living out the end of their lives. This second fact gave a particular richness and variety to the interviews because of the breadth of experience of the women I encountered; originating from Bari to Vicenza, from seamstresses to war nurses, no two interviewees are the same. The interviews were semi-structured, and participants knew only that I wished to know about their lives and work during the post-Second World War period.

The three convents I visited were somewhat different in character. Two of the convents are mother houses and retirement homes. As such, they welcome retired women who lived and worked both in Italy and abroad in community institutions and missions. The other convent is also a mother house, but follows a progressive ideology with sisters wearing a simplified modern version of the habit, and performing lay work such as factory or administrative labour. All of the communities are apostolic, rather than contemplative orders; an essential prerequisite for being able to study their work.[2]

Women's work and the Catholic Church

In post-Second World War Italian society, women's work was regarded as a sometimes-necessary activity which should be subordinate to women's roles as wives and mothers. Women's work was a source of tension outside of Catholicism, but the work of women religious was doubly controversial; first because of their gender, and second because of their status as religious. In the two General Congresses of the States of Perfection [*Congressi generali degli stati di perfezione*] in 1950 and 1957 preceding Vatican II, and indeed in Vatican II itself, the apostolic work of religious was a subject of debate. These congresses and the Church at large were concerned that work and faith were incompatible, and 'women's religious and moral vocation were reconciled uneasily with the notion of the female professional' (Gleadle 2001: 144). The notion that some women chose to become religious because of the professional opportunities it offered is extrapolated by Giancarlo Rocca, who asserts that 'no small proportion of [religious] considered religious life as just a way to better perform apostolic work' (2013: 145–46).

The very terms in which women religious' work was expressed indicate the tension around it. Work was 'vocation' or 'mission'. Even the contemporary term 'profession' has its etymological roots in the idea of a higher spiritual commitment. This etymological crossover highlights how the work of religious transformed over the nineteenth century from occupation to profession. Teaching and nursing professions, which women religious often dominated, are good examples of 'occupations upgraded to professional status' (Mangion 2005: 229) during the period in question.³ I argue that tension around women religious as professionals is evident in the oral histories examined in this chapter.

Women religious are counted by the Italian census as professionals, belonging to the group of *professioni tecniche* [technical professions], in the subgroup *tecnici delle attività religiose e di culto* [technicians in religious and faith activities] (ISTAT.it 2017).⁴ The turn to apostolic rather than enclosed orders – and thus to professional work studied in this book – came at the end of the 1800s (Valerio 2016: 185). In terms of what has happened to Catholic discourse around women and work since 1965, Vatican II does not appear to have changed the work of the women I interviewed. Vatican II saw an enthusiastic promotion of women's apostolic work, particularly by Cardinal Léon-Joseph Suenens (1963). Some of the decisions of Vatican II led to the restructuring of religious organizations, mirroring Europe's industrialization by making superiors managers and administrators rather than spiritual leaders (Rocca 2013: 131). All of the nuns with whom I spoke had worked 'in the world' both within lay and non-Catholic communities. Usually, the roles they fulfilled were nonetheless in Catholic organizations such as schools or hospitals frequented by laypeople.

Vocation and conversion narratives

Seeing work as vocation rather than profession was on the Catholic agenda at this time. Exemplifying this, the Treviso branch of Catholic Action Youth published a short work entitled 'Profession as Vocation' in 1959. This chapter makes a clear distinction between vocation, labour and profession. Vocation is known to be a 'species of the genus profession' (Cogan 1955: 106), and yet the two terms differ quite significantly in meaning. From the Latin *vocare*, vocation 'refers to a divine call in the sense of being fit for something, talented in something' (Coquillette 1994: 1271). In contrast, professional work refers to educated work, responsibility, self-organization and altruism (Cogan 1955: 106). Professions are class-bound, conventionally referring to white-collar work. Different again is labour, which Hannah Arendt defines as the activities necessary to fulfil basic needs, and associated with pain and hardship (1998: 80).

Nun's work, therefore, is best qualified as profession, yet this chapter underlines how it is described by women themselves as a vocation. What a profession has and a vocation lacks, according to Daniel Coquillette, is a sense of individual motivation and accountability: 'being called by your talent to a particular job does not require anything from you' (1994: 1272). This section explores the frequent accounts of interviewees' 'vocation moments' – their first recollections of desiring or deciding on their roles as religious – and how they attribute these moments to their communities or faith rather than claiming them as their own. Vocation stories support a narrative of nuns' labour being part of a higher calling in which they have little agency, blurring their identities as professionals and as religious. As one sister puts it, 'what we do is written in heaven [...] whether we do good or evil, it is all written up there' (Li 2017). Although it is neither my wish nor intention to demystify nuns' vocations, it is interesting to identify the recurrent features and descriptions of them.

Vocation also shares a border with conversion. Like vocation, conversion suggests a 'turning point, an event which marks a discontinuity between the biographical before and after' (Pannofino 2012: 1). Conversion narratives constitute a considerable literary corpus and span many religions. Yet, they exhibit consistent features, which lead some scholars to argue that they are often 'not so much composed as recited' and that 'the pattern is so plain as to give the experiences the appearance of a stereotype' (Morgan 1965: 71–72). The value of telling one's own religious story is contested between communities and religions. In seventeenth-century Baptist congregations, some believed 'to forget a work of God (a "crumb" that could be preserved) was offensive and sinful' (Adcock 2011: 212), whereas for the Benedictines, 'storytelling opportunities are few because narrative performances are discouraged' (Reidhead and Reidhead 2003: 193). O'Donaghue and Potts list numerous religious orders where religious are discouraged from telling personal stories (2004: 475). Maria Pia Di Bella looks at two historical examples of conversion in Italy and concludes that the act of speaking is a way of confirming one's religious belonging (2003: 90). The vocation stories told here reflect a desire to portray identity and work within a religious narrative. These vocation stories not only describe the individual but the community and institutions which formed them. They show the 'ways in which conversion [...] plays a major role in inserting the individual in [...] a collectivity' (Di Bella 2003: 85), 'mark[ing] the boundaries of the community' (Hovi 2004: 48), rather than the individual.

Most of the interviewees entered religious orders in their youth, the majority moving directly from the family to the convent. Some of the women held other jobs before they took vows, and a few had full-fledged careers as teachers or nurses before entering, but most developed their professions as religious. The average age at which my interviewees took their first vows was just over 18 years old, with a range of 14–34. Age was a significant aspect of women's accounts of their first vocations, especially in the cases of those who felt it was particularly early or late. Sister Ao exemplifies this: 'my dad says I was twelve when I started asking to become a novice. My mum says I was four and a half' (2017). Another sister outdoes this, saying:

> I was born with my vocation I think, because I was five when people started talking about how communists were killing priests, and at five years old I replied with such

certainty. [My mum] said 'are you sure you want to be a nun?', and I said 'Yes, I'm becoming a nun'.

(Pc 2017)

Accounts of interviewees choosing their occupation at a young age cast their decision as a calling rather than a choice.

Interviewees were attracted to religious life through direct contact with women religious. Sister Ao first affirms she doesn't know why she started asking to become a nun, but later asserts that 'there were a few nuns, friends who had already gone [into orders]' (2017). Although she evidently does not make the connection herself, this sister had been exposed to women religious at a young age. Sister Qo recounts a moving story of a Roman sister from her village who visited her village for the first time since the beginning of the war, to find that the German troops had destroyed the village's access to safe water. Arriving at the interviewee's house, the nun asked the interviewee's mother for a glass of water:

So Mother gave her some water and what did she do? She crossed herself before drinking, began to pray, and two tears slid down her face. Seeing this nun I felt like I had seen an angel. I said 'she's an angel come to save us from the war'. So I started saying 'I want to become a nun'.

(Qo 2017)

Another interviewee comments, 'I chose to go into a convent like my aunt, my father's sister, she was also a nun like me' (Ai 2017). These accounts attest to the powerful impact of other women religious as role models and evoke the community and family space as the background for professional inspiration.

The impact of female religious role models in the community is reiterated by those who went to school with nuns. In Italy, as in Ireland, nuns 'dominated and controlled women's health and education' (McKenna 2006a: 194), with around 200,000 male and female religious running schools (including sewing schools), hospitals, and charitable initiatives in the 1950s (Pollard 2008: 122). Many interviewees echo the sentiment of Sister Bo who says, 'I said to my mum "I want to become a nun like those ones there [at school]" [...]. [T]hey were all beautiful, calm, smiley. It made an impression on me [...] and I felt my vocation' (2017). Sisters also note the rural village as the backdrop to many vocations. For example, Sister Li tells of how a group of Franciscan monks visited her village, saying 'I wanted to listen to the Franciscans when I went back home in the evening. I went to listen to this priest, and my religious vocation came to me that way' (Li 2017). It is interesting to note that community spaces – family, school, village – take prominence in vocation narratives. Tuija Hovi notes of conversion narratives that 'to be converted, an individual must have already adequately internalized the tradition in question to be able to accept its explanatory models' and that this most often happens in local or familial spaces (Hovi 2004: 40–41).

The link between nuns' identities and their families is one of the clearest features of the interviews. Fifteen of the total sixteen interviewees mentioned their families, and the word *famiglia* [family] alone was uttered 75 times throughout the corpus. Often, the interviewee's family would be brought up immediately in response to an introductory question, such as 'when were you born?', eliciting responses like 'I was born in 1932 and I'm from a very poor family' (Qo 2017). Interviewees identified themselves carefully and explicitly within the family unit, explaining their choices and experiences in direct relation to other members of that unit. Parents, particularly, play a prominent role in these accounts; in the sixteen interviews, the word 'mother' is mentioned 174 times, and 'father' on 104 occasions.[5] In the case of the Dominican sisters, the community allowed nuns to visit and be visited by their families, something which was not common to all orders at the time. One woman explicitly says that this was the reason she chose that particular order, stating, 'I was very attached to my family' (Pz 2017). Here I study references to families in relation to women's vocations, and argue that the inclusion of the family in accounts of what was essentially a professional choice contributes to these stories becoming about a community rather than an individual, and about religion rather than profession.

Families are narrated as having given interviewees the example of piety which then inspired them to vocation. Sister Pt remembers 'my mother's tenderness towards those in need. […] [T]hat's what made me tell myself how much I'd like to be a nun!' (2017). The reaction of family members to their daughters' vocations also appears important to interviewees' vocation stories. The giving of parental permission was a feature of these accounts which emerged as a source of both inspiration and conflict. One woman explains how her mother tried to test her vocation when she first expressed it (Pc 2017). Several sisters tell tales of their parents despairing at their vocations:

> When I left home my mum fainted and said 'sweetheart, you've decreased my life expectancy by a hundred years', because I was the first child to leave home. […] The only thing my dad said was, 'sweetheart […] you don't understand anything about what you're going to do'. I replied, 'I'll learn to understand'.
>
> (Jp 2017)

These oral histories recount religious vocation as a communal, familial experience. Even in the cases where families were happy with their daughters' vocations, saying, for example 'go for it, we're happy for you, but think about it carefully'

(Ai 2017), interviewees foreground the family in their vocation stories. The prominence of families in vocation stories echoes Hovi's assertion of personal narratives of conversion that 'the way in which individuals experience something (and also the way they interpret their experiences) is constructed collectively' (Hovi 2004: 42).

Nowhere is this more evident than where accounts of family traumas influence or inspire interviewees' vocations, of which there is a surprising number. Sister Qo recounts the story of her father being captured by the Nazis. She details how he hid and fled from occupying Nazi forces for a prolonged period before he was finally captured and taken to a concentration camp:

> My father escaped and it took him four months to get back home. On foot. He walked night and day. [...] Today I am in awe of refugees. [...] When I see them I feel bad when I think my father was like that. [...] I say to myself 'look at everything we have here, our canteen. They can come and get something to eat, but my father [...]?'
>
> (Qo 2017)

Qo's testimony was recounted to demonstrate how a family trauma influenced her vocation to help others, as she does now providing charity to refugees of war. Qo directly linked this traumatic experience and her decision to do religious work, saying 'these are things that stay with you. And this is the terror of war, really the terror. Then I left for Africa after I became a nun' (2017). Again, the reason attributed to her professional zeal is located firmly in the familial. Several of my interviewees recall the deaths of their parents as having motivated their vocations. Crying, Sister Pc remembers how her mother died suddenly just weeks after Pc entered the convent:

> PC: After losing my mum I began to [...]. From that moment I, honestly my vocation became a serious one [...]. I worked hard. I'm getting emotional. [Crying] Because I told myself, 'I must be a sister'.
>
> INTERVIEWER: So you were motivated by this event?
>
> PC: Yes. I thought 'if mum knows anything of what's happening, well – I must be a nun, I must become a nun'. I worked hard. [...] I experienced my vocation sort of as a way to make my mum happy. [Crying] With the fact of being – I'm getting emotional, it's emotional stuff.
>
> (Pc 2017)

Another sister recalls how she had dreamt of her deceased mother after her first visit to the convent; 'on the bus I dreamt of my mother saying "have you gone to Rome?" [...]. And when was back in the South I started to swear that I wanted to become a sister' (Ao 2017). Recollections like these reinforce the impact of family trauma in memory, highlighting that it is indeed 'emotional stuff', perceived as significant enough to influence interviewees' professional choices. Trauma is also a classic inclusion in conversion narratives, which articulate vocation around 'a moment of epiphany, when a traumatic or seemingly chaotic past is revealed as the subtle handiwork of a benevolent God' (Buckser and Glazier 2003: xii). The effect of referencing family trauma – as is the case in conversion narratives – is that the vocation decision is portrayed as a spiritual one, influenced by faith and community.

There are those who recount their initial contact with, or calling to, the religious life as a struggle in itself, with the evocation of an 'internal turmoil' (Cd 2017) as typical. Several interviewees explain this as a result of negative experiences with nuns from their youth. Sister Jp describes:

> Since in those days nuns thought everything was a sin, I remember once at cathechism one of them told us that dancing was unintentionally sinful, stuff like that, that really hurt, not just irritated, us. We didn't want to hear those things because all that stuff was nice to us, we didn't see anything malicious in it. But back then it was like that unfortunately. So I didn't want to go to these nuns, I would say *'no Mamma, no Mamma, no'*.
>
> (Jp 2017)

Another sister remembers how she and her little brother went to a school run by nuns, much to his chagrin:

> At five years old I thought 'these sisters are so mean. If only they knew how much my brother and I are suffering'. Who would have thought that with this bad impression I would later have become a nun? Never. I still feel it now. But that was how it was at the time.
>
> (Pc 2017)

Acknowledging the unlikelihood of their subsequent vocations, these interviewees separate themselves temporally from these negative experiences with the words, 'back then it was like that' (Jp 2017), and 'that was how it was at the time' (Pc 2017), suggesting that their own vocations – although formed by these negative experiences – then broke with or departed from previous identities of women religious into something more positive and modern. Such descriptions echo Edmund Morgan's 'morphology of conversion', one stage of which sees a 'struggle between faith and doubt' (1965: 72), and Pannofino's description of the necessary 'rupture moment' (2012) in conversion narratives.

I was also interested to find numerous interviewees who describe the moral or practical struggle which they experienced in their first vocations. Contrasting strongly with the interviews which spoke of mystical spiritual callings at a young age, a number of women's tales were permeated with discomfort. The word *lotta* [struggle] and its grammatical derivatives were used in this context by four of the interviewees, in statements like:

> I was secular, secular in all senses. [...] And I really struggled to say yes, because I had a job I liked, because I had prepared for five years to work there, it was a great experience for me. [...] I didn't really know where this idea had come from, if I had thought it up myself. But the Lord has his own language, he shows you another path.
> (Az 2017)

This interview highlights that becoming a nun was not only a religious choice, but a practical one, which this sister ultimately valued over an existing and fulfilling career. Similarly, Sister Cd recounts, 'it was a bit of a struggle to take this decision. Because dedicating myself to the Lord in this way wasn't easy' (Cd 2017). Sister Jp, who previously stated 'I couldn't stand the sisters' (Jp 2017), also recalls her internal turmoil at hearing her calling:

> One wonderful day which still moves me to think about, I was at school and I asked a sister to go to the toilet. I go to the toilet and on the way there were the sisters who were at prayer. The Mother Superior was at the lectern and was making that very soft soft sound on the organ and under that sound the sisters were praying. And this triggered something inside me so that everything else seemed to fade almost. [...] I would go to listen to the sisters [...]. Then one day at church I was praying and crying and I heard someone knock at the door [blowing her nose], the Prioress called me and said 'listen, you seem so strange at the moment: sometimes you're angry, sometimes you laugh like a madwoman, other times you cry, or don't speak with anyone. What's going on, you're not yourself anymore?' [I replied] 'nothing, nothing, nothing'. There I was praying to the Lord to send me a sign, and yet saying 'nothing, nothing, nothing'. [...] After about a year the Prioress called me and said 'listen, I have to go to Rome because I've finished my mandate. If you're thinking about taking orders' – I had never talked about taking orders, but the fact of hearing that – 'What!' – and she said – 'to become a sister' – 'really??' And from that moment I just exploded, and no one could hold me back.
> (Jp 2017)

This highly sensory and emotive account suggests an astounding professional and personal fulfilment and a dramatic resolution to an existential struggle. Narratives of spiritual, moral and practical struggles in the oral histories provide a counterpoint to those who portray themselves as born to their vocation but still fit with canonical conversion accounts of 'faith in its proper imperfection' (Morgan 1965: 72).

Finally, discussions of love and romance also appear in a number of women's recollections of their vocations. Sister Ft explains that she first felt her vocation when 'I was teaching when two sisters passed by [...] and I spoke with them, and I fell in love with them' (2017). Similarly, another sister discusses seeing nuns in her village and says 'the sisters in my town had sown the seeds of prayer [...] always always always true love' (Pt 2017). Apart from this romantic lexis to describe other women religious, some of the interviewees recount tales of secular romance which led them to their vocations. As in the films of Chapter 8, romance is presented as the catalyst for religious vocation. Sister Ai mentions, 'I had a boyfriend, but I felt that it wasn't – I said to myself, "why don't I love him?" But I could feel that he loved me. It was certainly not my path' (2017). Another sister compares her romantic experiences with her religious calling, saying:

> There were three boys who tortured me: one was Beppe and he was perhaps the most sincere of them all because when our gazes met he would turn red as a pepper. And I think there was something strong there, something – well. Gino was the one who sat behind me and when I would get a poor grade and was ashamed he would realise because I would go red. He would take my hair in his hands – I had a ponytail down to here – and stroke it and tell me 'don't worry, I love you anyway'. [...] The third one taught me to dance [...]. He would put his hand on my shoulders and I felt all these butterflies inside and thought 'what's he doing?' [makes a panicked gesture]. [When later I felt my vocation] from then on [gestures to show everything moved on from there] I was burning up. I didn't think any more about Gino or Beppe. [...] A different satisfaction filled my heart, it wasn't superficial like the others. From that moment I tried to take some distance.
>
> (Anonymous 2017)[6]

There are many similarities between this statement and another testimony from Sister Cc, who describes a boy who was almost unknown to her trying to convince her parents that he must marry her, instead of her becoming a nun. Of this moment, Cc says 'that was the beginning. That was when I started to say "no, I don't want to marry, I want to be a nun"' (2017). Both interviewees express strong physical and psychological discomfort with romance in their descriptions of the 'butterflies inside' (Anonymous 2017), and body language of physically pushing against romance with the words 'I really avoided him' (Cc 2017). It is common for conversion narratives to describe faith as a sensual experience, exemplified by Mary Ann and Van Reidhead's study of a nun who recounted that 'her senses confirmed that she belonged' (2003: 187); here, the senses serve to convey the opposite impression. As in the films of Chapter 8, romance in these interviews is another example of the 'rupture moment', common to conversion stories (Pannofino 2012), from which women's religious identities were born. Like in the films, secular romance is portrayed as limiting for women. These stories, and those who described their interaction with other nuns, speak of vocation as an alternative, more fulfilling love, which was chosen rather than foisted upon women.

This section has argued that oral histories evidence interviewees' agency in choosing and pursuing their professions, yet this agency is consistently described as motivated by community or religion rather than ambition or independent choice. Their stories also echo conversion narratives, an established institutional narrative form. It is usual for women religious to be repeatedly interrogated about their vocations during their training, and it is possible that because of this, vocation stories '[take] recourse to a pre-existing corpus of organisational stories in order to construct and communicate [...] personal stories' (Linde in Pannofino 2012: 5).

Education

In this chapter, it becomes evident that the careers offered to women religious were frequently far more varied and exotic than the average woman could expect at this time – the period that Willson describes as the 'era of the housewife' (Willson 2010: 120). The first major difference to women's work that religious vows appear to make is a longer, more comprehensive education. Their role in teaching is one of the more developed areas of study regarding women religious. For a comprehensive historiography, see Raftery (2012). Nuns' access to education had long been on the Church's agenda, and Vatican II presented an opportunity for concessions to be made in favour of women. Discussing one of the preparatory texts for Vatican II, Rocca affirms, 'the fourth point concerned the training of women religious and the Sacred Congregation of Religious asked that Vatican II promoted the training of female "juniorates" and "scholars", in the same way as for male seminarians and scholars' (Rocca 2013: 142). As I listened to the interviewees, a clear system of progression emerged; women were accepted into orders as novices and were then allotted training or education which would lead them into a professional field.

There does not appear to have been much flexibility or choice in the pathways the women were given, nor did they necessarily fit with existing talents the novices may have had. For example, Sister Qo tells of how her profession was decided on the basis of her physique:

> they said 'get a vocation' and sent us to the clinic to see what it was like. Then they sent the ones who were a bit more feeble to school. I was pretty robust because I've always been a little chubby – you need to be strong to work.
>
> (2017)

Another sister tells of how her expectations were not met in the choice of her vocation, saying 'I really loved sewing, and so I said "I know how to embroider so maybe they will put me with the sisters to do darning, and then they'll send me out into the local community". That didn't happen' (Cc 2017). Sometimes, novices were deliberately allocated an occupation which did not fit their skills. This was known as 'talent-stripping' (Campbell-Jones 1979: 29).

Contrary to my expectations, many of the interviewees testified to having had little, and poor, education prior to religious profession. Some attributed this to the penury of their families, for example Sister Cd remarks:

> Since I was the youngest of seven – we were poor peasants – my brother who was three years older had begun his studies when I finished primary school and I said to my mum 'Mamma, can I study [too]?', and mum said 'if you go to school too we won't be able to get by. You go to work, and help us pay for your brother. At least one of you will have a full education'.
>
> (Cd 2017)

Other interviewees note the damage that war did to their educations. One sister recalled, 'since I grew up during wartime, we only had primary school' (Cc 2017). After her only teacher was killed in bombing in Foggia, she asserted 'I refused to continue into fifth grade' (Cc 2017). These anecdotes of war interrupting education are supported by historical and statistical evidence. Many schools were suspended or closed during the Second World War because of bombing or lack of resources. Reflecting this, ISTAT was unable to record statistics on education during this period, noting 'data collection usually published annually in the *Annuario statistico italiano* [Italian Statistical Annual] up until 1942–43 [...] was suspended because of the worsening of the World War (2011: 6). Religious institutions were a bulwark for wartime education, for students both within and outside of religious orders. Sister Pt explains that the only reason that she was able to go on studying at all during the war was because in the convent 'we had our own religious teachers who had already got their degrees' (2017). Religious orders emerge in these oral histories as the guardian angels of women's education, tallying with the findings of studies of nuns in different nations. The 1951 census records that only a third of pupils registered in middle and senior schools were girls. At university, those numbers drop to just 60,000 women enrolled nationwide, in comparison to 167,000 men (Cinquantamila.it 2014). Yet, women religious with the most basic of qualifications at entrance were provided with professional training courses, if not with access to higher education. The Annuario Pontificio for 1948 records 22 universities worldwide and twelve *Istituti di studi superiori* [Institutes of Higher Education] in Rome under pontifical rule. Many interviewees discussed education and training provided inside the convent. Perhaps the best example of the transformative education provided for women religious is Sister Cc's story:

> It's not like in those days girls studied, they did primary school and that was it [...] and then with the war, it was impossible. So some girls didn't know how to read, write, or even sign their name. [...] I remember when I did my postulancy they didn't know what to do with me because I'd only done fourth grade. So from the age of nineteen to thirty I did my studies up to a degree in English [...] all within the religious institute because we had schools and I could go with the girls and do the exams internally.
>
> (Cc 2017)

These interviewees underline the increased educational and professional opportunities religious life offered women. If interviewees remember their educations so forthrightly, it may be a testament to their unusualness both within communities, and in the wider secular context as we have seen in the case of both the *mondine* and *sarte*. This narrative also stands in contrast to interviewees' own initial humble origins. Memories of enhanced education highlight the professionalization of women religious' activity and their empowerment and distance from the traditional destinies of wife and mother.

Although this is a remarkable achievement of religious orders, we should be cautious. Cc goes on to stipulate:

> I'm not someone who had who-knows-what kind of ambitions as a nun. All these promotions that I had – I didn't ask for them, and plenty of my sister colleagues had wanted to study and hadn't been able to [...] for example there was another sister who entered with me, but stopped after primary school. Her brother, a doctor, had written a note to the Superior to ask 'why hasn't my sister continued her studies?', but it was no good. My parents didn't even know what I was studying, and I ended up with a degree in English!
>
> (Cc 2017)

It is true that religious institutions have historically provided education both for their own communities and also for non-Catholics and mission communities. However, it does appear that provision of education to sisters was patchy and sometimes seemingly random.

One of the most remarkable and unusual features of women religious' education regards their linguistic abilities. In the interviews themselves, I was often asked in which language I would prefer to speak, and, at one of the convents, the official language of the mother house was French. Among the languages spoken by the sisters interviewed were: Italian, English, French, Urdu, Punjabi, Swahili, Mandarin, German, and Arabic. Most of these languages were learned either during overseas missions or with them in mind. The emphasis given to languages reflects the transnationalism which characterizes most religious communities. Although interviewees often spoke of thorough linguistic training in recognized institutes, there are other accounts of sisters learning languages in rather improvised circumstances. Sister Cd provides an amusing example of this:

> I first went to Kenya. I didn't know how to speak French or English, because in Italy I had only gone to middle school, our education was very limited. But by praying in French – because there were other novices in Kenya from a number of francophone countries, so we did psalms in French. The *Osservatore Romano* would come to us in English, and we did confessions – if you want to have a laugh – with the sins already written out for us! We just tried to read them out because we didn't know – I'm telling you, it makes us laugh now, but at that time there were English missionary sisters in Africa and they would hand us a little script, and we would choose our sins off of it to read out at confession!
>
> (Cd 2017)

These memories speak of a highly vocational education which challenged women by putting them into unfamiliar circumstances with only partial preparation. In comparison to the domestic, agricultural or administrative jobs of most Italian working women (Willson 2010: 118), we can notice a significant difference. These accounts of education demonstrate the professional nature of women religious' training and testify to the 'regenerating' power of religious work.

Missions

Missionary work is not necessarily the vigorous evangelizing activity that is often imagined. In interviews, mission work was frequently described as an extension of the service and care work nuns often undertook in their home countries. All but one interviewee had been on at least one mission and exactly half of the interviewees had worked overseas. Most of the missionary sisters continued service work like nursing or teaching; however, this kind of work became exceptional because missionary life 'was often imagined to be "topsy-turvy", perhaps even dangerous' and, as such, 'the missions may also have been regarded as providing a space in which gender roles in *this* life might be negotiated or reinterpreted' (McKenna 2006a: 197). Destinations for missionary work among this group of subjects varied, although African countries featured strongly. The women often referred to their destination quite simply as 'Africa', for example, 'I spent thirty five years in Africa' (Qo 2017) and 'going to Africa or going to England, it was the same thing' (Cd 2017), rather than specifying the particular country. This feature recalls some of the criticisms which have been made of colonialism and of missionary work – that developing countries are not understood in their individuality; portrayed as 'other', a homogenous area identifiable only by its poverty and lack of sophistication in comparison to the West (Hall 2006). The problematizing of missionary sisters' presence in developing countries, or lack of it, is a subject to which this section returns.

Missionary work was central to the identity of women religious in both lay and faith communities at this time. As McKenna observes, 'many of the women discussed their attraction to religious life in terms of [...] a fascination for missionary work. Indeed, going "on the missions" was what first attracted most of the women to religious life' (2006a: 196). The same can be observed in my group of interviewees. Sister Ss recalls:

> My aunt – my dad's sister – was already on a mission. [...] Before she left, after the war, she came to see us. [...] I didn't say anything, and my aunt didn't ask me anything, so I kept my mouth shut. But, when I first turned fifteen or sixteen I started to say 'Mamma, you know, I'd like to become a-', [she replied] 'a what?', 'a nun, a nun'. That's when she started to think 'this girl wants to go on a mission'. And in the end I said it: 'I want to go on a mission'.
>
> (Ss 2017)

The reasons for feeling such an attraction to a missionary vocation are extrapolated by other sisters and are articulated around the idea of giving one's service in places of need. For example, 'there was a need for sisters in Vietnam, and I asked for Vietnam [...] there was the Vietnam war, this difficult situation, and that attracted me' (Be 2017). Sister Cd's testimony echoes this sentiment:

> After I took my perpetual vows I just made myself available, because I saw that when you're in a fraternity, whether you're in Africa or India, the whole world is yours – [...] why choose one country? I didn't choose I just wrote 'available'.
>
> (Cd 2017)

These statements recall missionary work as a calling to help and paint a picture of absolute charity. Like the protagonist of *Anna* (1951), the interviewees discuss an attraction to the work of helping and being present at personal risk, rather than to exotic travel and adventure, the highest goals of missionary work. This ties in with post-Second World War discourse about models of ideal femininity being based upon 'a model of an ultraconscious worker, a heroic apostle [...] a woman dedicated to heroism and sacrifice' (La Scuola 1988: 290).

The work which interviewees performed was most commonly the provision of medical aid or education, and often the danger and violence encountered in these missions are highlighted. For instance, Sister Qo remembers the civil war in Guinea-Bissau, saying:

> The missionaries would go out and pick up the poor, the ill, and the dead. They would take them to the house, throw them in the house and I had to take the dead, children, and elderly and sort one from the other. Sometimes my hands would be covered in blood because these people were coming from warfare, they were shooting each other, killing. A tribal war. This was the worst of it: they were killing mothers and children. And night and day I did this work.
>
> (Qo 2017)

Another sister recalls her experience of the 1965 revolution during her mission in the former Belgian Congo, saying, 'there was the revolution and the two of us were in prison for four years. In prison in our own homes, eh? They stole our cars. No one came to us because they were afraid. We had nothing left' (Pt 2017). Western presence, in the form of women religious, is depicted as paternalistic, addressing indigenous violence, supporting the comment that 'portrayals help to construct the West as parental, caring, generous, kind, helpful' (Cameron and Haanstra 2008: 1482), and Wendy Pojmann's observation that Italian women of this time 'remained part of a privileged western European culture [...] that reinforced ideas of European superiority' (Pojmann 2013: 11). They also recall the 'topsy-turvy' world of the missions, where sisters foreground the danger of their lives. These narratives allow women to enter the traditionally male roles of not only hero or adventurer but also colonizer.

Accounts of the provision of services can be found in other interviews, and relate not to war zones but places deemed to be in particular need or poverty. Sister Cd remembers working 'in a general hospital in Cameroon' and Sister Ss discusses how 'our house was in the desert. We had a clinic. Sick people came to us. They came for treatment, we gave them medicines' (2017). Many sisters were qualified medical professionals, but even where they were not, they worked to provide medical supplies, such as Sister Be, who told me:

> The work was bottle washing [laughing]. Yes, this was a bit strange. It was like that back then. Today it wouldn't be the same. But in those days bottles were collected in Saigon [sic], like Coca Cola bottles etc. and we would collect them in a pond. [...] It was manual labour. For six months. After another six months I went to a

pharmaceutical factory for children and it was simply mechanical: every morning you had to stamp 800–1000 bottles like this [gestures stamping and laughs].

(Be 2017)

This recollection recognizes that performing manual, unskilled labour was perhaps not the common imaginary of the nun.

Many of the interviewees had run or worked in mission schools. One, Sister Ft, had later become a diplomatic courier for the Vatican:

> After thirty years in Pakistan – because I spoke English – [...] I went to Nigeria. You could only enter Nigeria as a diplomat, and only if you spoke English. We had the Vatican Embassy. I lived there for two years [...]. *It was important for my life* because they would send me from that embassy all over the world with messages. [...] Internal messages from the embassies. Very, very secret, high-security. [...] Here and there, I made one hundred and eight flights.
>
> (Ft 2017, my emphasis).

Again, the importance and transformative power of languages, and the exceptional opportunities for travel and status which women religious had, come to the fore in discussions of missionary work.

It would, however, be wrong not to note criticisms of western colonialism, and the growing perspective that religious missionaries operated 'as an arm of imperialism' (Raftery 2012: 43). Works such as Ciro Poggiali's *Diario AOI* (1936–37) detail the brutality of Italian colonialism (Burdett 2011). Missionaries' involvement with colonial projects was often indirect; for example through establishing schools which educated them in the colonizer's language.[7] Especially in the light of burgeoning postcolonial theory, I was interested to see whether any of my interviewees would engage with the link between missions and imperialism. Although none of the subjects explicitly reference controversy or scandal, many of them highlighted the importance of harmonious relations with indigenous communities, stressing that religious imperialism was not the goal. Sister Az worked in Burundi as a nurse. She recalls:

> I got a lot of help from the people, with the language too, I needed a lot of help, and this brought us together [...] as equals. Because they needed my medical skills, but I needed their language skills, and so we formed a lovely bond [...]. Also because at that time there were very violent encounters between the Tutsi and the Hutu. So at that time my staff were all Hutu, and then there were the Tutsi, and we created an atmosphere of fraternity, of 'we can work together, we can live together'. Truly, for me it was a wonderful fraternal experience. It enriched me, yes.
>
> (Az 2017)

The picture that Az paints is one where missionaries, locals and warring factions are equal and work together for the greater good. She similarly remembers that when she was later working in Tunisia her Catholic community mixed peacefully with the Islamic community as 'an extended friendship'. Az highlights the potential for missionary work to create social links which overcome religious or political divide. Sister Ft, who directed a Catholic missionary school in Pakistan, repeats this theme, describing how she took over the school from two nuns who

> were afraid of the Muslims. And they kind of stayed in their little corner. But I opened my arms to the Muslims. [...] We really worked well together. [...] I was very happy with the local people, with the Muslims.
>
> (2017)

However, after this statement, she adds, 'the Muslim teachers felt honoured to work in our school' (2017). Without wishing to evaluate the veracity of this statement, it is nonetheless revelatory of the power play at work in missionary communities. Sister Pt describes the special treatment her community was given in the former Belgian Congo during its push for independence. Recalling the medical help which she provided in remote villages, she says:

> Four or five times we would go, by foot, about six kilometers at 2 pm. One time the governor's soldiers came across us. 'What a disgrace to send the sisters on foot!', and next thing a coach arrived, a coach with a paid driver, all the gas we wanted, for free!
>
> (Pt 2017)

This anecdote, set in the context of political upheaval in the former Belgian Congo, reveals the problematic presence and unequal treatment of missionary nuns abroad.

These unequal ethnic and power relations are something which only one interviewee acknowledges as problematic. In response to my question about how she found working with the local community, Sister Cd replies:

> I didn't know anything about tropical medicine. I did my studies here [in Italy] and so we studied a completely different kind of medicine. It was them [the locals] who taught me, and they had families, children, perhaps husbands, were paid less, and they were much better than me at the job. I felt bad about that, but not because they made me feel bad. [...] Sometimes I would ask myself 'what right do I have to a higher salary than them, when they are worth more than I am?'
>
> (Cd 2017)

That missionary women religious received special status or treatment was often the case, and it is an interesting nuance of memory that this is barely evoked in the interviews. The frequency of references to harmonious relations with the local community does, however, point towards this being a tension of which interviewees are aware. Women workers are portrayed as providing a unique opportunity for mediation and bridge-building in the shadow of more violent and turbulent male military colonialism.

Missionary work was a point of pride for the interviewees. Recollections concerning missionary work are overwhelmingly positive and assert their value. Descriptions of the missions as 'truly a marvellous lived experience' (Az 2017) are typical. Contact with other cultures and religions is remembered as having been a particularly valuable element of the work:

> It made me grow up, yes. Encountering a new culture, meeting those people, it was really a life school, in all senses, a cultural awakening, an awareness of different values [...] and from there *you can start to communicate, you can have a dialogue.*
>
> (Az 2017, my emphasis)

Interviewees principally describe missionary work as an ideal context in which feminine skills like communication and empathy can thrive. McKenna posits the missions as spaces in which gender roles might be flipped or changed (2006a: 197). Oral histories recalling mission work certainly foreground the exceptional opportunities that religious life gives women, in ways which are fairly uncritically presented by the subjects themselves, both in terms of gender and relations with indigenous peoples. Nuns' missionary work is recalled in terms of care and sacrifice, fitting into traditional feminine behaviours and lexis.

Pleasure and pain; Emotional labour

Michael Hardt describes labour which is immaterial such as care and service work, as affective, and notes how it is specifically feminine and corporeal (Hardt 1999: 96). It is useful to note that women religious are doubly 'vulnerable' to undertaking affective work because it is not only a gendered norm but a religious one. Catholicism makes the performance and regulation of emotion one of its foundational principles. For example, Colossians (3:12) entreats readers to 'put on, therefore, as the elect of God, holy and beloved, bowels of mercies, kindness, humbleness of mind, meekness, longsuffering' (King James Version 2011: 569).

It is not only missionary sisters who expressed pleasure and satisfaction with their work. However, interviewees' accounts of pleasure in their work are often tempered or intertwined with descriptions of obedience. Mary Magray comments that 'by the mid-nineteenth century, a new model of Catholic womanhood emerged which prized docility above most other qualities' (1998: 130). Certainly in post-Second World War Italy, this ideal was present in both religious and secular spheres. Catholic lay associations like the *Gioventù femminile* [Women's Youth] proposed certain ideal forms of womanhood, highlighting self-sacrifice and dedication to family, Church, and the community (La Scuola 1988: 290). Catholic discourse imagines an ideal of womanhood which ties together work, emotion, service, and sacrifice. I argue here that we can figure this discourse as a precursor to the contemporary theory of affective and emotional labour.

As we have already observed in Chapter 6, Arlie Hochschild's theory of emotional labour (1983) describes the 'effort, planning, and control needed to express organizationally desired emotions during interpersonal transactions' (Morris and Feldman 1996: 987). There is an evident crossover with affective work, and work in which emotions do not have to be produced but regulated, a common feature of oral histories of nuns. Hochschild distinguishes 'surface acting', where an emotion is displayed, but not felt, from 'active deep acting', when subjects try to truly feel a professionally desirable emotion in order to become an ideal worker (Zapf 2002: 244). Emotional work is gendered, since 'lacking other resources, women make a resource out of feeling' (Hochschild 1983: 163). We can therefore expect that women religious engage in active deep – rather than surface – acting by reminding themselves of religious doctrine and what it instructs God's servants to think and feel. Hochschild (1983) uses the example of an air hostess thinking of a difficult passenger as a child, not responsible for their own behaviour, in order to produce active deep acting which would allow her to feel the necessary emotions to deal with the passenger. Oral histories position the work of women religious in this lexis of deep acting for emotional labour. As well as emotional labour being very much female-gendered, it is also renowned for going unrecognized. The consequence of women religious describing their work in terms of emotional labour is that this has historically obscured its professional nature.

In some cases, interviewees describe their professional obedience and service as a continuation of what they experienced in the family space. Sister Pt describes her family, saying, 'there was obedience […], dad was the dad, mum should be helped. I had my service to perform from a young age' (2017). Here, description of family and convent space overlap. In response to the question of whether her vocation had changed her character, Sister Bo said, 'certainly. Let's say that I was obedient' (2017). McKenna states, the most important model of womanhood outside marriage and motherhood was to be found in religious life. Certainly, it was the only other form of womanhood the Church publicly espoused, fitting in, as it did, with Catholic ideologies of female self-sacrifice.

(2006a: 193–94)

A wider societal and institutional discourse around idealized femininity as self-denial can be seen to permeate these oral histories.

Obedience did not necessarily come easily; Sister My described how 'religious life, the way of life, influenced my character. It changed me, […] [causing me] to accept God's will. To accept things that went against my vision. But it took time' (My 2017). Similarly, Sister Ss says 'if I didn't like something, if I didn't want to eat something, I wouldn't say anything. You have to get used to it. You need to get used to a lot of things. If you didn't you'd never succeed' (2017). The dissonance between this 'ideal' femininity of sacrifice and self-effacement, and the lived reality for women was evoked by Sister Az, who tells of how she would hear others praise the convent,

saying 'how lovely' about a life of poverty. […] I would hear them say 'how lovely', because the fraternity evoked goodwill with those passing through, but I would boil up inside […]. We have to make ourselves small, stay in our place.

(Az 2017)

Another sister wept as she remembered how she was transferred from her community to another. She recalled how both the Prioress and the other sisters cried all day, before telling her '"Sister Jp it's your turn" […]. The tears I shed, because I had to go to this place which was really horrible to me' (Jp 2017). These oral histories consolidate the idea of religious work as necessitating deep-acting emotional labour and sacrifice and suggest that this was not necessarily the gendered or God-given characteristic that Catholic discourse would suggest.

The necessity for obedience is not only sometimes recounted pragmatically but also sometimes with explicit judgement and anger. We are left in no doubt that, occasionally, interviewees view obedience as a necessary evil, but an evil nonetheless. This is apparent again in a glimpse of one interview: 'they make you do something and you don't see [the reason]. Because it's one thing speaking with someone who says "do this", and to you *it seems stup-* that you don't want to, that's when obedience costs you' (My 2017, my emphasis). The half-utterance and then stifling of that word, *stupida* [stupid], tells of a judgement and resistance which is quashed both in reality and in testimony. While most interviewees reference obedience and sacrifice, some attribute it to established patterns, whereas others underline it as a learned – or forced – behaviour. All these comments describe emotional labour as an institutional lifestyle rather than a professional choice.

Similar to obedience is the forgetting, or burying, of the self. Statements such as 'you must, you manage to forget yourself' (Qo 2017) and 'difficult, it's difficult yes. There are sacrifices. A lot of self-abnegation in order to help others' (Ai 2017), evidence the importance of disregarding a sense of self. The notion of giving oneself to others and forgoing personal desires is also clear. For example, 'I wouldn't think about myself. I didn't think about it [...]. I've never refused, never thought of myself' (Qo 2017). Indeed, when selfish pleasure is experienced, some recall this as a moral dilemma:

> At the end of every school year the mums would praise me saying 'well done, my goodness!', and I would always ask forgiveness from the Lord after the school year. I would ask the Lord 'look, did I work for you, or for myself?' [becoming emotional]. [...] But it's not like you would go looking for them [the compliments].
>
> (Jp 2017)

It should not be a surprise that obedience and abnegation take such an important place in women religious' accounts of the self. These declarations fit with statements discussed earlier about prioritizing others' care at work. The three vows which sisters take when entering the convent – poverty, chastity and obedience – evidently permeate their identity construction and ideals. The oral histories here support the idea of institutions instating acceptable versions of the self. Post-Second World War society and the Church were clear in their idealization of so-called feminine gifts of maternalism and sacrifice. These 'gifts' are historical examples of emotional and affective labour and pervade oral histories.

Narratives of emotion in work were not all negative, however. Responses to the question of whether interviewees had liked their work typically echoed Li's words, 'wonderful, wonderful, I loved it' (2017). As with oral histories of seamstresses in this period, many women religious described their work as an act of love. In response to my comment that caring for the elderly must be a difficult job, Sister Ai replied, 'you need to love' (2017). Similarly, when discussing her work as a nurse, Sister Ao states,

> I loved the oldies [...], the only thing I found hard were sores [...], they moved me, I guess. [...] Not because [they disgusted me], they moved me, moved me. [...] You need to love a lot. A lot, a lot, a lot.
>
> (2017)

The performance of love and compassion (often conquering aversion) are gendered notions and, when a necessary part of a profession, recall women's making a professional resource of emotion (Hochschild 1983: 163).

Similarly, there is a certain belief that to be truly good at one's job, 'you have to be suited' (My 2017). Another sister commented, 'you need to work with passion. I think a teacher is born to the role. Because it's not simply a job' (Pz 2017). Observations of interviewees' professional roles are made such as, 'I think these talents, some people have them, some don't' (Ai 2017), 'it really fitted me', and the mystic notion that 'I found myself in my element' (Pc 2017). The idea that destinies are predetermined is an extension of the faith of some Catholics, and this is significant because it may be argued to affect how interviewees describe their skills. However, given the similarities between these statements and similar ones from seamstresses, it seems more likely that this kind of discussion of work is linked to gender discourse and the formation of ideal (working) femininity. For example, Sister Jp affirms of her work with children, 'I passed on to them a gift that the Lord had given me' (2017). Another sister argues, 'it's natural things that come out. I'm not very educated and haven't done goodness knows what training. No, no, it comes from the person who has these demands inside of them' (Pc 2017). Competence and contentment at work are expressed as the result of finding an occupation that corresponds to a supposedly innate ability, rather than because of women's commitment or skill.

Loving and giving are expressed as central concepts to the professional work of women religious in these oral histories. Sister Li states, 'you have to help others. You have to be there to help others. This, desire [...] to do something, to help. Otherwise, why become a nun, what for?' (2017). The notion of giving oneself to those in pain is important to many of the interviewees. Sisters recount, 'I always liked working among suffering [...]. I really felt successful because I was working with love' (Qo 2017), reflecting again a giving of the self to one's profession. Describing her work with drug addicts, Sister Pz describes how, 'there were surgeons, doctors, who would say to me "but Sister, why are you burning yourselves out with these guys?" [...] You can't joke around. You need some guts, because it's gutting work' (Pz 2017). This very physical vocabulary reflects the bodily aspect of giving with which women religious recount their work. As in the expression 'to give oneself body and soul', so do women religious recount the very physical experience of emotional labour.

Conclusion

These oral histories illustrate religious life as Valerio contends, offering unprecedented opportunities and self-realization for women (2017: 186). Such a notion speaks to Bonifazio's idea of work regenerating and empowering the male citizen (2011: 163), proving that it is also applicable to women. However, women religious engage in a number of strategies which cast their identities as collective, and their work as a vocation or emotional labour. Women religious tie their identities and memories to collective spaces such as the family or community. They draw upon conversion narratives to fit their own personal stories into a wider canon of religious experience. I argue that the reasons for this are institutional, social and political. My argument is supported by Mangion, who observes the unlikelihood of women religious self-identifying as professionals because of the secular overtones of such an identity (Mangion 2005: 234). We should also recall the position of the Catholic Church which saw in the demands of contemporary feminist movements the 'shipwrecking of the strongholds of the family and of society' (Valerio 2016: 176). It was impossible for Catholicism – and by that merit women religious themselves – to describe female workers as emancipated or independent. Consequently, the unique and innovative labour performed by nuns is widely unnoticed and unproblematized by women religious themselves in oral histories and more widely by secular society. Their labour is considered instead as part of a larger story of Catholic – and female – charity.

NOTES

1. *God Bless Our Pope/Full in the panting Heart of Rome* (Wiseman 1802–65).
2. Apostolic nuns work outside of the convent and are therefore more easily classifiable as workers than contemplative religious.
3. Nursing was a profession both recognized and celebrated by the Church, in occasions such as the International Congress of Catholic Nurses in 1936, suggesting that, in the period leading up to the one under study, it fits into both Fascist and Catholic ideals of acceptable female work (Pollard 2008: 96).
4. Let it be noted that this group includes monks and general *religiosi*, but is differentiated from *Specialisti in discipline religiose e teologiche* [specialists in religious and theological disciplines] who count among them *parroci, sacerdoti, vescovi*, and *abati* [parish priests, ministers, bishops, and abbots] – all positions currently barred to women in the Catholic church.
5. I have added together the numbers for the Italian terms *mamma* and *madre*, and *papà* and *padre* to reach my totals.
6. The names of the characters in this story have been changed, at the request of the interviewee, who asked to be anonymous.
7. For a discussion of the various involvements of religious in colonialism in a non-Italian context, see J. P. Daughton (2008), and the work edited by Dana L. Robert (2008).

Afterword

Did work empower and regenerate the female citizen in post-Second World War Italy? This is one of the central questions that this book has sought to address. Over the nine chapters, I have examined filmic representations of working women, and put these into dialogue with oral histories, asking how work is embedded in, and interacts with, gender norms and historical context. This book began by setting out three key areas from which the Italian working woman is absent in the post-war period: filmic representations, oral histories and scholarly enquiry. To redress these absences, I found and analyzed eight films featuring female working protagonists which span a range of years, directors and genres. I also collected and conducted original oral history interviews with women who worked between 1945 and 1965. The very act of uncovering and examining these sources is political and responds to oral history's aspiration to give voice to the silent. I have demonstrated the interaction between cultural representations and individual and collective memories of working women, observing how both oral and filmic sources refer to, build upon and reject dominant discourses. I selected the period between 1945 and 1965 because it is so significant in terms of women's work, where women were occupying increasingly visible roles, but were subject to discourse encouraging them back to traditional roles and spaces. This work is important because it responds to the absence of the working woman, because it critiques her representation where she appears, because it helps us to understand the role she played in post-war society and because its branches reach towards a wider enquiry into how society reacts to and values women's work.

This book consistently connects films and other cultural texts, collective memories and individual identity. The choice to examine film as a medium was crucial; as the most popular leisure pursuit of this time (Sorlin 1996: 74), cinema spoke to and of post-war Italy. Film was a cultural medium and a collective experience. A point arising from the analysis contained in Chapter 3 on the *mondine* demonstrates this phenomenon. A *mondina* recalls her experience of watching the film *Riso amaro* (De Santis 1949), saying:

> There is a scene where the girls were climbing a wall to go out one evening, and there was someone behind me who said: 'It's true, you know, they were all whores'. I got to my feet, I took him like this and I said: 'If you say that word again I will take you to the police and have you arrested! You ignorant idiot! There has never even been a frog who has wanted to kiss you!'
>
> (*Sorriso amaro* 2003)

Not only does this episode underline the interactivity of film and collective memory but it also shows what is at stake in portrayals of working women, and the depth of feeling of those women that cultural portrayals claim to represent.

One of the arteries of this book has been the symbolic connection between women's work and the Italian nation. In the first section addressing the *mondine*, I demonstrated the influence of films' political contexts on their portrayals of working women. The turmoil between the political Left and Right in post-war Italy plays out in the depiction of the *mondine* in *Riso amaro* (De Santis 1949) but is absent from the later *La risaia* (Matarazzo 1956), mirroring post-war Italy's move from political upheaval in 1949 to 'ideological complacency' in 1956 (Marcus 2000: 339). This reading connects with and enriches the analysis of other scholars who have pointed to women's political and national symbolism in post-war Italian films.[1] The section also reflected on the claim that women represent collectivity and linked this to the primacy given to the concept of *solidarismo* [solidarity] in post-war political discourse. Notions of solidarity and collectivity were drawn out both from the films of Chapter 2 and the oral histories of Chapter 3 and tied in with traditional ideas of women as maternal carriers of a nation. Although this section highlighted the privileged cultural space accorded to the *mondine*, it suggested that cultural memory of the *mondine* has instrumentalized them for their political symbolism and thus diminished their identity as workers. The case of Maria Margotti, evoked in Chapter 3, brings this argument into focus by highlighting how her memory was exploited by the Left; sometimes to the detriment of historical accuracy and the well-being of her surviving relatives.

The theme of social change being expressed through representations and oral histories of working women emerged again in the second section on seamstresses. Seamstresses provide an interesting counterpoint to the *mondine* because their work has associations with traditional female employment and supposedly feminine skills. This book has consistently engaged with the historical sexual division of labour, looking at how women in feminized sectors related differently to their employment. In Chapter 5, I observed how the films *Sorelle Materassi* (Poggioli 1943), *Le ragazze di piazza di Spagna* (Emmer 1952), and *Le amiche* (Antonioni 1955) show seamstresses occupying urban spaces, often with disastrous consequences. By considering the theories of feminist geographers, I argued that the urban space is shown as fraught with danger, an outlook which expresses postwar attitudes to women's work more generally. In oral histories with seamstresses discussed in Chapter 6, space was again evoked as fundamental to women's identities. Whether through the modern structure of the atelier or the increased social mobility of seamstresses themselves, interviewees narrate how their work allowed them to occupy new and potentially transgressive spaces. I contended that it is the feminized nature of seamstresses' work which allows them to enter such spaces without gaining renown as transgressive subjects.

Women religious, like seamstresses, inhabit an ambiguous territory between emancipated and traditional femininity. The final section on women religious underlined the inherently patriarchal context of the Church but set this as a counterpoint to the opportunities which religious life affords to women. Chapter 8 contended that filmic portrayals of women religious allowed new gender behaviours to be rehearsed and considered the role that genre plays in this. Melodrama, like pink neorealism and comedy, presents female professionals in new and transgressive professional roles but guards the possibility of returning them to reassuring structures like marriage, the domestic sphere, or the convent. The very real and unique opportunities bestowed on women religious are thrown into relief by the oral histories in Chapter 9. Bringing us back to the question of whether work empowered and regenerated the female citizen, interviewees testify to enhanced education, varied and satisfying careers, and the opportunity for self-determination. Yet, as in Chapter 6 on seamstresses, the career narratives of nuns reveal narratorial and linguistic features which gender their work. Interviewees deploy narrative strategies which link their professional choices to familial influence and describe their success in affective terms of love, passion, and care.

Drawing together the various threads of this book is my contention that work was, to a greater or lesser extent depending on the sector, traditionally considered to be unfeminine. In order to be made visible, it is therefore feminized in film and oral history in a number of ways. These include sexualizing women, making them symbolic of the collective or rendering their work essentially emotional. This reflects the failings and urgent importance of scholarly enquiry into women's work; we need to recognize their activity as work before we can value and inscribe women into (labour) history.

This book is not a conclusion, but a contribution, to enquiry into cultural representations and memory of women's work. It is also one of the few projects which bring filmic representations, oral histories and archival material into contact. In the course of this book, I have sought out other scholars who conduct oral histories with women workers and have found a majority of researchers looking at contemporary case studies.² This is perhaps unsurprising because contemporary working women are both more numerous and more accessible. Yet, this is the very reason for the urgency of interviewing women who worked in the past. All of the sectors investigated in this book are disappearing; the *mondine* ceased to exist in the early 1960s, made-to-measure clothing has been almost obliterated by ready-to-wear fashion and secularization has reduced the number of women religious worldwide by almost 25 per cent over twenty years (Rocca 2013: 152). To understand how women's work is valued today, it is crucial to critically assess its cultural and collective memory.

Inevitably, this study has opened up paths of enquiry without being able to travel to their conclusions. This project selects women's work sectors which are portrayed in film, which present the possibility of interviewing workers and constitute an original area of research. This multidimensional brief meant that some paths of enquiry fell by the wayside. Professions like factory, shop and office work, dancing, politics and teaching would constitute fascinating extensions of my research on women's work in post-war Italy. However, it was often the case that an area of work which featured in film would not have presented an easily reachable group of interviewees. Office workers, for example, feature in a number of comedies, like *L'impiegato* (Puccini 1960). Yet, given financial and time restraints, it was not possible to assemble a sufficient body of interview subjects who had worked in offices. There are, therefore, a number of meaningful projects to be undertaken in the area of women's work in post-Second World War Italy but which would have to narrow their focus to either filmic or oral history sources.

The sector which most captured my academic interest was that of post-war women religious. As previously mentioned, their ambiguous status as professionals, as well as the proliferating academic and popular interest in their contributions, makes them ripe figures for further study.³ There is also particular appeal in the transnational nature of the work of women religious. As Chapter 9 highlighted, their work crosses geographical and linguistic expanses. They are also interesting figures in terms of how they reflect social change; despite being inhabitants of a transnational institution, they also come from, and go out into, local and national communities. For these reasons, their oral histories are rich sources for the study of religious, institutional and national change. Research into how women religious have responded to contemporary institutional and social change would undoubtedly be fascinating. Specifically, I plan to conduct a transnational oral history study into how women religious responded to the changes resulting from Vatican II.

There are also meaningful transnational and interdisciplinary offshoots to be made from this book's enquiry into women and work. This was evidenced by a paper that I gave at the University of Warwick Centre for the study of women and gender in the department of sociology. In tandem with my own paper on the labour of nuns, sociologist Asiya Islam presented her oral histories of Indian women working in the service sector. She highlighted how Arlie Hochschild's concept of the 'time bind' (Hochschild 1997), where women blur home and work environments in their narratives of work, was relevant to both our research. This crossover highlights just one of the ways in which a transnational and interdisciplinary project on women's work would present a fascinating and original contribution.

This book has contributed original analysis, new voices, innovative methodological approaches, and promising future pathways in the cultural study of women's work. Setting out with the intention to recognize women in post-war Italy's labour landscape, it has drawn attention to critical and representational absences and critiqued cultural and collective memories which come to constitute the identities of working women. As a final reflection, I wish to underline the personal and political value of this book. This research allowed me to meet and exchange with subjects who were at the early stages of what subsequently became women's mass entry into the workforce. It enriches our understanding of the role of work in gender relations and social power, and, as such, is of ongoing relevance both in Italy and beyond.

NOTES

1. See Hipkins (2006a, 2006b, 2007, 2014, 2016); Wood (2005, 2006); Ben-Ghiat (1999); and Marcus (2000).
2. See, for example, the academic journal *Gender, Work, and Organisation*, and sociologist Asiya Islam's doctoral research on women's work in urban India (for example 2016).
3. For a fuller discussion of the interest of studying contemporary women's religious life, see my article (Derounian 2018b).

Bibliography

Adcock, Rachel (2011), '"Gather Up the Fragments, That Nothing Be Lost": Memorable women's conversion narratives', *Early Modern Women: An Interdisciplinary Journal*, 6, pp. 209–15.

Ahmed, Sara (2004), *The Cultural Politics of Emotion*, Edinburgh: Edinburgh University Press.

Alexander, Lynn M. (2003), *Women, Work and Representation: Needlewomen in Victorian Art and Literature*, Athens: Ohio University Press.

Allum, Percy (1990), 'Uniformity undone: Aspects of Catholic culture in post-war Italy', in Z. G. Baranski and R. Lumley (eds), *Culture and Conflict in Post-War Italy: Essays on Mass and Popular Culture*, Basingstoke: Macmillan.

Alsop, Elisabeth (2014), 'The imaginary crowd: Neorealism and the uses of *Coralità*', *The Velvet Light Trap*, 74, pp. 27–41.

Amelio, Gianni (2004), *Il vizio del cinema: Vedere, amare, fare un film*, Turin: Einaudi.

Amendola, Giulio (1968), *La classe operaia italiana. Con uno scritto sulla lezione della FIAT e un saggio di Giulio Sapelli*, s.l.: goWare.

Anghel, L. (1949), 'Maria Margotti', *Noi Donne*, May.

Anna, Alberto Lattuada (dir.) (1951) [Film], s.l.: s.n.

Anon. (1951), 'Incontro in risaia tra pittore e mondine', *L'Unità Edizione Piemontese*. s.l.: s.n.

Anon. (1957), 'Il mestiere del critico', *Cinema Nuovo*, 75, 25 January, p. 59.

Anonymous (2017), interview with anonymous.

ANPI (1949), *Lettera riguardante le figlie di Maria Margotti*, Rome, Bologna: s.n.

Aprà, Adriano (2009), *Alberto Lattuada: Il cinema e i film*, Padua: Marsilio.

Archivio Storico Udi di Ferrara (2014), *Paolina con le donne: Tra il fare e il pensare*, Ferrara: UDI.

Arendt, Hannah (1998), *The Human Condition*, 2nd ed., Chicago: University of Chicago Press.

Assemblea Costituente (1946), *Costituzione della Repubblica Italiana*, Rome: Senato della Repubblica.

Assmann, Jan (1992), *Das kulturelle Gedächtnis: Schrift, Erinnerung und politische Identität in frühen Hochkulturen*, Berlin: Verlag.

Assman, Jan and Czaplicka, John (1995), 'Collective memory and cultural identity', *New German Critique*, 65, Spring–Summer, pp. 125–33.

Avveduto, Sveva (ed.) (2012), *Italia 150 anni: Popolazione, welfare, scienza e società*, Rome: Gangemi Editore.

Babini, Elisabetta (2012), 'The representation of nurses in 1950s melodrama', *Nursing Outlook*, 60, pp. s27–s35.

Baldini, G. and Siroli, A. (1998), interview with Giuseppina Baldini, 11 December.

Barberis, Eduardo (2015), interview with Eduardo Barberis for the Italian Cinema Audiences Project.

Bayman, Louis (2004), *The Operatic and the Everyday in Post-War Italian Film Melodrama*, Edinburgh: Edinburgh University Press.

Bayman, Louis (ed.) (2011), *Directory of World Cinema: Italy*, Bristol: Intellect.

Bayman, Louis (2014), 'Something else besides a man: Melodrama and the Maschietto in post-war Italian cinema', in D. Hipkins and R. Pitt (eds), *New Visions of the Child in Italian Cinema*, Bern: Peter Lang, pp. 169–88.

Beccari, G., Fiorentini, L., and Fantuz, A. (2009), interview with Giuseppina (Pina) Beccari, Lucia Fiorentini, Antonia Fantuz, 4 August.

Bellizzi, Matteo (2005), *Note di regia del documentario* Sorriso Amaro, https://www.cinemaitaliano.info/news/01371/note-di-regia-del-documentario-sorriso-amaro.html. Accessed 9 February 2018.

Ben-Ghiat, Ruth (1999), 'Liberation, Italian cinema and the Fascist past, 1945–1955', in R. J. B. Bosworth and P. Dogliani (eds), *Italian Fascism: History, Memory and Representation*, Basingstoke: Palgrave Macmillan, pp. 83–101.

Ben-Ghiat, Ruth (2005), 'Unmaking the Fascist man: Film, masculinity, and the transition from dictatorship', *Journal of Modern Italian Studies*, 10:3, pp. 336–65.

Bertuzzi, L., Romagnoli, G. and Zappaterra, G. (1999), *Incontro collettivo*, 2 February.

Betti, Eloisa (2013), 'Gli archivi dell'UDI come fonti per la storia del lavoro nell'Italia dell'Age d'Or (1945–75)', in S. Chemotti and M. C. L. Rocca (eds), *Il Genere nella Ricerca Storica*, Padua-Venice: Il Poligrafo, pp. 485–509.

Betti, Eloisa (2015), 'Making working women visible in the 1950s Italian labour conflict. The case of the Ducati factory', in K. H. Nordberg, H. Roll-Hansen, E. Sandmo, and H. Sandvik (eds), *Mindighet og Medborgerskap*, Oslo: Novus, pp. 311–22.

Betti, Eloisa (2016), *Donne e città nella guerra fredda*, Bologna, Unpublished conference paper, 26 May.

Bettio, Francesca (1988), *The Sexual Division of Labour: The Italian Case*, Oxford: Clarendon Press.

Betz, Mark (2013), 'High and low and in between', *Screen*, 54:4, pp. 495–513.

Biavati, V. and Biavati, E. (1999), interview with Velia and Edma Biavati, 22 January.

Binetti, Vincenzo (2003), 'Contextualizing marginality: Urban landscape and female communities in Cesare Pavese's *Among Women Only*', in D. Valentini and J. L. Smarr (eds), *Italian Women and the City*, London: Associate University Presses, pp. 201–14.

Birnbaum, Lucia Chiavola (1986), *Liberazione della donna: Feminism in Italy*, Middletown: Wesleyan University Press.

Bisoni, Claudio (2015), '"Io posso offrirle soltanto l'immenso calore del mio affetto": Masculinity in Italian cinematic melodrama', *The Italianist*, 35:2, pp. 234–47.

Bondanella, Peter (2001), 'Exploring the boundaries of neorealism', in *Italian Cinema: From Neorealism to the Present*, 3rd ed., New York, London: Continuum, pp. 74–102.

Boneschi, Marta (1999), *Santa Pazienza: La storia delle donne italiane dal dopoguerra ad oggi*, Milan: Mondadori.

Bonifazio, Paola (2011), 'Work, welfare, bio-politics: Italian and American film propaganda of the Reconstruction in the age of neorealism', *The Italianist*, 31:2, pp. 155–80.

Borgato, Renata (2015), 'Maria Margotti', http://www.enciclopediadelledonne.it/biografie/maria-margotti/. Accessed 24 June 2015.

Bosio, Gianni (ed.) (1996), *I Giorni Cantati: Ricerche, Riproposte, Verifiche del Gruppo Padano di Piàdena*, Modena: Ala Bianca.

Bossaglia, Rossana (1984), *Sorelle Fontana*, Parma: CSAC dell'Università.

Bothma, Chris, Khapova, Svetlana, and Lloyd, Sandra (2015), 'Work identity: Clarifying the concept', in P. G. Jansen and G. Roodt (eds), *Conceptualising and Measuring Work Identity: South-African Perspectives and Findings*, Dordrecht: Springer, pp. 23–51.

Bourdieu, Pierre (1979), 'Les trois états du capital culturel', *Actes de la recherche en sciences sociales*, 30, pp. 3–6.

Bourdieu, Pierre (1985), 'The forms of capital', in J. Richardson (ed.), *Handbook of Theory and Research for the Sociology of Education*, New York: Greenwood, pp. 241–58.

Bourdieu, Pierre (1996), *Physical Space, Social Space and Habitus*, Oslo: University of Oslo.

Brandolini, P. et al. (1998), *Incontro collettivo*, 28 November.

Bravo, Anna and Bruzzone, Anna Maria (2000), *In guerra senza armi: Storie di donne, 1940–1945*, Rome: Laterza.

Broghi, Alessandro (2011), *Confronting America: The Cold War between the United States and the Communists in France and Italy*, Chapel Hill: University of North Carolina Press.

Brooks, Peter (1984), *Reading for the Plot: Design and Intention in Narrative*, New York: Knopf.

Brooks, Peter (1995), *The Melodramatic Imagination: Balzac, Henry James, Melodrama, and the Mode of Excess*, New Haven: Yale University Press.

Buckley, Réka (2006), 'Elsa martinelli: Italy's Audrey Hepburn', *Historical Journal of Film, Radio and Television*, 26:3, pp. 327–40.

Buckley, Réka (2008), 'Glamour and the Italian female film stars of the 1950s', *Historical Journal of Film, Radio and Television*, 23:3, pp. 267–89.

Buckley, Réka (2013), 'Dressing the part: "Made in Italy" goes to the movies with Lucia Bosè in chronicle of a love affair', in L. Bayman and S. Rigoletto (eds), *Popular Italian Cinema*, New York: Palgrave Macmillan, pp. 163–82.

Buckser, Andrew and Glazier, Stephen (eds) (2003), *The Anthropology of Religious Conversion*, Oxford: Rowman & Littlefield Publishers, Inc.

Caldwell, Lesley (2000), 'What about women? Italian films and their concerns', in U. Seiglohr (ed.), *Heroines Without Heroes: Reconstructing Female and National Identities in European Cinema 1945–51*, London: Cassell, pp. 131–46.

Caldwell, Lesley (2006), 'What do mothers want? Takes on motherhood in *Bellissima, Il Grido*, and *Mamma Roma*', in P. Morris (ed.), *Women in Italy, 1945–1960: An Interdisciplinary Study*, New York: Palgrave Macmillan, pp. 225–37.

Cameron, John and Haanstra, Anna (2008), 'Development made sexy: How it happened and what it means', *Third World Quarterly*, 29:8, pp. 1475–89.

Cammet, John M. (1967), *Antonio Gramsci and the Origins of Italian Communism*, Palo Alto: Stanford University Press.

Campbell-Jones, Susan (1979), *In Habit: An Anthropoligical Study of Working Nuns*, London: Faber & Faber.

Cardone, Lucia (2012), *Il melodramma*, Milan: Editrice Il Castoro.

Carmini, Roberta Di (2013), 'Comedy "Italian Style" and *I soliti ignoti (Big Deal on Madonna Street*, 1958)', in A. Horton (ed.), *A Companion to Film Comedy*, Chichester: John Wiley & Sons, pp. 454–74.

Carotti, Carlo (2011), *Le donne, la famiglia, il lavoro nel cinema di Pietro Germi*, Milan: Lampi di stampa.

Casadio, Gianfranco (1990), *Adultere, fedifraghe, innocenti. La donna del 'Neorealismo popolare' nel cinema italiano degli anni Cinquanta*, Ravenna: Angelo Longo Editore.

Castelli, Franco, Jona, Emilio, and Lovatto, Alberto (2005), *Senti le rane che cantano: Canzoni e vissuti popolari della risaia*, Roma: Donzelli Editore.

Centro Cattolico Cinematografico (1956), *Segnalazioni cinematografiche*, Roma: s.n.

CGIL (1949), 'Figure della settimana', *Lavoro*, 22–28 May.

Chapman, James, Harper, Sue, and Glancy, Mark (eds) (2007), *The New Film History*, London: Palgrave Macmillan.

Chatman, Seymore (1985), *Antonioni, or, the Surface of the World*, Berkeley: University of California Press.

Chiti, Roberto and Pioppi, Roberto (1991), *Dizionario del cinema italiano: I film, Vol. 2 1945–59*, Rome: Gremese Editore.

Cinquantamila.it (2014), 'Cinquantamila.it', http://cinquantamila.corriere.it/storyTellerThread.php?threadId=censimento1951. Accessed 12 June 2017.

Cogan, Morris L. (1955), 'The problem of defining a profession', *The Annals of the American Academy of Political and Social Science*, 297, January, pp. 105–11.

Cohen, Laurie (2014), *Imagining Women's Careers*, Oxford: Oxford Scholarship Online.

Cohen, Louis, Mannion, Lawrence, and Morrison, Keith (eds) (2011), *Research Methods in Education*, 7th ed., Oxon, New York: Routledge.

Colombi, Marchesa (1878), *In Risaia*, Milano: Lampi di Stampa.

Coppola, G. (2016), interview with Giuseppina Coppola, 13 May.
Coquillette, Daniel R. (1994), 'Professionalism: The deep theory', *North Carolina Law Review*, 72, pp. 1271–78.
Cortese, Giuseppe (1953), 'Intervento al Senato: 26 marzo 1953', s.l.: s.n.
Cosulich, Callisto (1985), *I film di Alberto Lattuada*, Rome: Gremese.
Cowie, Elisabeth (1997), *Representing the Woman: Cinema and Psychoanalysis*, Basingstoke: Macmillan.
Crainz, Guido (1994), *Padania: Il mondo dei braccianti dall'Ottocento alla fuga dalle campagne*, Rome: Donzelli Editore.
Crane, Diana (2001), *Fashion and Its Social Agendas: Class, Gender, and Identity in Clothing*, Chicago: University of Chicago Press.
Culhane, Sarah (2017), 'Street cries and street fights: Anna Magnani, Sophia Loren and the *popolana*', *The Italianist*, 37:2, pp. 254–62.
Dalle Vacche, Angela (1992), *The Body in the Mirror: Shapes of History in Italian Cinema*, Oxford: Princeton University Press.
Dalle Vacche, Angela (1996), *Cinema and Painting: How Art is Used in Film*, London: University of Texas Press.
Dawes, Helen (2014), *Catholic Women's Movements in Liberal and Fascist Italy*, New York: Palgrave Macmillan.
De Grazia, Vittoria (1992), *How Fascism Ruled Women: Italy 1922–1945*, Berkeley: University of California Press.
De Lacroix, Joelle (1971), 'Les mondine: premier mouvement syndical féminin en Italie', Thesis, Paris: s.n.
De Santis, Giuseppe (1987), 'Il Guttuso di *Riso amaro*', *Bianco & Nero*, pp. 119–22.
Derounian, Flora (2018a), 'How women rice weeders in Italy took on Fascism and became heroines of the Left', *The Conversation*, 7, March.
Derounian, Flora (2018b), 'The invisible work of women religious: The Italian case', *Studies: An Irish Quarterly Review*, 107:427, pp. 314–25.
Derrida, Jacques (1995), *Archive Fever: A Freudian Impression*, Chicago: University of Chicago Press.
Di Bella, Maria Pia (2003), 'Conversion and marginality in southern Italy', in A. Buckser and S. D. Glazer (eds), *The Anthropology of Religious Conversion*, Oxford: Rowman & Littlefield Publishers, pp. 85–94.
Di madre in figlia, Andrea Zambelli (dir.) (2008) [Film], Italy: s.n.
Dines, Gail and Humez, Jean M. (2002), *Gender, Race, and Class in Media: A Text-Reader*, Thousand Oaks: SAGE Publications.
Dipartimento di Pedagogia dell'Università Cattolica di Milano (1988), *Chiesa e progetto educativo nell'Italia del secondo dopoguerra (1945–58)*, Brescia: La Scuola.
Duggan, Christopher (1995), *Italy in the Cold War: Politics, Culture and Society 1948–58*, Oxford: Berg.

Dunnage, Jonathan (1999), 'Policing and politics in the southern Italian community, 1943–48', in J. Dunnage (ed.), *After the War: Violence, Justice, Continuity and Renewal in Italian Society*, Market Harborough: Troubador, pp. 32–47.

Dunnett, Jane (2002), 'Foreign literature in Fascist Italy: Circulation and censorship', *TTR: Traduction, Terminologie, Rédaction*, 15:2, pp. 97–123.

Dyer, Richard (1998), *Stars*, London: British Film Institute.

Eller, Cynthia (1995), *Living in the Lap of the Goddess*, Boston: Beacon Press.

Ellis, Jacqueline (1998), *Silent Witnesses: Representations of Working-Class Women in the United States*, Bowling Green: Bowling Green State University Popular Press.

Ente Nazionale Prevenzione Infortuni (1959), *Mondine, difendetevi dai pericoli!*, s.l.: s.n.

Erll, Astrid (2011), *Memory in Culture*, Hampshire: Palgrave Macmillan.

Erll, Astrid and Nunning, Ansgar (eds) (2010), *Cultural Memory Studies: An International and Interdisciplinary Handbook*, Berlin: Walter de Gruyter & Co.

Erll, Astrid and Rigney, Ann (eds) (2009), *Mediation, Remediation, and the Dynamics of Cultural Memory*, Berlin: Walter de Gruyter.

Erll, Astrid and Young, Sara B. (eds) (2011), *Memory in Culture*, Hampshire: Palgrave Macmillan.

Fondazione 'Emanuela Zancan' (2011), *Per carità e per giustizia. Il contributo degli istituti religiosi alla costruzione del welfare italiano, Padova, Fondazione E. Zancan Onlus-Centro Studi e Ricerca sociale 2011*, Padova: Fondazione 'Emanuela Zancan' Onlus.

Fontana, Micol (1991), *Uno specchio a tre luci*, Rome: RAI Edizioni.

Foot, John (2008), 'Words, songs and books. Oral history in Italy. A review and discussion', *Journal of Modern Italian Studies*, 3:2, pp. 164–74.

Forgacs, David and Gundle, Stephen (2008), 'Practices of the self: Intimacy, sexuality, sport, fashion', in S. Gundle and D. Forgacs (eds), *Mass Culture and Italian Society from Fascism to the Cold War*, Bloomington: Indiana University Press, pp. 63–91.

Foucault, Michel (1977), *Discipline and Punish: The Birth of the Prison*, New York: Vintage Books.

Foucault, Michel (1979), *The History of Sexuality: An Introduction*, London: Allen Lane.

Franco, Massimo (2008), *Andreotti: La Vita di un Uomo Politico, La Storia di un'Epoca*, Milan: Mondadori.

Fullwood, Natalie (2015), *Cinema, Gender, and Everyday Space: Comedy Italian Style*, New York: Palgrave Macmillan.

Gabrielli, Patrizia (2007), *Scenari di guerra, parole di donna: Diari e memorie nell'Italia della seconda guerra mondiale*, Bologna: Mulino.

Gadda, Carlo Emilio (1937), *La Gazzetta del Popolo*.

Garagnani, L. (2016), interview with Lucia Garagnani, 16 May.

Gavioli, Micaela (1999), 'La costruzione delle memorie. La morte di Maria Margotti nei racconti delle donne', in L. Zaganoni (ed.), *Le donne, le lotte, la memoria 1949–1999 a cinquant'anni della morte di Maria Margotti*, Ferrara: Il Globo.

Gavioli, Micaela (2015), e-mail correspondance with Micaela Gavioli.

Gennari, Daniela Treveri (2009), *Post-War Italian Cinema: American Intervention, Vatican Interests*, New York: Routledge.

Gennari, Daniela, Treveri Hipkins, Danielle, O'Rawe, Catherine, and Dibeltulo, Sara (2013–16), *Italian Cinema Audiences*, s.l.: s.n.

Gennari, Daniela Treveri et al. (2016), '"Un Mondo Che Pensavo Impossibile": Al Cinema Negli Anni Cinquanta', *Cinema e Storia*, 5, pp. 215–27.

Ghirardini, Cristina (2012), *Noi siam le canterine antifasciste. I canti delle mondine di Lavezzola*, Santa Vittoria, Udine: Nota.

Ghirardini, Cristina and Venturi, Susanna (2011), *Siamo tutte d'un sentimento: Il coro delle mondine di Medicina tra passato e presente*, Udine: Nota.

Ghirardini, R. and Zagatti, A. (1998), interview with Rina Ghirardini and Alves Zagatti, 3 December.

Gini, Al (1998), 'Work, identity and self: How we are formed by the work we do', *Journal of Business Ethics*, 17:7, pp. 707–14.

Ginsborg, Paul (1990), *A History of Contemporary Italy: Society and Politics, 1943–88*, London: Penguin Books.

Ginsborg, Paul (2001), *Italy and Its Discontents 1980–2001*, London: Penguin.

Giordano, L. (2016), interview with Lina Giordano, 24 May.

Gleadle, Kathryn (2001), *British Women in the Nineteenth Century*, Basingstoke: Palgrave.

Gluck, Sherna Berger (2014), 'Why do we call it oral history? Refocusing on orality/aurality in the digital age', in D. A. Boys and M. Larson (eds), *Oral History and Digital Humanities*, New York: Palgrave Macmillan, pp. 35–52.

Gramsci, Antonio (1975), *I Quaderni: Passato e presente*, Rome: Riuniti.

Gramsci, Antonio (1978), *Selections from the* Prison Notebooks, New York: International Publishers.

Gramsci, Antonio (2014), *Quaderni dal carcere: Edizione critica dell'Istituto Gramsci (Quaderno 13)*, Bologna: ET Biblioteca.

Gribaldo, Alessandro and Zapperi, Giovanna (2010), *Lo schermo del potere: Femminismo e regime della visibilità*, Verona: Ombre Corte.

Gribaudi, Maurizio (1987), *Mondo operaio e mito operaio: Spazi e percorsi sociali a Torino nel primo Novecento*, Turin: G. Einaudi.

Grignaffini, Giovanna (1982), 'Verità e poesia: Ancora di Silvana e del cinema italiano', *Cinema e cinema: materiali di studio e di intervento cinematografici*, 9, pp. 41–46.

Grignaffini, Giovanna (1999), 'Sisters and saints on the screen', in G. Zarri and L. Scaraffia (eds), *Women and Faith: Catholic Religious Life in Italy from Late Antiquity to the Present*, Cambridge: Harvard University Press.

Gundle, Stephen (1999), 'Feminine beauty, national identity and political conflict in postwar Italy, 1945–54', *Contemporary European History*, 8:3, pp. 359–78.

Gundle, Stephen (2007), *Bellissima: Feminine Beauty and the Idea of Italy*, London: Yale University Press.

Günsberg, Maggie (2005), *Italian Cinema: Gender and Genre*, New York: Palgrave Macmillan.

Halbwachs, Maurice (1925), *Les cadres sociaux de la mémoire*, 1st ed., Paris: Éditions Alcan.

Halbwachs, Maurice (1980), *The Collective Memory*, New York: Harper & Row.

Hall, Stuart (2006), 'The West and the rest: Discourse and power', in R. Maaka and C. Anderson (eds), *The Indigenous Experience: Global Perspectives*, Ontario: Canadian Scholars' Press, pp. 165–73.

Hardt, Michael (1999), 'Affective labor', *Boundary*, 2:26, pp. 89–100.

Hardt, Michael (2006), 'Laboratory Italy', in P. Virno and M. Hardy (eds), *Radical Thought in Italy*, Minneapolis: University of Minnesota Press, pp. 2–10.

Helauwick (1952), *Anna ou plus exactement riz (golade) amere une annerie*, Paris: Noir et Blanc.

Hipkins, Danielle (2006a), 'Francesca's salvation or damnation?: Resisting recognition of the prostitute in Roberto Rossellini's *Paisà* (1946)', *Studies in European Cinema*, 3:2, pp. 153–68.

Hipkins, Danielle (2006b), '"I don't want to die": Prostitution and narrative disruption in Visconti's *Rocco and his brothers*', in P. Morris (ed.), *Women in Italy 1946–1960*, New York: Palgrave Macmillan, pp. 193–210.

Hipkins, Danielle (2007), 'Were sisters doing it for themselves? Prostitutes, brothels and discredited masculinity in postwar Italian cinema', in D. Hipkins and G. Plain. (eds), *War-Torn Tales: Literature, Film and Gender in the Aftermath of World War*, Oxford: Peter Lang, pp. 81–103.

Hipkins, Danielle (2011), 'Melodrama', in L. Bayman (ed.), *Directory of World Cinema: Italy*, Bristol: Intellect.

Hipkins, Danielle (2014), 'The fantasy harem: Prostitution and the battle of the sexes in Italian film comedy of the early to mid-1960s', *Cinergie*, 5, pp. 45–57.

Hipkins, Danielle (2016), *Italy's Other Women: Gender and Prostitution in Italian Cinema, 1940–1965*, Bern: Peter Lang.

Hipkins, Danielle and Plain, Gill (eds) (2007), *War-Torn Tales: Literature, Film and Gender at the end of World War Two*, Oxford: Peter Lang.

Hochschild, Arlie (1997), *The Time Bind: When Work Becomes Home and Home Becomes Work*, New York: Henry Holt and Company.

Hochschild, Arlie (1983), *The Managed Heart: Commercialization of Human Feeling*, Berkeley: University of California Press.

Hoskins, Andrew (2009), 'Digital network memory', in A. Erll and A. Rigney (eds), *Mediation, Remediation, and the Dynamics of Cultural Memory*, Berlin: Walter De Gruyter, pp. 91–108.

Hovi, Tuija (2004), 'Religious conviction shaped and maintained by narration', *Archive for the Psychology of Religion*, 26:1, pp. 35–50.

Hughes, Howard (2011), *Cinema Italiano: The Complete Guide from Classics to Cult*, London: I.B. Tauris.

Il maggio delle mondine, Francesco Marano (dir.) (2011) [Film], Italy: s.n.

Imbergamo, Barbara (2003–04), 'Mondine e Resistenza: Gli eventi e il "discorso" politico', in D. Gagliani (ed.), *Guerra Resistenza Politica: Storie di donne*, Reggio Emilia: Aliberti Editore.

Imbergamo, Barbara (2003), *Mondine in Campo: Dinamiche e retoriche di un lavoro del Novecento*, Firenze: Edit Press.

Imbergamo, Barbara (2014), *Mondine in Campo: Dinamiche e retoriche di un lavoro del novecento*, Florence: Edit Press.

Imprenti, Fiorella (2007), *Operaie e socialismo: Milano, le leghe femminili, la camera del lavoro (1891–1918)*, Milan: Francoangeli.

Insenghi, Mario (2011), *I Luoghi della Memoria: Simboli e Miti dell'Italia Unita*, Bari: Laterza.

Intervista collettiva (2009), 'Intervista collettiva per il progetto sulle mondine di Medicina', 4 August.

Irigaray, Luce (1985), *Speculum of the Other Woman*, s.l.: Cornell University Press.

ISTAT.it (2017), *Technici delle attività religiose e di culto*, http://nup2006.istat.it/scheda.php?id=3.4.5.7.0. Accessed 7 July 2017.

Istituto Luce (1960), *Italia: Pascal Petit, diva tascabile*, Rome: s.n.

Italia Taglia (2018), *Le amiche*, http://www.italiataglia.it/search/dettaglio_opera. Accessed 25 May 2018.

James, Nicky (1989), 'Emotional labour: Skill and work in the social regulation of feelings', *The Sociological Review*, 37:1, pp. 15–42.

Jeannet, Angela M. (2003), 'A myth reclaimed: Rome in twentieth-century women's writings', in: *Italian Women and the City*, London: Associated University Press, pp. 98–125.

Jori, F. (1990), *Dalla fabbrica al territorio. Cinquant'anni di pastorale del lavoro a Padova*, Padua: Gregoriana Libreria Editrice.

Kawamura, Yuniya (2004), *Fashion-ology: An Introduction to Fashion Studies (Dress, Body, Culture Series)*, Oxford: Berg.

Kezich, Tullio and Levantesi, Alessandra (2001), *Dino De Laurentiis, la vita e i film*, Rome: Feltrinelli.

Kitzinger, Celia (1987), *The Social Construction of Lesbianism*, London: Sage Publications.

Krips, Henry (2010), 'The politics of the gaze: Foucault, Lacan and Žižek', *Culture Unbound*, 2, pp. 91–102.

Kubacki, Marie-Lucile (2018), 'Il lavoro (quasi) gratuito delle suore', *L'osservatore romano*, 66, March, pp. 10–15.

Kuhn, Annette (2002), *An Everyday Magic: Cinema and Cultural Memory*, London, New York: I.B. Tauris Publishers.

La donna del fiume, Mario Soldati (dir.) (1954) [Film], Italy: s.n.

La novice, Alberto Lattuada (dir.) (1960) [Film], s.l.: s.n.

La risaia, Raffaello Matarazzo (dir.) (1956) [Film], Italy: s.n.

La Scuola (1988), *Chiesa e Progetto Educativo Nell'Italia del Secondo Dopoguerra 1945–1958*, Brescia: La Scuola.

La Voce di Molinella (1949), 'Come una pietra miliare', *La Voce di Molinella*, 9, October.

Labanyi, Jo (2007), 'Cinema and the mediation of everyday life in 1940s and 1950s Spain', *New Readings*, 8, pp. 1–24.

Lacan, Jacques (1981), *The Four Fundamental Concepts of Psychoanalysis*, New York: Norton.

Ladri di biciclette, Vittorio De Sica (dir.) (1948) [Film], Italy: s.n.

Landy, Marcia (1992), *Fascism in Film: The Italian Commercial Cinema, 1931–1943*, Princeton: Princeton University Press.

Landy, Marcia (1994), *Film, Politics, and Gramsci*, Minneapolis: University of Minnesota Press.

Landy, Marcia (2002), 'Theatricality and impersonation: The politics of style in the cinema of the Italian fascist era', in J. Reich and P. Garofalo (eds), *Re-viewing Fascism: Italian Cinema, 1922–1943*, Bloomington: Indiana University Press, pp. 250–75.

Lapointe, Kirsi (2010), 'Narrating career, positioning identity: Career identity as a narrative practice', *Journal of Vocational Behavior*, 77:1, pp. 1–9.

Le amiche, Michelangelo Antonioni (dir.) (1955) [Film], Italy: s.n.

Le ragazze di piazza di Spagna, Alberto Lattuada (dir.) (1952) [Film], Italy: s.n.

Le ragazze di San Frediano, Valerio Zurlini (dir.) (1955) [Film], Italy: s.n.

Levi, Primo (1989), *The Drowned and the Saved*, New York: Knopf Doubleday Publishing Group.

Lizzani, Carlo (2009), Riso amaro. *Dalla scrittura alla regia*, Rome: Bulzoni.

L'onorevole Angelina, Luigi Zampa (dir.) (1947), [Film], Italy: s.n.

MacCurtain, Margaret (1997), 'Godly burden: Catholic sisterhoods in twentieth-century Ireland', in A. Bradley and M. G. Valiulis (eds), *Gender and Sexuality in Modern Ireland*, Amhurst: University of Massachusetts, pp. 245–56.

Madges, William (2003), 'What it means to be Church: Formulating a new understanding of Church', in W. Madges and M. J. Daley (eds), *Vatican II: 50 Personal Stories*, New York: Orbis Books, pp. 85–94.

Magray, Mary Peckham (1998), *The Transforming Power of the Nuns: Women, Religion and Cultural Change in Ireland, 1750–1900*, New York: Oxford University Press.

Maher, Vanessa (1987), 'Sewing the seams of society: Dressmakers and seamstresses in Turin between the wars', in J. F. Collier and S. J. Yanagisako (eds), *Gender and Kinship: Essays Toward a Unified Analysis*, Palo Alto: Stanford University Press, pp. 132–61.

Maher, Vanessa (2007), *Tenere la fila: Sarte, sartine e cambiamento sociale, 1860–1960*, Turin: Rosenberg & Sellier.

Mammarella, Giuseppe (1966), *Italy after Fascism: A Political History 1943–65*, s.l.: University of Notre Dame Press.

Mangion, Carmen M. (2005), '"Good Teacher" or "Good Religious"? The professional identity of Catholic women religious in nineteenth-century England and Wales', *Women's History Review*, 14:2, pp. 223–42.

Marano, Francesco (2018), e-mail correspondance with Francesco Marano, 9 February.

Marcus, Millicent (2000), 'The Italian body politic is a woman: Feminized national identity in postwar Italian film', in D. E. Stewart and A. Cornish (eds), *Sparks and Seeds: Medieval Literature and its Afterlife. Essays in Honor of John Freccero*, Turnhout: Brepols Publishers, pp. 329–47.

Marx, Karl (1976), *Capital (Volume 1)*, 1st ed., London: Penguin Books.

Masi, Stefano and Lancia, Enrico (1998), *Les Seductrices du Cinema Italien*, Rome: Gremese.

Massey, Doreen (1994), *Space, Place and Gender*, Cambridge: Polity Press.

McCarthy, Patrick (2000), *Italy since 1945*, Oxford: Oxford University Press.

McKenna, Yvonne (2006a), 'Entering religious life, claiming subjectivity: Irish nuns, 1930s–1960s', *Women's History Review*, 15:2, pp. 189–211.

McKenna, Yvonne (2006b), *Made Holy: Irish Women Religious at Home and Abroad*, Kildare: Irish Academic Press.

Meccoli, D. (1952), '*Le ragazze di piazza di Spagna*', *Epocha*, 8, March.

Meek, David (2015), 'Learning as territoriality: The political ecology of education in the Brazilian landless workers' movement', *The Journal of Peasant Studies*, 42:6, pp. 1179–200.

Meisenbach, Rebecca J. (2010), 'The female breadwinner: Phenomenological experience and gendered identity in work/family spaces', *Sex Roles*, 62, pp. 2–19.

Michelone, Guido (2009), Riso amaro; *La storia di un cult movie*, Milan: Lampi di stampa.

Millar, E. A. (ed.) (1989), *The Legacy of Fascism: Lectures Delivered at the University of Glasgow*, Glasgow: University of Glasgow.

Miss Italia, Duilio Coletti (dir.) (1950) [Film], Italy: s.n.

Morgan, Edmund S. (1965), *Visible Saints: The History of a Puritan Idea*, Ithaca: Cornell University Press.

Morgenstern, Aliyah (2014), 'Children's multimodal language development: Manual of language acquisition', in C. Facke (ed.), *Manual of Language Acquisition*, Berlin: Mouton de Gruyter, pp. 123–42.

Morreale, Emilio (2011), *Così Piangevano: Il cinema melò nell'Italia degli anni Cinquanta*, Rome: Donzelli Editore.

Morris, J. Andrew and Feldman, Daniel C. (1996), 'The dimensions, antecedents, and consequences of emotional labor', *Academy of Management Journal*, 21, pp. 989–1010.

Morris, Penelope (2006a), 'The Harem exposed: Gabriella Parca's *Le italiane si confessano*', in *Women in Italy 1945–1960*, New York: Palgrave Macmillan, pp. 109–30.

Morris, Penelope (2006b), *Women in Italy 1945–1960*, New York: Palgrave Macmillan.

Mulvey, Laura (1975), 'Visual pleasure and narrative cinema', *Screen*, 16:3, pp. 6–18.

Mulvey, Laura (1999), 'Visual pleasure and narrative cinema', in L. Braudy and M. Cohen (eds), *Film Theory and Criticism: Introductory Readings*, New York: Oxford University Press, pp. 833–44.

Nakahara, Tamao (2004), 'Barred nuns: Italian nunsploitation films', in E. Mathijs (ed.), *Alternative Europe: Eurotrash and Exploitation Cinema Since 1945*, New York: Wallflower Press, pp. 124–133.

Nakahara, Tamao (2005), *Bawdy Tales and Veils: The Exploitation of Sex in Post-War Italian Cinema (1949–1979)*, s.l.: s.n.

Negrello, Dolores (2000), *A pugno chiuso: Il Partito comunista padovano dal biennio rosso alla stagione dei movimenti*, Milan: FrancoAngeli.

Negrello, Dolores (2006), *Donne venete: Dalla grande emigrazione alla Resistenza*, Padova: Centro Studi Ettore Luccini.

Nerenberg, Ellen (2001), *Prison Terms: Representing Confinement During and After Italian Fascism*, Toronto: Toronto University Press.

Neri, O. (2016), interview with Oriana Neri, 18 May.
Nichols, Bill (1992), *Representing Reality: Issues and Concepts in Documentary*, Bloomington: Indiana University Press.
Noce, Teresa (1977), *Rivoluzionaria Professionale*, Milan: Bompiani.
Non c'è pace tra gli ulivi, Giuseppe De Santis (dir.) (1950) [Film], Italy: s.n.
Nora, Pierre (1989), 'Between memory and history: Les Lieux de Mémoire', *Representations*, 26, Spring, p. 724.
Nora, Pierre (1999), *Re-thinking France: Les Lieux de Mémoire*, Paris: Gallimard.
Nora, Pierre (2006), *Re-thinking France: Les Lieux de Mémoire*, Paris: Gallimard.
Nora, Pierre (2009), *Re-thinking France: Les Lieux de Mémoire*, Paris: Gallmard.
Nora, Pierre (2010), *Re-thinking France: Les Lieux de Mémoire*, Paris: Gallimard.
Nora, Pierre and Kritzman, Lawrence D. (1996), *Realms of Memory*, New York: Colombia University Press.
Noto, Paolo (2011), *Dal Bozzetto ai Generi. Il Cinema Italiano dei Primi Anni Cinquanta*, Turin: Kaplan.
O'Donaghue, Tom and Potts, Anthony (2004), 'Researching the lives of Catholic teachers who were members of religious orders: Historiographical considerations', *Journal of the History of Education Society*, 33:4, pp. 469–81.
O'Rawe, Catherine (2010), 'Gender, genre and stardom: Fatality in Italian neorealist cinema', in H. Hanson and C. O'Rawe (eds), *The Femme Fatale: Images, Histories, Contexts*, Basingstoke: Palgrave Macmillan.
O'Rawe, Catherine (2010), 'Italian star studies', *Italian Studies*, 65:2, pp. 286–92.
O'Rawe, Catherine (2014), *Stars and Masculinities in Contemporary Italian Cinema*, New York: Palgrave Macmillan.
O'Rawe, Catherine (2017), 'Back for good: Melodrama and the returning soldier in post-war Italian cinema', *Modern Italy*, 22, pp. 123–42.
Pannofino, Nicola (2012), 'Quando le Storie Funzionano: Simbolizzazione del Sé nelle Narrazioni di Conversione Religiosa', M@gm@, 10:1.
Passerini, Luisa (1984), *Torino operaia e fascismo: Una storia orale*, Turin: Laterza.
Passerini, Luisa (1987), *Fascism in Popular Memory: The Cultural Experience of the Turin Working Class*, Cambridge: Cambridge University Press.
Passerini, Luisa (1988), *Storia e soggettività. Le fonti orali, la memoria*, Florence: La Nuova Italia.
Passerini, Luisa (1992), 'A memory for women's history: Problems of method and interpretation', *Social Science History*, 16:4, pp. 669–92.
Passerini, Luisa (2011), 'Historic passion: A passion for memory', *History Workshop Journal*, 72:1, pp. 241–50.
Pateman, Carole (1989), *The Disorder of Women: Democracy, Feminism and Political Theory*, Cambridge: Polity Press.
Patriarca, Silvana (2010), *Italian Vices: Nation and Character from the Risorgimento to the Republic*, Cambridge: Cambridge University Press.

Paulicelli, Eugenia (2015), 'Italian fashion: Yesterday, today and tomorrow', *Journal of Modern Italian Studies*, 20:1, pp. 1–9.

Perks, Robert and Thomson, Alistair (eds) (1998), *The Oral History Reader*, Abingdon: Routledge.

Pierson, Inga (2008), 'Towards a poetics of neorealism: Tragedy in the Italian cinema 1942–1948', Thesis, s.l.: ProQuest Dissertations Publishing.

Pioppi, Roberto (1991), *Dizionario del cinema italiano: I film, Vol. 2 1945–59*, Rome: Gremese.

Plummer, Ken (2001), *Documents of Life 2: An Invitation to a Critical Humanism*, London: Sage.

Pojmann, Wendy (2013), *Italian Women and International Cold War Politics, 1944–1968*, New York: Fordham University Press.

Pollard, John (2008), *Catholicism in Modern Italy: Religion, Society and Politics since 1861*, New York: Routledge.

Portelli, Alessandro (1981), 'The peculiarities of oral history', *History Workshop Journal*, 12:1, pp. 96–107.

Portelli, Alessandro (1991), *The Death of Luigi Trastulli and Other Stories: Form and Meaning in Oral History*, Albany: State University of New York Press.

Portelli, Alessandro (1997), *The Battle of Valle Giulia: Oral History and the Art of Dialogue*, Madison: University of Wisconsin Press.

Portes, Alejandro (1998), 'Social capital: Its origins and applications in modern sociology', *Annual Review of Sociology*, 24, pp. 1–24.

Raftery, Deirdre (2012), 'Religions and the history of education: A historiography', *History of Education*, 41:1, pp. 41–56.

Reidhead, Mary Ann and Reidhead, Van A. (2003), 'From Jehova's witness to benedictine nun: The roles of experience and context in a double conversion', in A. Buckner and S. D. Glazier (eds), *The Anthropology of Conversion*, Oxford: Rowman & Littlefield Publishers, pp. 183–97.

Riccardi, Andrea (1988), *Chiesa e progetto educativo nell'Italia del secondo dopoguerra 1945–1958*, Brescia: La Scuola.

Riso amaro, Giuseppe De Santis (dir.) (1949) [Film], Italy: s.n.

Rocca, Giancarlo (1992), *Donne Religiose: Contributo a una storia della condizione femminile in Italia nei secoli XIX-XX*, Roma: Edizioni Paoline.

Rocca, Giancarlo (1999), *Donne Religiose: Contributo a una storia della condizione femminile in Italia nei secoli 19-20*, Rome: Edizioni Paoline.

Rocca, Giancarlo (2013), 'La vita religiosa verso il Concilio Vaticano II', *Chiesa e Storia*, 3, pp. 129–78.

Ropa, Rossella and Venturoli, Cinzia (2010), *Donna e Lavoro: Un'identità difficile*, Bologna: Editrice Compositori.

Rose, Gillian (1993), *Feminism & Geography: The Limits of Geographical Knowledge*, Cambridge: Polity Press.

Rossi-Doria, Anna (2000), 'L'invisibilità politica delle donne: Alcune riflessioni', in D. Gagliani, L. Mariani, F. Tarozzi, and E. Guerra (eds), *Donne, guerra, politica*, Bologna: Universitaria Editrice Bologna, pp. 361–66.

Rossi, V. and Pilotto, G. (2014), interview with Simone Massimiliano, Paola Ruffino, Tiziana Caserta for 'Affetti personali. Storie di Donne e di Moda', https://www.youtube.com/watch?v=3uxkDUXtYII&list=PLtDxEiG2hUztSU2b9qmw. Accessed 25 July 2018.

Ruberto, Laura (1998), 'La contadina si ribella: Gendered resistance in *L'Agnese va a morire*', *Romance Language Annual*, 9, pp. 328–35.

Ruberto, Laura (2003), 'Grains of truth: Rice, labor, and cultural identity', in E. G. Messina (ed.), *In our Own Voices: Multidisciplinary Perspectives on Italian and Italian-American Women*, Boca Raton: Bordighiera Press, pp. 3–20.

Ruberto, Laura (2008), *Gramsci, Migration, and the Representation of Women's Work in Italy and the U.S.*, Lanham: Lexington Books.

Sabine, Maureen (2013), *Veiled Desires: Intimate Portrayals of Nuns in Postwar Anglo-American Film*, New York: Fordham University Press.

Sangster, Joan (1994), 'Telling our stories: Feminist debates and the use of oral history', *Women's History Review*, 31:1, pp. 5–28.

Saraceno, Chiara (1988), 'La famiglia: I paradossi della costruzione del privato', in P. Aries and G. Duby (eds), *La vita privata*, Rome and Bari: Laterza, pp. 33–78.

Scaraffia, Lucetta and Zarri, Gabriela (eds) (1999), *Women and Faith: Catholic Religious Life in Italy from Late Antiquity to the Present*, Cambridge: Harvard University Press.

Scott, Joan Wallach (2018), *Gender and the Politics of History*, New York: Colombia University Press.

Shilling, Chris (2012), *The Body and Social Theory*, 3rd ed., London: Sage Publications.

Siamo donne (Quattro attrici, una speranza – primo episodio), Alfredo Guarini (dir.) (1953) [Film], Italy: s.n.

Simmel, George (1957), 'Fashion', *American Journal of Sociology*, 62:6, pp. 541–58.

Sipe, Dan (1991), 'The future of oral history and moving images', *The Oral History Review*, 19:1&2, pp. 75–87.

Small, Pauline (2009), *Sophia Loren: Moulding the Star*, Bristol: Intellect Books.

Sorelle Materassi, Fernando De Poggioli (dir.) (1943) [Film], Italy: s.n.

Sorlin, Pierre (1996), *Italian National Cinema 1896–1996*, London: Routledge.

Sorriso amaro, Matteo Bellizzi (dir.) (2003) [Film], Italy: s.n.

Sorriso amaro, Maite Carpio (dir.) (2009) [Film], Italy: Rai Due.

Spinazzola, Vittorio (1985), *Cinema e pubblico: Lo spettacolo filmico in Italia 1945–1965*, Milano: Bulzoni.

Stacey, Jackie (1994), *Star Gazing*, New York: Routledge.

Stanfill, Sonnet (2014), 'The role of the *sartoria* in post-war Italy', *Journal of Modern Italian Studies*, 20:1, pp. 83–91.

Starhawk, (1993), *Dreaming the Dark: Magic, Sex and Politics*, Boston: Beacon Press.

Suenens, Cardinal Leo Joseph (1963a), *The Nun in the World*, s.l.: s.n.

Suenens, Cardinal Leo Joseph (1963b), *The Nun in the World*, Westminster: The Newman Press.

Suor Letizia, Mario Camerini (dir.) (1956) [Film], s.l.: s.n.

Tambor, Molly (2014), *The Lost Wave: Women and Democracy in Postwar Italy*, Oxford: University of Oxford Press.

Tassoni, N. (2016), interview with Norma Tassoni, 12 June.

Taylor, Diana (2003), *The Archive and the Repertoire: Performing Cultural Memory in the Americas*, Durham: Duke University Press.

Tinti, A. (2016), interview with Anna Tinti, 27 May.

Togliatti, Palmiro (1973), *Opere, 3(2) 1929–1935*, Rome: Editori Riuniti.

Tomka, Béla (2013), *A Social History of Twentieth-Century Europe*, Oxford: Routledge.

Toplin, Robert B. (1996), *History by Hollywood: The Use and Abuse of the American Past*, Urbana, Chicago: University of Illinois Press.

Torri, L. (2016), interview with Luciana Torri, 10 May.

Trombetti, G. and Fortini, G. (1999), interview with Giuseppina Trombetti and Gina Fortini, 2 February.

Turner, Graeme (1988), *Film as Film*, London: Routledge.

Uffreduzzi, Elisa (2017), 'Mambo and *Maggiorate*: Italian female stardom in the 1950s', in V. Picchietti and L. Salsini (eds), *Writing and Performing Female Identity in Italian Culture*, s.l.: Palgrave Macmillan, pp. 61–80.

Un americano in vacanza, Luigi Zampa (dir.) (1946) [Film], Italy: s.n.

Valerio, Adriana (2016), *Donne e chiesa; Una storia di genere*, Rome: Carrocci Editore.

Vecchio, Giorgio (ed.) (2010), *Le suore e la Resistenza*, Milan: Ambrosianeum.

Verzelli, Angela (2000), 'Le mondine tra Resistenza e partecipazione politica', in D. Gagliani (ed.), *Donne, guerra, politica: esperienze e memorie della Resistenza*, Bologna: CLUEB.

Verzelli, A. and Zappaterra, Paola (2001), *La vita, il lavoro, le lotte: Le mondine di Medicina negli anni Cinquanta*, Bologna: Edizioni Aspasia.

Viganò, Renata (1952), *Le Mondine*, Modena: Arti Grafiche Modenesi.

Viganò, Renata (1967), *L'Agnese va a morire*, Turin: Einaudi.

Villa Borghese, Alberto De Sica, Gianni Franciolini (dir.) (1953) [Film], Italy: s.n.

Vitti, Antonio (2011), *Giuseppe De Santis e il cinema italiano del dopoguerra*, Pesaro: Metauro.

Warner, Marina (1990), *Alone of All Her Sex: The Myth and the Cult of the Virgin Mary*, Oxford: Oxford University Press.

West, Rebecca (2006), '"What" as ideal and "Who" as real: Portraits of wives and mothers in Italian postwar domestic manuals, fiction, and film', in *Women in Italy 1945–60: An Interdisciplinary Study*, New York: Palgrave Macmillan, pp. 21–34.

Wickham, Chris and Fentress, James J. (1992), *Social Memory: New Perspectives on the Past*, Oxford: Blackwell.

Wikipedia (2017), 'Maria Margotti', https//it.wikipedia.org/w/index.php?title=Maria_Margotti&oldid=87138275. Accessed 21 February 2018.

Willson, Perry (1993), *The Clockwork Factory: Women and Work in Fascist Italy*, Oxford: Clarendon Press.

Willson, Perry (1999), 'Saints and heroines: Rewriting the history of Italian women in the Resistance', in T. Kirk and A. McElligott (eds), *Opposing Fascism: Community, Authority and Resistance in Europe*, Cambridge: Cambridge University Press, pp. 180–98.

Willson, Perry (2002), *Peasant Women and Politics in Fascist Italy: The Massaie Rurali*, London: Routledge.

Willson, Perry (2010a), *Italiane: Biografia del Novecento*, Bari: Editori Laterza.

Willson, Perry (2010b), *Women in Twentieth-Century Italy*, London and Basingstoke: Palgrave Macmillan.

Wilson, Elizabeth (1991), *The Sphinx in the City: Urban Life, the Control of Disorder, and Women*, London: Virago Press.

Wood, Mary (2000), 'Woman of Rome: Anna Magnani', in U. Sieglohr (ed.), *Heroines Without Heroes: Reconstructing Female and National Identities in European Cinema, 1945–51*, New York: Cassell, pp. 149–62.

Wood, Mary (2004), '"Pink" neorealism and the rehearsal of gender roles', in P. Powrie, A. Davies, and B. Babington (eds), *The Trouble With Men: Masculinities in European and Hollywood Cinema*, New York: Wallflower Press, pp. 134–43.

Wood, Mary (2005), *Italian Cinema*, Oxford: Berg.

Wood, Mary (2006), 'From bust to boom: Women and representations of prosperity in Italian cinema of the late 1940s and 1950s', in P. Morris (ed.), *Women in Italy 1945–1960*, New York: Palgrave Macmillan, pp. 51–63.

Wood, Mary (2010), 'Chiaroscuro: The half-glimpsed femme fatale of Italian film noir', in H. Hanson and C. O'Rawe (eds), *The Femme Fatale: Images, Histories, Contexts*, New York: Palgrave, pp. 157–69.

Yuval-Davis, Nira (1997), *Gender & Nation*, London: Sage Publications.

Zagagnoni, Liviana (1999), *Le donne, le lotte, la memoria: 1949–1999 a cinquant'anni dalla morte di Maria Margotti*, Ferrara: Il Globo.

Zagatti, A., Ghirardini, R., Gessi, F., and Siroli, E. (1998), interview with Alves Zagatti and Rina Ghirardini, Fernanda Gessi and Elva Siroli, 3 December.

Zapf, Dieter (2002), 'Emotion work and psychological well-being; A review of the literature and some conceptual considerations', *Human Resource Management Review*, 12, pp. 237–68.

Zappi, Elda G. (1991), *If Eight Hours Seem Too Few: Mobilization of Women Workers in the Italian Rice Fields*, Albany: State University of New York Press.

Zini, N. and Sangiorgi, F. (2009), interview with Neves Giorgi, 3 May.

Filmography

Mondine
Di madre in figlia, Andrea Zambelli (dir.) (2008) [Documentary], Italy: Rossofuoco.
Il maggio delle mondine, Francesco Marano (dir.) (2011) [Documentary], Italy: Francesco Marano.
La risaia, Raffaello Matarazzo (dir.) (1956) [Film], Italy: Minerva.
Riso amaro, Giuseppe De Santis (dir.) (1949) [Film], Italy: LUX.
Sorriso amaro, Matteo Bellizzi (dir.) (2003) [Documentary], Italy: Stefilm International, YLE TV1, YLE Teema, RSI Radiotelevisione svizzera.

Sarte
Le amiche, Michelangelo Antonioni (dir.) (1955) [Film], Italy: Trionfalcine.
Le ragazze di piazza di Spagna, Alberto Lattuada (dir.) (1952) [Film], Italy: Cine Produzione Astoria.
Sorelle Materassi, Fernando De Poggioli (dir.) (1943) [Film], Italy: Cines.

Religiose
Anna, Alberto Lattuada (dir.) (1951) [Film], Italy: LUX.
La Novice/Lettere di una novizia, Alberto Lattuada (dir.) (1960) [Film], Italy: Euro International Films.
Suor Letizia, Mario Camerini (dir.) (1956) [Film], Italy: Cineriz.

Other Media Cited
Caterina da Siena, Oreste Palella (dir.) (1947) [Film], Italy: Cigna.
Cercasi bionda bella presenza, Pina Renzi (dir.) (1942) [Film], Italy: S.A.C.I.T.E.R., Sovrania Film.
Cielo sulla palude, Augusto Genina (dir.) (1949) [Film], Italy: ARX, Film Bassoli.
Coco Before Chanel, Anne Fontaine (dir.) (2009) [Film], France: Haut et Court, Ciné.

Domenica d'Agosto, Luciano Emmer (dir.) (1950) [Film], Italy: Colonna Film.
Due lettere anonime, Mario Camerini (dir.) (1945) [Film], Italy: LUX, Ninfa.
Fiamme sulla laguna, Giuseppe Maria Scotese (dir.) (1949) [Film], Italy: Arga Film.
Giovanna d'Arco al rogo, Roberto Rossellini (dir.) (1954) [Film], Italy: Produzioni Cinematografiche Associate, Franco London Films.
I bambini ci amano, Enzo Della Santa (dir.) (1954) [Film], Italy: M. Braga.
I figli non si vendono, Mario Bonnard (dir.) (1952) [Film], Italy: Schermi Associati, Zeus.
Il lupo della sila, Vittorio De Sica (dir.) (1949) [Film], Italy: LUX.
Il suo più grande amore, Antonio Leonviola (dir.) (1956) [Film], Italy: Glomer Film.
Io, Caterina, Oreste Palella (dir.) (1957) [Film], Italy: Arciere, Arena Cin.ca.
La Casa de Papel, Álex Pina (dir.) (2017) [TV], Spain: Atresmedia, Vancouver Media.
L'angelo bianco, Raffaello Mattarazzo (dir.) (1955) [Film], Italy: Titanus, Labor Films.
La ciociara, Vittorio De Sica (dir.) (1960) [Film], Italy: Compagnia Cinematografica Champion, Cocinor, Les Films Marceau, Société Générale de Cinématographie.
La donna del fiume, Mario Soldati (dir.) (1954) [Film], Italy: Excelsa Film, Les Films du Centaure, Ponti-De Laurentiis Cinematografica.
La maestrina, Giorgio Bianchi (dir.) (1942) [Film], Italy: Nembo Film.
La monaca di Monza, Raffaello Paccini (dir.) (1947) [Film], Italy: A.C.I.F.
La monaca di Monza, Carmine Gallone (dir.) (1962) [Film], Italy: Globe, Paris Elysées Films, Paris Film, Produzione Gallone.
Ladri di biciclette, Vittorio De Sica (dir.) (1948) [Film], Italy: Produzioni De Sica.
Le ragazze di piazza di Spagna, José Maria Sánchez (dir.) (1998) [Film], Italy, RAI Radiotelevisione Italiana.
Le ragazze di San Frediano, Valerio Zurlini (dir.) (1955) [Film], Italy: LUX.
L'impiegato, Gianni Puccini (dir.) (1960) [Film], Italy: Ajace Produzioni Cinematografiche.
L'onorevole Angelina, Luigi Zampa (dir.) (1947) [Film], Italy: LUX, Ora Film.
Luisa Spagnoli, Lodovico Gasparini (dir.) (2016) [TV Film], Italy: Moviheart.
Mambo, Robert Rossen (dir.) (1954) [Film], Italy: Ponti-De Laurentiis Conematografica.
Malacarne, Pino Mercanti (dir.) (1946) [Film], Italy: Organizzazione Filmistica Siciliana.
Margherita da Cortona, Mario Bonnard (dir.) (1950) [Film], Italy: Scalera Film, Secolo Film.
Miss Italia, Duilio Coletti (dir.) (1950) [Film], Italy: ATA.
Noi peccatori, Guido Brignone (dir.) (1953) [Film], Italy: Titanus.
Noi vivi, Goffredo Alessandrini (dir.) (1942) [Film], Italy: Era Film, Scalera Film.
Non c'è pace tra gli ulivi, Giuseppe De Santis (dir.) (1950) [Film], Italy: LUX.
Siamo donne (Quattro attrici, una speranza – primo episodio), Alfredo Guarini (dir.) (1953) [Film], Italy: Titanus, Film Costellazione Produzione.
Sorelle Fontana, Riccardo Milani (dir.) (2011) [TV], Italy: Lux Vide, Rai Fiction.
Sorriso amaro, Maite Carpio (dir.) (2009) [TV], Italy: RAI Educational.
Teresa Venerdì, Vittorio De Sica (dir.) (1941) [Film], Italy: Alleanza Cinematografica Italiana, Europa Film.

Tre storie proibite, Augusto Genina (dir.) (1951) [Film], Italy: Electra Film Productions.
Un americano in vacanza, Luigi Zampa (dir.) (1946) [Film], Italy: Castrignano Film, LUX.
Un giorno nella vita, Alessandro Blasetti (dir.) (1946) [Film], Italy: Orbis Films.
Velvet, Ramón Campos and Gema R. Neira (dir.) (2013) [TV], Spain: Bambú Producciones.
Villa Borghese, Alberto De Sica and Gianni Franciolini (dir.) (1953) [Film], Italy: Cine Produzione Astoria, Productions Sigma-Vog.

Index of Interviews

Mondine

Baldini, G. and Siroli, A. (1998), interview with Giuseppina Baldini, 11 December.
Beccari, G., Fiorentini, L., and Fantuz, A. (2009), interview with Giuseppina (Pina) Beccari, Lucia Fiorentini, Antonia Fantuz, 4 August.
Bertuzzi, L., Romagnoli, G., and Zappaterra, G. (1999) Incontro collettivo, 2 February.
Biavati, V. and Biavati, E. (1999), interview with Velia e Edma Biavati, 22 January.
Brandolini, P. et al. (1998), Incontro collettivo, 28 November.
Gessi, F. and Siroli, E. (1998) interview with Fernanda Gessi and Elva Siroli, 3 December.
Ghirardini, R. and Zagatti, A. (1998), interview with Rina Ghirardini and Alves Zagatti, 3 December.
Intervista collettiva (2009), Intervista collettiva per il progetto sulle mondine di Medicina, 4 August.
Martina, B. (1999), interview with Biagia Martini, 22 January.
Trombetti, G. and Fortini, G. (1999), interview with Giuseppina Trombetti and Gina Fortini, 2 February.
Zagatti, A., Ghirardini, R., Gessi, F., and Siroli, E. (1998) interview with Alves Zagatti and Rina Ghirardini, Fernanda Gessi and Elva Siroli, 3 December.
Zini, N. and Sangiorgi, F. (2009), interview with Neves Giorgi, 3 May.

Sarte

Coppola, G. (2016), interview with Giuseppina Coppola.
Garagnani, L. (2016), interview with Lucia Garagnani, 16 May.
Giordano, L. (2016), interview with Lina Giordano, 24 May.
Neri, O. (2016), interview with Oriana Neri, 18 May.
Tassoni, N. (2016), interview with Norma Tassoni, 12 June.
Tinti, A. (2016), interview with Anna Tinti, 27 May.
Torri, L. (2016), interview with Luciana Torri, 10 May.

Religiose

Ai, S. C. (2017), interview with Sister Ai, 21 January.
Anonymous (2017), interview with anonymous, 21 January.

Ao, S. C. (2017), interview with Sister Ao, 21 January.
Az, S. G. (2017), interview with Sister Az, 21 January.
Be, S. M. B. (2017), interview with Sister Be, 22 January.
Bo, S. M. P. (2017), interview with Sister Bo, 21 January.
Cc, S. R. (2017), interview with Sister Cc, 23 January.
Cd, S. M. (2017), interview with Sister Cd, 22 January.
Ft, S. I. (2017), interview with Sister Ft, 21 January.
Jp, S. L. (2017), interview with Sister Jp, 21 January.
Li, S. M.-L. (2017), interview with Sister Li, 21 January.
My, S. A. (2017), interview with Sister My, 21 January.
Pc, S. C. (2017), interview with Sister Pc, 21 January.
Pt, S. V. (2017), interview with Sister Pt, 22 January.
Pz, S. P. (2017), interview with Sister Pz, 21 January.
Qo, S. E. (2017), interview with Sister Qo, 22 January.
Ss, S. L. (2017), interview with Sister Ss, 21 January.

Milton Keynes UK
Ingram Content Group UK Ltd.
UKHW020746280324
440254UK00010B/79